"I laughed until I stopped"

Happy Xmas 2007

Glen, Máirín & Conal

Silent Comedy

Silent Comedy

Paul Merton

Published by Random House Books 2007

2 4 6 8 10 9 7 5 3 1

First published in Great Britain in 2007 by Random House Books
Random House, 20 Vauxhall Bridge Road, London SW1V 2SA

www.rbooks.co.uk

Addresses for companies within The Random House Group Limited can be found at:
www.randomhouse.co.uk/offices.htm

The Random House Group Limited Reg. No. 954009

A CIP catalogue record for this book is available from the British Library

ISBN 9781905211708

The Random House Group Limited makes every effort to ensure that the papers used in its books
are made from trees that have been legally sourced from well-managed and credibly certified forests.
Our paper procurement policy can be found at: www.rbooks.co.uk/environment

Printed in Great Britain by Butler & Tanner, Frome

Publishing Director: Nigel Wilcockson
Editorial: Emily Rhodes, Charlie Taylor
Copy-editor: Lydia Darbyshire
Proof-reader: Sarah Barlow
Index: Geraldine Beare
Design: Two Associates
Picture researcher: Felicity Page
Cover: Glenn O'Neill
Production: Simon Rhodes

‘All I need to make a comedy is a park, a policeman and a pretty girl’

– Charlie Chaplin

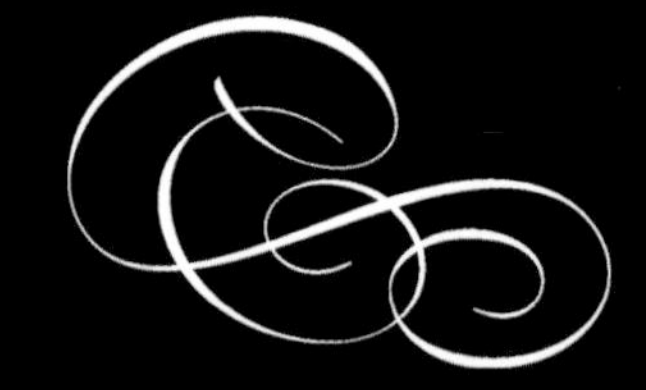
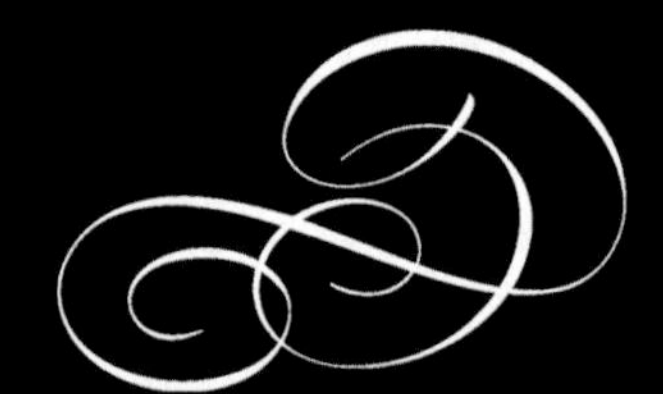

"Contents"

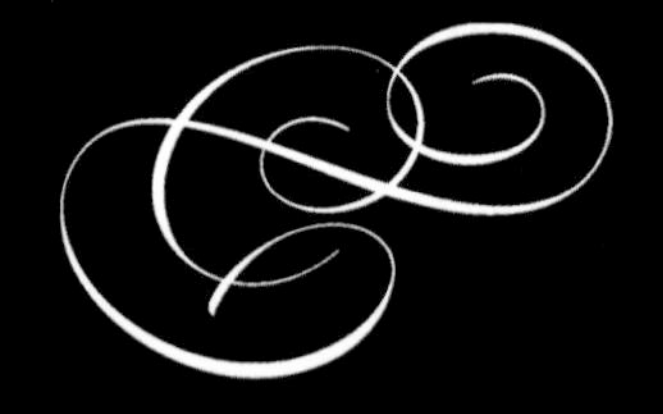
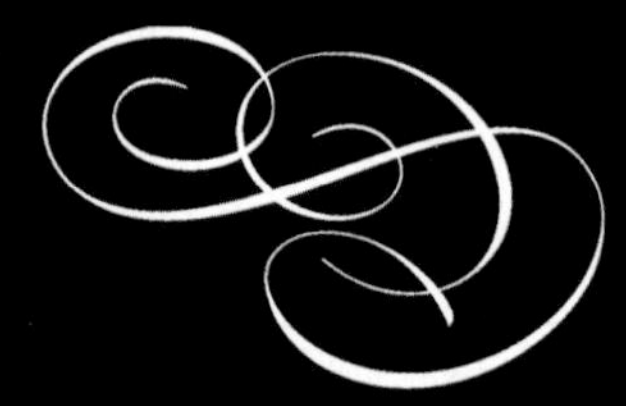

‘Like anyone else I enjoy being called a genius. But I cannot take it seriously’

– Buster Keaton

Acknowledgements

I must first thank David Robinson whose 1969 book about Buster Keaton gave such vivid descriptions of films that were then very difficult to see. Also David's masterly biography *Charlie Chaplin – His Life and Art* made a big impact with me. It was given to me as a birthday present in 1985 when I had few possessions and was living in a bedsit. I've read and re-read that book over the years and it's still marvellous to dip into every now and again.

I must also thank Kevin Brownlow who, together with David Gill, produced a series of documentaries about silent comedians for Thames Television which introduced new generations to the work of Chaplin, Keaton and Lloyd. *The Unknown Chaplin* series narrated by James Mason and featuring never-before-seen outtakes is particularly fascinating. Occasionally I have shown Episode One to people who claimed not to 'get' Chaplin and each one of them has been easily converted.

I must also thank Glenn Mitchell, film historian, broadcaster and author of *The Chaplin Encyclopaedia* and *The A–Z of Silent Film Comedy*, both of which are essential reference books for students of the period; and also Simon Louvish whose excellent Laurel and Hardy book provided much-appreciated early biographical material.

My thanks to Jessica Tipping for her immaculate research, enthusiasm and sympathetic editing, particularly in the first half of the book. I thank my parents Albert and Mary Martin and my sister Angela for enjoying silent comedies with me in my teenage years. And I thank Suki for sharing them with me now.

But the biggest thank you is reserved for Charlie, Buster, Harold, Stan and Ollie. No comedians will ever be as big again.

Introduction

I've always enjoyed visual comedy. When I was five I was taken to Bertram Mills' Circus. At that age the leggy, glamorous trapeze artiste held no sway over me, but ah, the clowns, what an impression they made! Colourfully clothed adults, with painted faces, unfeasibly large boots, driving easily collapsible cars and throwing buckets of whitewash over each other – I was filled with rapturous glee. It was a major revelation in my life to discover that adults got up to this level of silliness. I still recall the all-embracing sound of a big top filled with laughter, the intoxicating roar of happy people. At that moment was born a desire to live in that laughter, somehow to be part of its creation, to engender that sound in people, to flood their brains with endorphins.

At my urging, my mother bought a plastic clown mask as a memento. I wore it more or less constantly over the next few days. It was a crude, moulded face that tore easily, exposing sharp edges to my young skin. Even though it hurt, I still put it on. I'm aware of the massive symbolism now, but then it was just a torn clown mask that caused a bearable amount of irritation as I tumbled behind and across the sofa. I easily recall the difficulty of breathing through the rudimentary nose – two holes, optimistically, but inaccurately, placed somewhere in the vague vicinity of a child's nostrils.

A thirst for comedy led me to Charlie Chaplin, whose early Keystone films were shown on television in a puzzling world of black and white shadows. My grandfather told me that Charlie Chaplin had been the funniest man in the world, yet there seemed little evidence on the screen in front of me: the poor quality print was too dark to reveal what was happening. Shown at the wrong speed with awful, unsympathetic music, it just didn't give Charlie a chance.

A programme called *Mad Movies*, hosted by the comedian Bob Monkhouse, appeared on British television in 1965. It introduced me to more Chaplin, Laurel and Hardy, Mack Sennett, Harry Langdon, Mabel Normand, Roscoe Arbuckle and cross-eyed Ben Turpin. Then in 1968 the comedian and life-adventurer Michael Bentine presented the *Golden Silents* on the BBC. The ex-Goon had a passion for visual humour, and for the first time I saw Buster Keaton, who had been kept out of the *Mad Movies* series by contractual problems. Seeing Keaton's

Above **An essential element of every knock-about film. Here Charlie Chaplin receives a well-placed foot in his backside during the filming of *Kid Auto Races at Venice*.**

I saw my first silent comedy on a big screen with a live accompaniment when Buster Keaton's *The General* was shown at the Academy Cinema in Oxford Street. It was a tremendous eye-opener

work was a revelation. I thought I was an eleven-year-old kid who knew a fair amount about silent comedy. I wasn't. I was an eleven-year-old who had never seen Buster Keaton: his incredible acrobatic abilities; his stillness; his extraordinary stunts; his surrealism; his dedication to his work; his comedy.

The *Golden Silents* inspired in me a desire to collect silent comedies – in those days they were on a film format called Super 8. I had a projector in my bedroom and a sheet on the wall, but very few films were available. Three years later, I saw my first silent comedy on a big screen with a live accompaniment when Buster Keaton's *The General* was shown at the Academy Cinema in Oxford Street. It was a tremendous eye-opener: silent, visual comedy on the big screen comes alive in a way that television struggles to match. The presence of a large, appreciative audience creates an atmosphere of laughter.

Indeed, broadcasting history was made when, in a unique experiment on 26 September 1925, the BBC transmitted a live recording from the Tivoli, Strand, of the audience's laughter during Chaplin's film *The Gold Rush*. The marathon outburst occurred during the climactic scene in which the log cabin, housing Charlie and Mack Swain, teeters on the edge of a precipice. Ten minutes of continual laughter filled the airwaves. It was announced in newspapers across the UK: '7.30 p.m. Interlude of Laughter. Ten Minutes with Charlie Chaplin and his audience at the Tivoli.' I wonder what corner of outer space has now been reached by those delirious radio signals. About ten years ago I saw a screening of *The Gold Rush* at the Royal Festival Hall, London, and the log cabin sequence got the same response.

The tiresomely idiotic debate on Keaton versus Chaplin is, in my experience, overwhelmingly used by proponents of Buster to attempt to rubbish Charlie. It's an appealing mind-set for some people, who say: 'We've all heard that Charlie Chaplin was meant to be the greatest comedian in the world, but my preference for Buster Keaton demonstrates *my* ability to think for myself. Chaplin was overly sentimental, but Keaton's coolness and cynical eye chime exactly with our modern times.'

Well, the good news is that they are both fantastic. There's no need to choose between them. Enjoy them both! That's one of the main aims of this book. I shall examine the films of Charlie Chaplin and Buster Keaton, not in isolation, as has been the usual practice, but showing how they influenced each other in a creative rivalry that also featured Harold Lloyd (the man hanging off the clock). This rivalry and desire to make better and better comedies ensured a stream of high-quality pictures. Great works of art were created.

In the past it was often very difficult to track down watchable versions of many of the silent greats. Charlie Chaplin's early work, for example, was mangled, distorted and rendered worse than unwatchable by repeated re-issues. The image was often incredibly dark, and horribly inappropriate music was used. Sometimes it's not even music. I have a DVD that features a Chaplin Keystone with a jazz vocalist saying: 'Hi there everybody and welcome to the club! Tonight the band wants to play for you the hottest numbers. Let's go!' All this accompanies visuals of somebody in darkness doing something that we can't see and then jumping up and down. Luckily, the overall picture is now far rosier. The DVD format has revolutionized the availability of the greatest comedies of the silent era. Shoddy copies of Chaplin's Keystones aside, Chaplin's career is beautifully represented from 1915 onwards. Not one film is missing. Keaton also has an excellent survival rate. The same applies to Harold Lloyd, at least as far as his post-1918 comedies are concerned. Only one of the thirty-three silent films of Laurel and Hardy's career is missing. All these films and many more are available on DVD.

So, here we go. This book is a guide through the silent comedy jungle. Using my experience of watching silent films with appropriate music, on a big screen with a big audience and big laughs, I hope to pinpoint the towering artistic achievements of the era. Some of them involve people being kicked up the arse.

So, here we go. This book is a guide through the silent comedy jungle. I hope to pinpoint the towering artistic achievements of the era. Some of them involve people being kicked up the arse

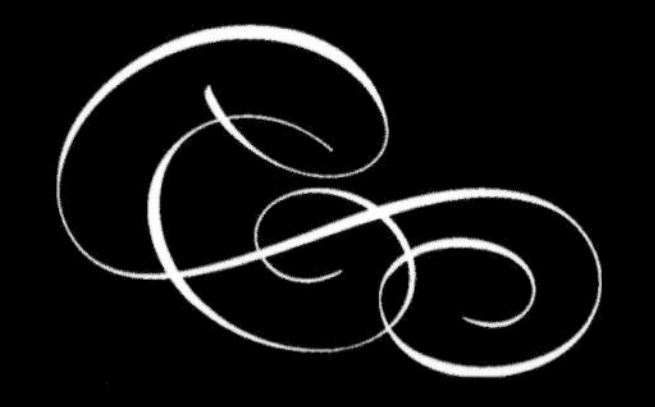

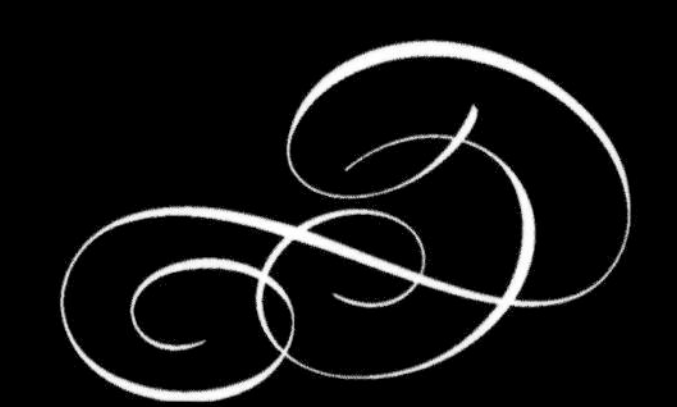

Chapter 1
"Starting Out"

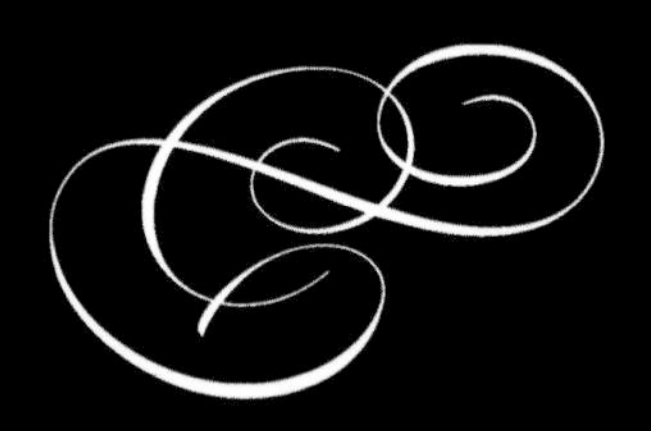

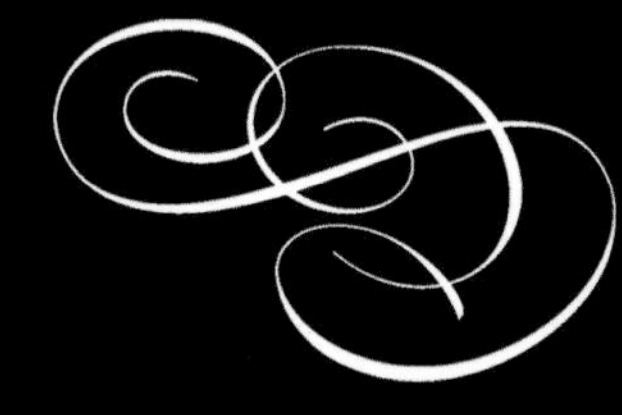

This is the great picture upon which the famous comedian has worked a whole year.
6 reels of Joy.
Charles Chaplin
IN
"THE KID"
Written and directed by Charles Chaplin
A First National Attraction

Starting Out

Our story begins on 16 April 1889 in a small upstairs room in East Street, Walworth, South London. Here, at eight o'clock in the evening a baby was born to Hannah Chaplin, a singer and a dancer on the music hall stage. In her late twenties, she already had an older son, Sydney, by another man, and her new baby was named after his father, Charlie, who, like Hannah, was a successful music hall performer.

It took courage, staying power and talent to thrive on the music hall circuit. At many venues a performer could expect a volatile crowd because often the audience would be enthusiastically drunk. A song with a pretty uplifting melody or a melancholic moan about the iniquities of life was standard fare of the day, and Chaplin senior was successful enough to commission songwriters to write specifically for him. Song sheets were printed up and purchased by the public to take home and play on the piano, for in an era before it was possible to reproduce music electronically in the home, people relied on the real thing – musical instruments.

Being a successful music hall act had many advantages. The money was good and so were the hours; the working conditions were warm and well lit; and if the audience loved you, you walked off the stage feeling ten feet tall. The management expected the acts to mix with the customers in the bar afterwards. A jovial patron slaps you on the back, buys you a drink and tells you he's never laughed so much or cried so much and 'come and meet the missus'. It sounds idyllic.

The downside to this picture is that it was easy to develop a taste for the booze because you're in the bar after every performance, drinking in the applause … and the drink. 'Some theatres made more profit from the bar than from the box office, and a number of stars were paid large salaries not alone for their talent but because they spent most of their money at the theatre bar,' wrote Charlie Chaplin. 'Many an artist was ruined by drink – my father was one of them. He died of alcoholic excess at the age of thirty-seven.'[1]

Charlie's mother, Hannah, separated from Charlie's father a year after Charlie's birth. At her peak as a music hall artist she had earned £25 a week at a time when the average national weekly wage was under £1.50, but she began having trouble with her throat. She had attacks of laryngitis, which lasted for weeks, and in the middle ofa song she would suddenly lose her voice, and what had been an appreciative audience would start to jeer and boo. She couldn't afford not to work, but when she did she put additional strain on her voice, which led to further humiliating performances.

In *My Autobiography* Charlie Chaplin recalls the night he made his first appearance onstage. He was five years old. His mother was 'playing the

Right **Charlie Chaplin's mother, Hannah, was at one time a popular musical performer. As her star waned, she found herself upstaged by her five-year-old son.**

Inset **Charles Chaplin senior separated from Hannah when Charles junior was only a year old. A successful music act, like his wife, his career was destroyed by drink.**

3

1894 found Joe Keaton joining the Cutlers' travelling medicine show. Myra Cutler, the owner's daughter, played the cornet and saxophone – she was reported to be America's first female saxophonist

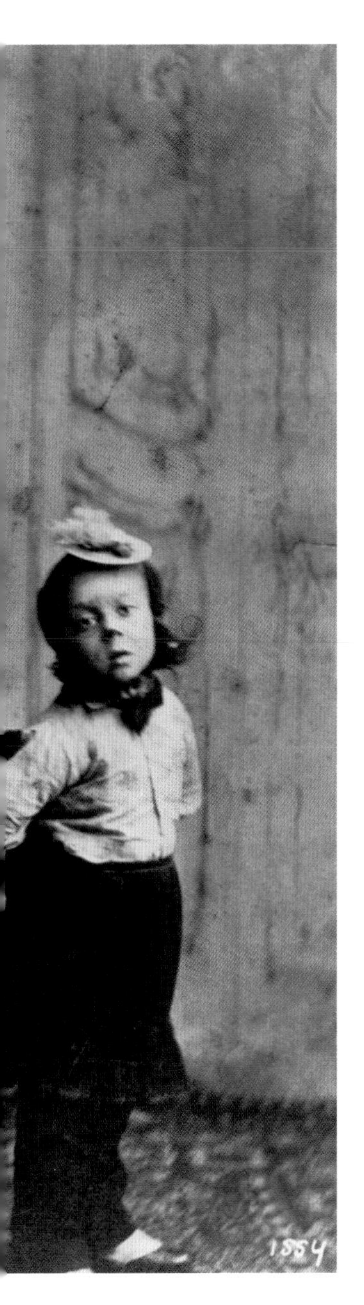

Left Buster Keaton makes an early appearance in his parents' vaudeville act. His ability to survive being thrown around the stage by his father was one of the highlights of their performance.

Canteen at Aldershot at the time, a grubby, mean theatre catering mostly to soldiers. They were a rowdy lot and wanted little excuse to deride and ridicule. To performers, Aldershot was a week of terror.'[2] I know what that terror's like. In the 1980s I worked as a stand-up comic on the London comedy circuit, and I absolutely dreaded the Saturday midnight show at the Comedy Store. I'd start worrying about the Saturday performance on the Tuesday. A drunk, easily bored audience could be won over, but you needed good jokes, luck, attitude – and a voice. Hannah's voice cracked onstage that night in Aldershot in 1894 and became a whisper. There was no amplification in those days – no microphones, no loudspeakers – and you stood on the stage and sang with the band. If the audience couldn't hear you, you would soon hear them. Hannah was forced offstage by the catcalls and general booing. Her son, Charlie, was standing in the wings, and he witnessed her distress and her argument with the stage manager. The manager suggested that Charlie went on in her place – he'd seen Charlie entertain his mother's friends – and he took Charlie by the hand, led him onto the stage and explained the situation to the audience. The manager then walked offstage, leaving the five-year-old alone

> before a glare of footlights and faces in smoke, I started to sing, accompanied by the orchestra, which fiddled about until it found my key ... Halfway through, a shower of money poured onto the stage. Immediately I stopped and announced that I would pick up the money first and sing afterwards. This caused much laughter ... I was quite at home. I talked to the audience, danced and did several imitations, including one of Mother singing ... And in repeating the chorus, in all innocence I imitated Mother's voice cracking and was surprised at the impact it had on the audience. There was laughter and cheers, then more money-throwing; and when Mother came on the stage to carry me off, her presence evoked tremendous applause. That night was my first appearance on the stage, and Mother's last.[3]

On the other side of the Atlantic, 1894 found Joe Keaton joining the Cutlers' travelling medicine show. Myra Cutler, the owner's daughter, played the cornet and saxophone – she was reported to be America's first female saxophonist – and Joe was an actor, an eccentric dancer, who often performed in blackface, the old minstrel tradition.

Working in a travelling medicine show involved pitching up in a town, getting a licence from the local sheriff, setting up a rudimentary stage, enter-

'I ignored any bumps or bruises I may have got at first on hearing audiences gasp, laugh and applaud. There is one more thing: little kids when they fall haven't very far to go' – Buster Keaton

taining a gathering crowd with music and spectacle, then selling them 'medicine' in bottles designed to cure earache, backache, gout, baldness and everything else. The 'medicine' was normally alcoholic.

When Joe and Myra's first child was born on 4 October 1895 he turned out to be Buster Keaton, originally named Joseph Frank Keaton. When he was six months old he tumbled down a flight of stairs in a theatrical boarding house, and Harry Houdini, who was in the same company, was the first to reach him. He picked up the child, who astonished everyone by laughing! According to Myra Keaton, 'Houdini gasped and said, "That's some buster your baby took." Joe looked down and said, "Well, Buster, looks like Uncle Harry has named you." He's been Buster ever since.'[4] Buster himself told this story on more than one occasion, and it has appeared in countless books and magazine articles: Buster Keaton named by Harry Houdini. The only thing is, it's not true. Joe Keaton was a wonderful publicist, and his implausible tales became gospel through repetition. If Buster did fall down a flight of stairs when he was six months old, it certainly hadn't been witnessed by Harry Houdini. Yes, Houdini had once been in the same company as the Keatons, but that had been many years before. A newspaper clipping from 22 July 1901 states that 'the name Buster was conferred on him by members of the company with which his parents were then touring'.[5] No mention of Houdini who, at this point, was one of the biggest stars in vaudeville. Joe Keaton was a publicity genius, and surely Houdini would have been mentioned if he had been there.

Buster, like Charlie Chaplin, made his first stage appearance at a very early age:

> If I say I officially joined my folks' act in 1899 it is because my father always insisted that I'd been trying to get into the family act unofficially – meaning unasked, unwanted and unbilled – practically from the day I was born ... According to him, the moment I could crawl, I headed for the footlights. 'And when Buster learned to walk,' he always proudly explained to all who were interested and many who weren't, 'there was no holding him. He would jump up and down in the wings, make plenty of noise, and get in everyone's way. It seemed easier to let him come out with us on the stage where we could keep an eye on him. At first I told him not to move. He was to lean against the side wall and stay there. But one day I got the idea of dressing him up like myself as a stage Irishman with a fright wig, slugger whiskers, fancy vest and over-size pants. Soon he was imitating everything I did, and getting laughs.'[6]

Buster was learning how to take falls. His father would carry him out onstage and then drop him. 'When I gave no sign of minding this he began throwing me through the scenery, out onto the wings, and dropping me down on the bass drum in the orchestra pit.'[7] Although the act was heavily rough and tumble, the young Buster loved it. 'I ignored any bumps or bruises I may have got at first on hearing audiences gasp, laugh and applaud. There is one more thing: little kids when they fall haven't very far to go.'[8]

Buster made a major discovery one night at the beginning of his career. 'One of the first things I noticed was that whenever I smiled or let the audience suspect how much I was enjoying myself they didn't seem to laugh as much as usual.'[9]

So there we have it. Buster Keaton at the age of five, or thereabouts, successfully finding and defining the comic style that will make him the world famous subject of countless books and documentaries, and whose greatest films are enjoyed and applauded by cinema audiences over eighty years after their first appearance.

Opposite The young Buster Keaton, complete with cut-down adult clothes and pipe, poses as a small gentleman. The disguise was part of his act, but it also helped to throw welfare agencies concerned with child exploitation off the scent.

Charlie Chaplin's theatrical debut had saved the show in Aldershot when his mother's voice cracked alarmingly. He'd found himself the cause of laughter – an exhilarating experience for a five-year-old – but the next few years were to be among the hardest of his life, for his mother's voice never fully recovered. Perhaps the humiliation was too much, standing onstage, experiencing the audience turn against her, but she couldn't work, and the money she had saved dwindled away. The family moved from three comfortable rooms into two, then into one. As Charlie says in his autobiography:

> Jobs were hard to find and Mother, untutored in everything but the stage, was further handicapped. She was small, dainty and sensitive, fighting against terrific odds in a Victorian era in which wealth and poverty were extreme, and poorer class women had little choice but to do menial work or to be the drudges of sweatshops.[10]

Hannah turned to religion as the money dribbled away, while Charles Chaplin senior's drinking led to him losing work, which meant he couldn't keep up the ten shillings maintenance due to Hannah each week. For a while Hannah worked as a seamstress, but she couldn't maintain the payments on her sewing machine. A single mother with two children, she sought advice from a solicitor, who advised her to throw herself and her family on the support of the Lambeth Borough authorities. In Charlie's own words, 'there was no alternative: she was

'One of the first things I noticed was that whenever I smiled or let the audience suspect how much I was enjoying myself they didn't seem to laugh as much as usual' – Buster Keaton

Above The grim Lambeth Workhouse where a six-year-old Charlie Chaplin, his half-brother Sydney and his mother were forced to live when the family ran out of money.

Opposite Charlie at school in Kennington, aged seven and a half. Unlike Buster Keaton's, his childhood was marked by poverty and family unhappiness.

burdened with two children, and in poor health; and so she decided that the three of us should enter the Lambeth workhouse'.[11] More humiliation.

The Lambeth Workhouse was a big, grim building crammed with defeated humanity. The two Chaplin brothers (in fact, they were half-brothers) were separated from their mother and transferred to the Hanwell Schools for Orphans and Destitute Children, some 12 miles outside London. After a few days, Charlie and Sydney were parted: 'We slept in different ward blocks, so we seldom saw each other. I was little over six years old and alone, which made me feel quite abject.'[12]

Almost a year later Hannah's circumstances improved, and she, Charlie and Sydney moved into a room at the back of Kennington Park. But this proved to be the beginning of a desperate period, and soon they were back in the workhouse, from where they were transferred to Norwood Schools. One day the boys were told that their mother had gone insane and had been sent to Cane Hill lunatic asylum. Charlie and Sydney spent a couple of months living with Charlie's father and his girlfriend, Louise, who were both heavy drinkers, and scenes of drunkenness and physical violence were not uncommon. One night, Charlie couldn't get into the house. Nobody was in and it was approaching midnight, so he sat on a kerb at the corner of Kennington Cross, feeling wretched. From the nearby White Hart public house he heard 'The Honeysuckle and the Bee' played by two musicians on the harmonium and clarinet:

> I had never been conscious of melody before, but this one was beautiful and lyrical, so blithe and gay, so warm and reassuring. I forgot my despair and crossed the road to where the musicians were.[13]

Later that night, Charlie, his father and Louise were all back in the house. The adults quarrelled, and Chaplin senior threw a heavy clothes brush violently into Louise's face, knocking her unconscious. Imagine young Charlie's emotional journey that night, from despair, to joy, to terror.

'On a Sunday morning, when he had not been drinking, he would breakfast with us and tell Louise about the vaudeville acts that were working with him, and have us all enthralled' – Charlie Chaplin

There were happier times when he did see a genuine, tender love between Louise and his father: 'On a Sunday morning, when he had not been drinking, he would breakfast with us and tell Louise about the vaudeville acts that were working with him, and have us all enthralled. I would watch him like a hawk, absorbing every action.'[14] On other occasions, Charlie would look on with astonishment as his father swallowed six raw eggs in port wine before leaving for work in the theatre.

After several months Hannah Chaplin was released from the asylum. She rented a room in Methney Street near the Hayward's pickle factory. At one end of the street was a slaughterhouse, and it was usual practice for sheep to be herded past the Chaplins' front door on the way to be butchered. As Charlie recalls:

> I remember one escaped and ran down the street to the amusement of onlookers. Some tried to grab it and others tripped over themselves. I had giggled with delight at its lambent capering and panic, it seemed so comic. But when it was caught and carried back into the slaughterhouse, the reality of the tragedy came over me, and I ran indoors, screaming and weeping to Mother: 'They're going to kill it! They're going to kill it!' That stark, spring afternoon and that comedy chase stayed with me for days; and I wonder if that episode did not establish the premise of my future films – the combination of the tragic and the comic.[15]

His mother's fluctuating health, both mental and physical, made for a continually unstable existence. When times were good, Hannah was well and fascinated the young Charlie with her theatrical stories. During one childhood illness, Hannah enthralled Charlie with readings from the New Testament, and sometimes mother and son would look out of the window at the passers-by while Hannah made up stories about them:

> Then a man would pass slowly, moping along. 'Hm, he's going home to have stew and parsnips for dinner, which he hates' ... Then another with a fast gait would streak past. 'That gentleman has just taken Eno's!' And so she would go on, sending me into gales of laughter.[16]

The young Charlie's own career in the music hall began towards the end of 1898, when he joined a clog-dancing troupe called the Eight Lancashire Lads. Clog-dancing was very popular during the late nineteenth century, and Charlie toured with the act until December 1900.

At the age of eleven, Charlie was standing on the edge of a new century. So was a five-year-old Buster Keaton, the star of the Three Keatons. The year before, the Keatons had graduated from the travelling medicine shows onto the vaudeville circuit. Vaudeville in America, like the music hall in Britain, was thriving, and audiences flocked in their millions to see live entertainment. Young performers like Chaplin and Keaton were not only performing regularly in front of live audiences, but they were also studying the other more established acts from the wings. Both Buster and Charlie were destined to enjoy the fruits of their intense apprenticeships, and once they became filmmakers, their sure instincts as to what made audiences laugh proved invaluable. Performing live is how they learned their craft.

Buster's early childhood, unlike Charlie's, was a cavalcade of fun. He adored working with his parents, and in his autobiography he speaks of his father with enormous affection. Over the years, modern eyes with today's sensibilities have suggested that Buster's childhood was abusive. It's true that his mother once sewed a suitcase handle into Buster's coat to make it easier for his father to pick him up and throw him across the stage, and for a while he was billed as 'The Human Mop', but this was not abuse, it was part of the act. Literally throwing himself into show business, Buster loved performing, getting the laughs and mixing with the other acts backstage. There were agencies around at the time that were concerned with child welfare, and prominent among them was the Gerry Society, formed to ensure that no child was exploited on the stage. To throw them off the scent, the young Buster happily posed as a 'midget' adult, wearing cut-down adult clothes offstage as well as on.

As the years progressed, the Three Keatons became one of the biggest acts in vaudeville. The chief ingredients were father and son's rough-and-tumble slapstick, while mother Myra played the saxophone. This was Buster's life, and he loved it. Travelling from town to town, he went to school only once, for just a day, when he enlivened normal school proceedings by repeating gags he'd seen on the vaudeville stage:

> The teacher called the roll:
> 'Smith?'
> 'Here'
> 'Johnson?'
> 'Here.'
> 'Keaton?'
> 'I couldn't come today.'
> That sent the class into an uproar and even won an appreciative smile from

Buster's early childhood, unlike Charlie's, was a cavalcade of fun. He adored working with his parents, and in his autobiography he speaks of his father with enormous affection

From music hall to silver screen

Below A poster advertising Marie Lloyd, one of the biggest stars of British music hall before the First World War. Her mixture of sentimental songs ('The Boy I Love is up in the Gallery') and risqué ones ('A Little of What You Fancy Does You Good'), and her skills as a comedienne won her an adoring following.

Music hall, where Charlie Chaplin made his first public appearance aged only five, had its roots in the song and supper rooms that became popular in the first thirty years of the nineteenth century. These were establishments serving food and drink but also providing music in the form of a song from the landlord or one of his regular customers. As time passed, more professional singers and other types of act were introduced into the mix. The audience sat at tables eating and drinking while the performers, by now on a small stage, battled to engage their attention. Singers of popular songs had an inbuilt advantage, and communal singing remained a feature of music hall throughout its existence.

Music hall was traditionally a working-class entertainment, but over time the owners built more lavish theatres to attract a middle-class and more affluent audience. Yet despite their efforts, music hall always remained a rougher entertainment than its counterpart, 'legitimate' theatre. The theatres didn't sell alcohol, but the music halls thrived on it. In the theatre the actors pretended there was a fourth wall and that the audience wasn't really there. In the music hall the performers stood on the stage and talked directly at the audience. But competing against other distractions meant they needed a strong personality to get their act across. Marie Lloyd became immensely popular with such comedy songs as 'My Old Man Said Follow the Van', and Dan Leno won great acclaim for his character-based monologues and clog-dancing.

The American vaudeville scene was in some ways quite similar to music hall, and the big names from music hall also played the vaudeville circuit in America. The traffic went the other way as well. W.C. Fields played in London, as did the Three Keatons. A popular act might well have played five music halls in a single evening, with a cab driver

Left ***The Music Hall*** **by Walter Sickert, who was fascinated by the world of the music hall.**

Below **Charlie Chaplin's contract of employment with Fred Karno's company.**

waiting at each stage door to whisk the performer to the next venue.

Music hall and vaudeville performers proved disparaging of cinema at first – even Charlie Chaplin initially regarded film-acting only as a way to boost his stage career – but those, such as Charlie and Buster Keaton, who made the transition were able on film to build on the skills they had developed in the theatre.

FRED KARNO'S COMPANIES.

Permanent Address:
VAUGHAN ROAD, CAMBERWELL.
LONDON. S.E.

Agreement made this 25th day of July 190 8
between FRED KARNO, hereinafter called the Manager of the one part, and
Chas. Chaplin
hereinafter called the Artiste of the other part.

The Manager engages the Artiste for Comedian & Pantomimist in Troupe or any other part or parts for which he may be required at a salary of £3 : 10 : 0 per week to include all performances, in any of Mr. Karno's Cos. that is for such days and nights only as the theatre shall be open for theatrical performances. The Artiste to rehearse and perform to the best of his skill and ability at any theatre or place of amusement in the United Kingdom or anywhere the Manager may direct, as often as he shall be warned to do so by the Manager or any other person or persons duly authorised by him on his behalf.

This engagement to commence on or about February 10th 1908 but the Artiste shall be bound to attend previous rehearsals, of not less than time required, such rehearsals to be given free.

The engagement to be for a period of one year at above mentioned salary and one year at the salary of £4 per week and in consideration of such engagement the Manager shall have the option of retaining the Artiste ~~through the ensuing Christmas (190)~~, at the ~~aforesaid~~ last mentioned salary. for a further period of twelve months.

The Artiste shall observe the rules of the Management attached, the same being deemed part of the agreement.

The Manager shall find all necessary special dresses, except tights, wigs, and shoes or modern wardrobe.

~~No salary shall be paid for any occasion when the Artiste does not perform, whatever the cause of such non-performance.~~

~~This engagement may be terminated by one of the parties thereto giving to the other in writing notice, such notice to be given on any day, unless otherwise specially specified.~~

Fire or other public calamity to put an end to this engagement on the Manager's side at his option.

As witness the hands of the said parties the day and the year first above written.

> the teacher. Enchanted that going to school meant only putting on an extra show each day, I could hardly wait for the next opportunity to spin my fellow scholars out into the aisles.[17]

As the onstage act developed and Buster grew older, the act became progressively rougher. Although it wasn't called improvisation at the time, the Keatons specialized in doing something different every night. 'We never bothered to do the same routines twice in a row. We found it much more fun to surprise one another by pulling any crazy wild stunt that came into our heads.'[18] One routine consisted of Joe lathering his face before shaving with a cut-throat razor, while Buster, who had previously attached a thick rubber rope above Joe's shaving mirror, would walk backwards holding a basketball tied to the other end of the rope:

> With each step I took, the audience screamed, expecting the rubber rope to break and snap against his head. When the rubber rope was stretched as tautly as possible, I let it go. As Pop was shaving his throat with his old-fashioned open razor, the basketball would sock him in the head and push his lathered face into the mirror. With the audience shrieking, Mom placidly continued playing her saxophone.[19]

What school could compete with that? Here's the choice: reciting your five

Below **A typical vaudeville theatre of *c.*1909. The Keaton family toured the vaudeville circuit relentlessly throughout Buster's childhood, a period he recalls with great affection in his autobiography.**

times table in a draughty classroom or getting huge laughs with a basketball on a piece of elastic.

From 1909 onwards the Keatons took summer off from the relentless grind of the vaudeville circuit. Joe Keaton had bought a cottage at Lake Muskegon where, soon after, an actors' colony was established. Buster delighted in the rural setting and the opportunity it gave him to build various humorous and ingenious gadgets. One of the simplest was called the Clown Pole. He would stick a bamboo fishing pole upright between two planks of the wooden pier situated opposite the clubhouse. A line from the pole led to the water and a red cork bobber. Instead of ending with a hook and bait, the line went back underwater, around a pulley under the pier, and then up and through the clubhouse window. When a stranger walked along the pier, they'd notice the bamboo fishing pole. Somebody inside the clubhouse would grasp the line, making it twitch at the other end to convince the stranger that a fish had been hooked. Naturally, the stranger couldn't resist picking up the pole and attempting to land his prize. So, the battle would commence, and an informal crowd would gather, offering advice and encouragement. The stranger would struggle for several minutes until, finally, the prankster in the clubhouse, with one big tug, would yank the fishing pole out of the victim's hands and into the water. The victim was invited into the clubhouse, given a wooden medal and encouraged to buy drinks all round.

This practical joking was taken on the road with equal good-hearted gusto:

> Laughs, laughs, day and night. I remember them all. Those practical jokes that went on and on like movie serials. Like the trunkful of cats. Why did I ever start that? A hundred cats lived in that theatre in Buffalo, barely holding their own against the rats. So I fill the Leightons' prop trunk with assorted cats. Nice and dark and cosy, so they all go to sleep. The trunk was a part of the act, so when they open it onstage, out fly the cats, all over the Leightons, up the scenery, even out into the audience.[20]

But if Chaplin and Keaton had performing in their blood, this wasn't true of all the future silent comedians. Harold Clayton Lloyd, for example, was a member of a noticeably untheatrical family. He was born in Burchard, California, on 20 April 1893; his parents, Foxy and Elizabeth, were serial movers, who took Harold and his older brother Gaylord to a new town every time one of his father's business enterprises didn't work out. Reflecting on those days in *An American Comedy*, the autobiography he wrote in collaboration with Wesley W. Stout, Harold saw himself as typical of the time:

> Supposing Atlantic City had been holding Average American Boy contests, with beauty waived, I might have been Master America most any year between 1893 and 1910. This is assuming that the average boy before the war was moderately poor, that his folks moved a good deal and that he worked for his spending money at any job that offered.[21]

Harold's early childhood games revolved around playing theatre. At an aunt's house he would gather together all the caps and hats and lay them across the floor, inventing characters and lines for them

However, Harold did see something exceptional in his 'single-tracked ambition' to be on the stage:

> As far back as memory goes, and to the exclusion of all else, I was stage crazy. There is no accounting for its strength and persistence, for it began before I ever saw a play, and there were no actors, so far as we know, in either my father's or mother's family.[22]

Harold's early childhood games revolved around playing theatre. At an aunt's house he would gather together all the caps and hats and lay them across the floor, inventing characters and lines for them. A couple of years later, Harold immersed himself in magic, tricks and mechanical puzzles: 'I went at them with that whole-souled devotion that characterized all my enthusiasms.'[23]

Harold also discovered an early flair for business. Whereas in Omaha he had a job as a paperboy delivering newspapers, in Denver he *owned* the route, which, he says, enabled him to discover 'responsibility and initiative'.[24] The route was run down when he bought it. He built it up, eventually needing to employ two other boys, and then sold it at a profit when they moved again.

Harold's sense of responsibility was tested to the utmost when, just thirteen years old, he took a trip to Colorado Springs with an alcoholic friend of the family. In his autobiography Harold discreetly gives him the fictional name of Joe Morgan. Let's hope his real name wasn't *Jim* Morgan. The trouble began before they even reached Colorado:

> In Denver Mr Morgan had been militantly sober, but before the train stopped at Palmer Lake for luncheon he had bought a bottle of whisky from the train porter and soon was limp with liquor.[25]

When they arrived at their hotel in Colorado Springs, Harold undressed Joe and put him to bed. The next morning he hid Joe's shoes and went off to explore some far-off caves. When he returned he discovered Joe drunk and shoeless. After a couple of days Harold had had enough: 'I wired to Denver to come and get him. As a moral lesson it was worth ten thousand temperance tracts to a boy. It was never needful to warn me away from the flying hoofs of the Brewers' Big Horses.'[26] He would remain teetotal throughout his life.

Harold saw his first film in 1903 when he was ten years old. It was *The Great Train Robbery*, a famous landmark in the early history of American cinema, and soon he was going to see movies on a regular basis, although in his autobiography

Opposite Dressed to the nines – the young Harold Lloyd.

he says he didn't at first make the connection between cinema and acting. Looking up at the screen he saw the actors as puppets, not as human beings.

One fateful day in Omaha in 1906 he met John Lane Connor, leading man with the Burwood Stock Company. Connor spotted Harold staring at an astrologer's shop window and was impressed that, unlike the rest of the town, he wasn't distracted by a local fire wagon haring off to a blaze. On hearing that Connor was looking for a place to lodge, Harold invited him to stay with his family. Fortunately, his mother agreed as the extra money was welcome, and Connor became a regular boarder. Knowing of Harold's passion for the stage, he would offer him a part with the Burwood Company whenever a boy's role came up.

Harold threw himself wholeheartedly into the study of theatrical make-up, quizzing the character actors he met backstage. They taught him about moustaches and beards and how to disguise his real eyebrows with putty, and they even explained how to make 'a dead or grotesque eye' by 'setting half a walnut shell over my own eye, building it into the socket with putty and glue, concealed by flesh paint, then painting the walnut shell to the desired effect'.[27]

Once Harold's voice began to break, his acting career came to a standstill. He was too old for child parts but not yet old enough to play the juvenile leads.

In 1911 his father Foxy was run down by a brewery truck and severely injured. When the case went to court Foxy won $3,000, and another move was contemplated: 'New York tempted me, for it meant Broadway; but Connor had moved to San Diego, where he was playing in stock and running a dramatic school.'[28]

In San Diego Harold spent most of his time at Connor's dramatic school where he 'played characters in four local stock companies and was assistant stage manager of one; gave Shakespearean readings before high-school English and elocution classes; worked as stage hand at the Spreckels, the road-show theatre. Many, if not most, of these activities were concurrent.'[29]

When a fellow player's nose began to bleed during a collegiate farce, *Going Some*, Harold reckoned his great opportunity had come:

> He walked off the stage, leaving me to conduct a monologue, and I got away with it. I had come back with great relish and yearning to the stage after four years and, where I had been a humble apprentice among professionals, I was now the fair-haired boy among amateurs.[30]

The next morning Harold expected to be lauded and applauded. Instead, Connor merely said hello. Determined to draw some adulation out of him, Harold suggested, 'Not so bad last night, was I?' Connor reluctantly replied:

> Harold, I was very much disappointed in you. After all, you're not an amateur in his first play – not that I would have known it at times last night ... How many times have I told you to get the full value out of a laugh? Of course you got the laughs. The laughs were in the lines and the situations. Half the time, though, you choked them to death before they were well started.[31]

In truth, Harold, at this stage in his career, had no flair for comedy.

Another star-to-be with a decidedly non-theatrical background but an early fascination with cinema was Oliver Hardy, who was born on 18 January 1892 to Oliver and Emily Hardy in the town of Harlem, Georgia. He was originally named Norvell Hardy, Norvell being Emily's maiden name. His father, Oliver, was a veteran of the American Civil War, who, by the 1870s, had risen to the height of Tax Collector for Columbia County.

Oliver was a popular politician but by the late 1880s had been voted out of office around the time that his second wife, Cornelia, died. On 12 March 1890 he married Emily Norvell Tant, herself recently bereaved and with four small children. Not long before Norvell's birth, Oliver sold the family farm and became a hotelier in Madison, about 80 miles west of Atlanta. Emily went back to Atlanta for the birth, returning a few days later. Then fate struck a bitter blow. On 22 November 1892 Oliver Hardy suddenly dropped dead, and Emily became a widow for the second time, but now with five children. Unfortunately, Oliver hadn't left a will, and Emily's desire to continue running the hotel was rebuffed, so she set out in business on her own, opening her own hotel on West Jefferson Street, which she ran for the next four years.

Below **Unmistakably Oliver Hardy as a baby.**

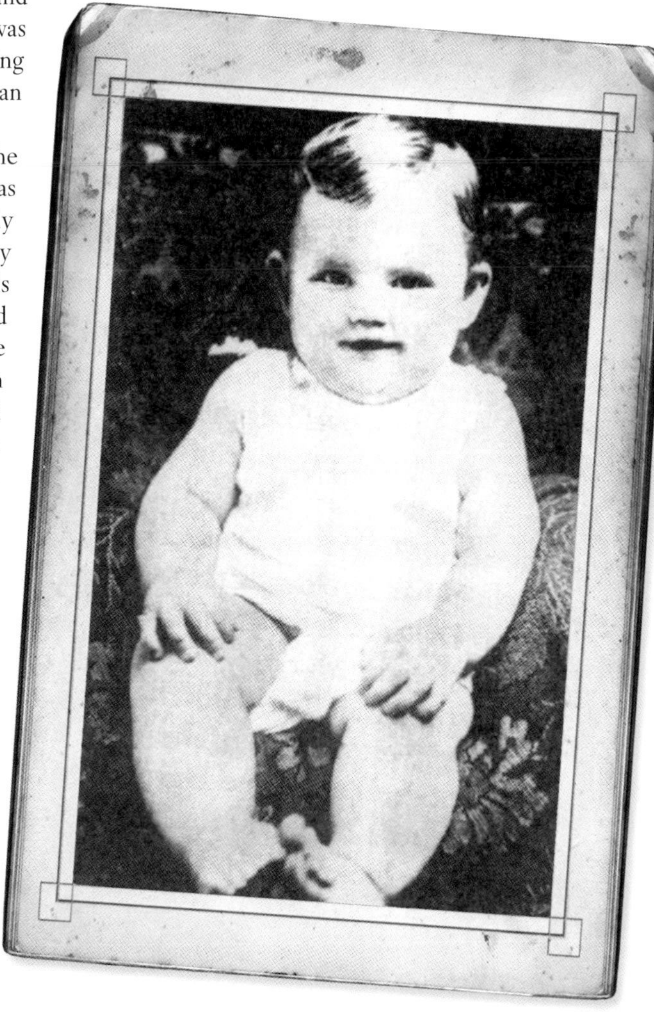

In late 1894 Emily bought a piano and, from the outset, Norvell, who had a beautiful singing voice, was fascinated by it. While the other children in the family were off creating mischief, Norvell, a rather chubby youngster, was more of a loner. As he grew into his teens Norvell adopted his father's name, Oliver, and became Oliver Norvell Hardy. Emily moved the family to Milledgeville, where she ran the Baldwin Hotel. Oliver, as we now must call him, was teased relentlessly over his size, and classmates called him 'Fatty'. Mid-teens is a vulnerable age, and in an attempt to get her son the best education possible Emily enrolled him in Georgia Military College. He weighed over 200 pounds at this point and must have dreaded the obstacle courses. He pleaded with his mother to be transferred somewhere else, and he ended up attending an institution called a 'progressive mountain school'.

In late 1909 or early 1910 the first cinema in Milledgeville was opened. It was called the Electric Theater, and Oliver became its projectionist and also helped in its general running. He stayed for three years. No doubt he would have particularly identified with one of the great stars of the time – Fatty Arbuckle. Here was somebody much admired and with the same label as himself, 'Fatty'. A big man on a big screen.

Back in Edwardian London, Charlie had found work playing Billy, the page boy, in a stage version of *Sherlock Holmes*. After Charlie's father died, Hannah Chaplin was readmitted to Cane Hill Asylum, where she remained for several years. The doctor's diagnosis included malnutrition, brought on by undernourishment. Charlie continued with *Sherlock Holmes* until 1906, and in that same year his half-brother Sydney was signed up by Fred Karno, the biggest comedy impresario of the British music hall.

Karno was a hugely influential figure. He had started out as an acrobat but developed into a fine comedian and writer of comedy sketches. He was also a very good businessman and had built up a number of successful touring companies, all bearing his name. At the time, 'Fred Karno' was a term widely used to describe something chaotic, but onstage chaos often needs a lot of practice, and Karno insisted on rigorous rehearsals and attention to detail. He also liked to mix pathos with the comedy, telling his comedians to 'keep it wistful … we want sympathy with the laughter.' Sydney Chaplin did well with Karno and recommended his younger brother, Charlie, at every opportunity. Eventually, Fred agreed to meet Charlie, who was then seventeen years old. Karno needed to replace a comedian working with Harry Weldon in a sketch called *The Football Match*, but he was worried that Charlie was very young and looked even younger. Charlie recalls: 'I shrugged off-handedly. "That's a question of make-up." Karno laughed. That shrug, he told Sydney later, got me the job.'[32] This was a big opportunity. Initially, it was a trial engagement for a fortnight but with the possibility of a year's contract. Charlie had recently suffered the humiliation of being booed offstage and having coins and orange peel thrown at him during the first night of a proposed trial week at the Forester's Music Hall. Situated just off the Mile End Road, the Forester's was in a predominantly Jewish part of London, and the audience hated Charlie's awful jokes (gleaned from an American joke book), which, to them, seemed anti-Semitic. His reception had knocked his self-confidence as a performer. A comedian thrives on laughter, and maintaining a level of confidence is essential, even in the middle of a bad show. Once a rough audience smells blood, it can destroy a performer: some people walk off the stage and never come back.

Opposite Fred Karno, the best-known comedy impresario of the British music hall, who gave the young Charlie Chaplin his first big break.

Charlie had a week to study his role in *The Football Match*. The man he was replacing had been uninspiring in the part, and traditionally there were no laughs until Harry Weldon, the main comedian, made his entrance. Charlie, as the first onstage, was determined to change that:

> On the opening night at the Coliseum my nerves were wound tight like a clock. That night meant re-establishing my confidence and wiping out the disgrace of that nightmare at the Forester's … In an emotional chaos I went on. One either rises to an occasion or succumbs to it. The moment I walked on to the stage I was relieved, everything was clear. I entered with my back to the audience – an idea of my own. From the back I looked immaculate, dressed in a frock-coat, top hat, cane and spats – a typical Edwardian villain. Then I turned, showing my red nose. There was a laugh … I was relaxed and full of

At the time, 'Fred Karno' was a term widely used to describe something chaotic, but onstage chaos often needs a lot of practice, and Karno insisted on rigorous rehearsals and attention to detail

> invention ... In the midst of my villainous strutting my trousers began to fall down. I had lost a button. I began looking for it. I picked up an imaginary something, then indignantly threw it aside; 'Those confounded rabbits!' Another laugh.[33]

That night, Charlie walked home flushed with joy. He stood on Westminster Bridge and gazed into the dark currents of the Thames, then walked all the way home to Kennington, stopping off for a cup of tea at the Elephant and Castle.

In 1982 I played at the Comedy Store, then situated in the heart of Soho. On my second time there, I performed a sketch about a policeman giving evidence in a courtroom and revealing, through his testimony, the details of a hallucinogenic trip he's unwittingly undergone. The Comedy Store was a tough audience, but that night I triumphed. I remember a particularly big laugh on the line, 'I observed Constable Parish approaching me disguised as a fortnight's holiday in Benidorm.' I stormed it. People were shrieking for more, but I didn't have any more, so I did the policeman sketch again. On my way home I stood on Westminster Bridge and looked into the Thames. I was twenty-four years old, and my boyhood dream of becoming a comedian had rapidly and unexpectedly come true. I'd endeavoured to make each line a joke or a set-up for a joke. Even though it was very early days for me as a performer, the strength of the material got me through. I remember that night so clearly: it was proof that I could make an audience laugh. I had no idea that Charlie Chaplin had looked into the river from the same bridge seventy-odd years earlier, feeling at last he was on his way. That night I felt the same. I walked home from Soho to my bedsit in Streatham, floating above the pavement.

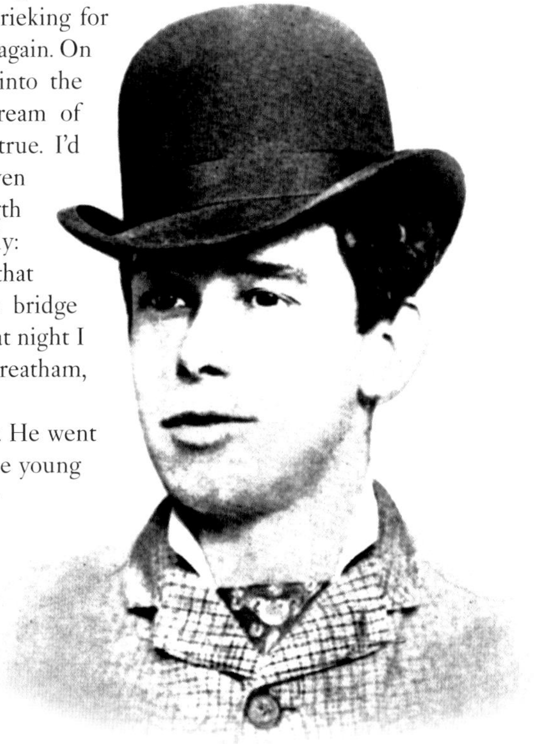

Fred Karno caught Charlie's performance two nights later. He went back to the dressing room after the show and congratulated the young man, offering him a year's contract at £4 a week, a healthy salary for a relative newcomer. For the next six months Charlie did bits and pieces in various Karno sketches, many of which proved the basis for several of his early films. *Skating*, a sketch written by Sydney, inspired *The Rink* (1916), and another sketch, *The Dentist*, became an early Keystone called *Laughing Gas* (1914).

Charlie also appeared in *Mumming Birds*, one of Karno's

A parade of acts were then heckled in various comic ways. A female vocalist was showered with cracker crumbs spat out by Charlie, who would then throw oranges at her

greatest creations. It took the form of a show-within-a-show: a steady succession of deliberately bad acts would be heckled by a drunk from one of the private boxes, situated on the stage. Charlie would enter the box in immaculate evening dress and, in a drunken haze, attempt to light his cigarette from a lightbulb. A young boy would offer a match, but, in reaching for it, Charlie would tumble out of the box and onto the stage. This would have got a big roar from contemporary audiences. It's important that the drunk is well dressed – he has his status and dignity to lose, whereas a drunk in workman's clothes is not such an obvious figure of fun in this situation. The sketch also places the protagonist inside a private box, which would have cost many times the weekly wage of the working man or woman.

A parade of acts were then heckled in various comic ways. A female vocalist was showered with cracker crumbs spat out by Charlie, who would then throw oranges at her. Next was an awful magic act, followed by a singer of patriotic songs. The final act was a thin, wasted individual called the Terrible Turk, and the management would offer the hefty sum of £100 to anyone who was willing to take him on. Amid a sea of hands going up, the 'plant' in the audience would be summoned onto the stage. Instead of fighting the Turk, the newcomer found himself fending off Charlie, who, by now, had stripped down to some brightly coloured underwear. Charlie then turned his attention to the Terrible Turk and tickled him into submission. No wonder this sketch was so popular: because the live theatre audience is encouraged to boo the deliberately awful acts, a raucous atmosphere can be generated that is no threat to the sketch itself. It's a great showcase for the lead comedian, too. Charlie's comic energy, invention and superb acrobatic control marked him out as a star.

Another comic had also recently joined the Karno Company. He was Arthur Stanley Jefferson, who was born on 16 June 1890 in Ulverston in northwest England. Nobody ever called him Arthur. His mother Margaret, known as Madge, was an actress who had met her husband Arthur Jefferson when he was the actor-manager of a small theatre in Ulverston called the Hippodrome. Arthur Senior, known as A.J., was a man of great enthusiasms, and he divided his work between writing long dramatic plays and managing theatres. Madge made a big contribution to the business by acting in his dramas, helping to run the theatres and providing excellent advice on designs and decor, and together they renovated and reopened theatres in the area. In August 1892 the *Consett Guardian* reported A.J.'s opening-night speech:

Left **The six-year-old Stan Jefferson – destined never to achieve stardom with this name.**

> Previous to the raising of the curtain, Mr Jefferson stepped to front and in a few brief words explained to the audience his intentions for the ensuing season, and having made up his mind that the comfort of his friends and patrons should be secured he had determined that on no account whatever would he permit smoking in the theatre.

A.J. cared for the welfare of his audience in other ways, too, arranging matinées for the poor and handing out gifts of packets of sugar, tea and tobacco.

He also toured his own plays in Bury and North Shields. They were typical Victorian melodramas, which were usually dependent on young men gambling away family fortunes and virtuous women fighting off the attentions of leering landlords.

Stan had not been particularly well as a child, and this prompted his parents to leave him with Madge's parents rather than subject him to life on the road. Many years later A.J. recalled:

> As Stan grew older, it became increasingly apparent that his young mind was obsessed with the idea of one day 'following in father's footsteps'; spending all his pocket money on toy theatres, Punch and Judy shows, marionettes, shadowgraphs, magic lanterns etc. ... When about nine years of age, Stan begged me to convert the attic of our home in North Shields ... into a miniature theatre, to which I agreed.[34]

A.J. was as good as his word. He built 'a perfect replica of the average small theatre of the period. Stan, assisted by several "dying to act" boys and girls, was hard at work inaugurating the "Stanley Jefferson Amateur Dramatic Society" – featuring said S.J. as Director, Manager, Stage Manager, Author, Producer, and Leading Man.'[35]

In 1905 the Jeffersons moved to Glasgow to enable A.J. to pay more attention to the Metropole Theatre, the mainstay of his empire, while he left his many other theatres in the hands of local managers. The following year, at the age of sixteen, Stan made his stage debut at Glasgow's Britannia Theatre. He didn't tell his dad, but A.J. found out anyway when he popped into the Britannia to chat with the manager only to be told that his son was due onstage in five minutes. According to A.J.'s later account, Stan came onstage

> wearing a pair of baggy patched trousers (new trousers of mine, cut down, patches added) and also my best frock coat and silk hat ... He got a very good reception and scored a genuine success, finishing up to loud laughter and applause and even shouts of 'encore!' The shouts brought him back ... but, in bowing his acknowledgements he spotted me.[36]

Stan rushed back to the Metropole Theatre but his father was already there waiting for him. As Stan himself recounted:

> He called me into his office where, for what seemed like several minutes, neither of us spoke ... Slowly, he rose to his feet. 'Have a whisky and soda?' he asked quite casually. At first I could not believe my ears. But when it dawned on me, I seemed to grow six inches in as many seconds. My boyhood was behind me – Dad was accepting me as a man! Then I did the silliest thing – I burst out crying.[37]

A.J. used his professional contacts to find Stan a job with Levy and Cardwell, a company that produced Christmas pantomimes, and he toured for six months

'Briefly I explained that I wanted a job as a comedian. "Are you funny?" he asked. I told him of my youthful experience. He nodded. "Very well," he said, "I'll try you out at £2 a week"' – Stan Jefferson

in *Sleeping Beauty*. In the summer of 1908 Stan was touring again, but this time with some of his father's comic sketches, A.J. having abandoned writing long melodramas in recent years and turning his hand instead to creating short sketches.

In December of that year Stan's mother Madge died. In her obituary the Glasgow publication *Victualling Trades' Review* reported: '[A.J.] attributes much of his early success to her artistic taste … as well as her business tact.'

In November 1909 Fred Karno was producing *Mother Goose* at the Grand Theatre, Glasgow. Stan went backstage one night and presented his business card:

> A gentle-voiced little man came forward to meet me. 'Well Mr Jefferson Junior,' he said, 'What can I do for you?' I told him I wanted to see Mr Karno. 'You're seeing him now,' he replied quietly. It was quite a shock and such a relief to find him such a pleasant, friendly man. Briefly I explained that I wanted a job as a comedian. 'Are you funny?' he asked. I told him of my youthful experience. He nodded. 'Very well,' he said, 'I'll try you out at £2 a week.' … Bewildered at the suddenness of it all, I blurted out my thanks and staggered into the street in a daze. I'd achieved the height of every budding comedian's ambition – I was one of Fred Karno's Comedians.[38]

Stan appeared in four sketches during the subsequent tour: *Mumming Birds*, *Skating*, *Jimmy the Fearless* and *The Wow-Wows*.

In *Jimmy the Fearless* Stan found himself playing the leading role. Karno had initially given the role to Chaplin, but a disagreement over how the part should be played led to Fred giving it to Stan instead. Karno was, no doubt, teaching Charlie a lesson by giving the role to the newest, most junior member of the troupe, and Stan made a real success of it, receiving five curtain calls and, more importantly, a great boost to his confidence. For a young comic this was an invaluable experience. Fred must have been delighted that his attempt to put Charlie in his place had worked so well. There were no bad feelings when Charlie replaced Stan in the star part, and Stan was destined never to see the name 'Stan Jefferson' in lights. He later remarked that he thought the origins of Charlie's tramp character were to be found in *Jimmy the Fearless*.

The following year both Charlie and Stan were picked by Fred to join a Karno troupe touring America. This was a step up and hugely exciting, for very few people travelled abroad in 1910. Charlie and Stan roomed together on the tour, and they often broke the lodging-house rules by cooking food in their rooms. Each room had a gas light, essential before the lightbulb became global,

'Chaplin sat at a small table and ate soda crackers, one after another ... A fine stream of cracker dust was coming out of his mouth. He kept that up for exactly fifteen minutes' – Groucho Marx

Below Fred Karno's troupe on board ship to the US for their first American tour. Charlie Chaplin is in the lifebelt; Stan Jefferson is on the extreme left. Standing top left is Albert Austin, who went on to appear in various Chaplin films, including *One A.M.* and *The Pawnshop.*

and Stan would cook chops over the gas flame while Charlie played his mandolin by the door, attempting to drown out the noise of cooking from inquisitive landladies. Stan's recollections of Charlie at this time are invaluable. He remembers him as 'the ringleader in everything. Even then we all felt there was something in him which was different from other men. We didn't know what it was; we couldn't put our finger on it; but it was there.'[39] The tour was very successful, lasting several months, and then, after a brief sojourn back in England, both Charlie and Stan embarked on another Karno tour of America.

Unexpectedly, Groucho Marx was a huge Charlie Chaplin fan. Normally never much of a devotee of other comedians, he could be characteristically withering, homing in on a rival's perceived weak spot. He was always scathing about Bob Hope's need to surround himself with dozens of writers, for example, and when he heard that Hope was doing a radio show with only four writers, Groucho remarked, 'Only *four*? For Bob Hope, that's practically ad libbing.' On Charlie's second tour of North America with Fred Karno in 1913, Groucho caught the show during one of its Canadian dates, the Sullivan–Considine Theater in Winnipeg. He'd gone in to see one of the other acts, but instead was overwhelmed by Charlie: 'Chaplin sat at a small table and ate soda crackers, one after another. A woman up front was singing all the while, but nobody heard a single note I'm sure. They were too intent on Chaplin's every move. A fine stream of cracker dust was coming out of his mouth. He kept that up for exactly fifteen minutes … I know there will never be anyone like him. He's in a class all by himself, just as he always has been.'[40]

It was on that same tour that Mack Sennett, head of Keystone studios, also saw Charlie onstage. Keystone was a highly successful film studio and the first in the world to dedicate itself exclusively to the production of comedies. Sennett, who was looking to replace one of his star comedians, offered Charlie double his Karno salary of $75 a week.

This represented a considerable sum of money (after all, the average US wage at the time was only $750 a year), but it wouldn't have been that surprising if Charlie had turned it down. Many on the vaudeville stage were highly suspicious of the movies, and Buster Keaton's father, Joe, had even once rejected an offer from the newspaper publisher William Randolph Hearst to make a two-reeler film with the words, 'We work for years perfecting an act, and you want to show it, a nickel a head, on a dirty sheet?'[41] As it was, Charlie decided to accept the offer, reckoning that a year or so making films would enable him to return to the stage as a headliner, a top-of-the-bill act.

Chapter 2
"First Steps in Hollywood"

PARAMOUNT-ARBUCKLE COMEDIES

JOSEPH M·SCHENCK
PRESENTS

Roscoe "FATTY" Arbuckle

IN

OUT WEST

PRODUCED BY
COMIQUE FILM CORPORATION
RELEASED EXCLUSIVELY THRU
PARAMOUNT PICTURES CORP.

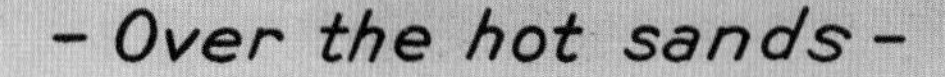

-Over the hot sands-

First Steps in Hollywood

The film industry that Charlie Chaplin joined in 1914 may have been in its infancy (filmmaking in California, for example, had started only four years earlier), but moving pictures were certainly nothing particularly new. Magic lanterns – early slide projectors capable of projecting an image onto a screen for a public audience – had been around since the seventeenth century. They used an elaborate system of levers and pulleys to create the illusion of movement, and the addition of a second, or even a third, lens to the original single-lens design meant that more complex effects, such as dissolves and editing, could be achieved. The magic lantern was quickly adapted to photographic use in the 1850s.

In 1893 Thomas Edison invented a peep show machine, known as a kinetoscope, which ran films on loops, which one person at a time could watch through an eye-piece. However, the first films to be projected onto a screen, in front of public audiences, were those of the Lumière brothers in Paris in 1895, and in the following year Edison projected films onto a screen at Koster and Bial's Music Hall, New York. Films were very basic and had no elaborate plots. Not much more than thirty seconds long, they typically featured scenes of actual events, such as people walking out of a factory or a train pulling into a station. The latter famously frightened the more sensitive audience members into believing they were about to be hit by a locomotive. Yes, that's right, a black and white, two-dimensional, silent train. Now we don't pause to think about the miracle of moving photographs that walk and talk, but when this technology was new some people were frightened.

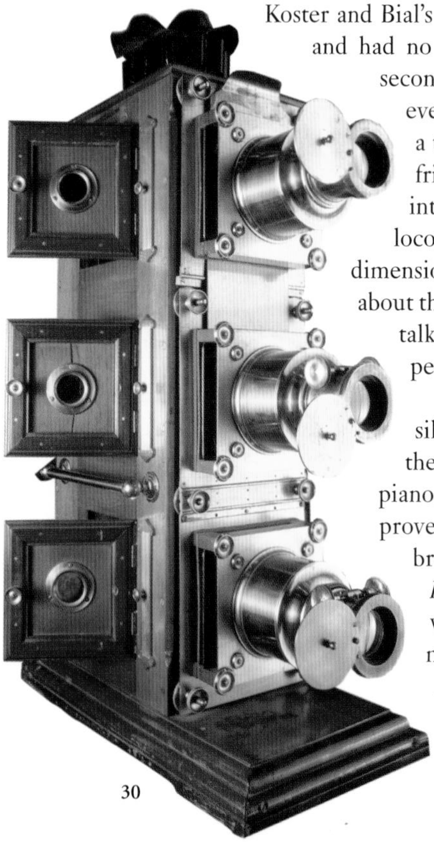

Films didn't talk yet, but although they were silent, they were never shown in silence. From the beginning musicians accompanied them with piano, drums, violin … whatever was handy. Comedy proved to be an early favourite. The Lumière brothers in France produced, among other films, *L'Arroseur arrosé* (*The Sprinkler Sprinkled*) (1895), which lasts for fifty-four seconds and shows a man watering a garden with a hose-pipe. Another man runs into the scene behind the luckless gardener and steps onto the hose,

Above A magic lantern show, forerunner of the cinema. This particular one was given in 1889 for 1,450 poor children at the Fulham Liberal Club in London.

Left A state-of-the-art three-lens magic lantern. Sophisticated magic lanterns could give the illusion of movement and achieve a range of special effects.

Above The Frenchman Max Linder, the most popular of early film comedy actors, in the guise of a rich, drunk toff. Some of his drunken mannerisms were later used by Charlie Chaplin, particularly in the 1916 short *One A.M.*

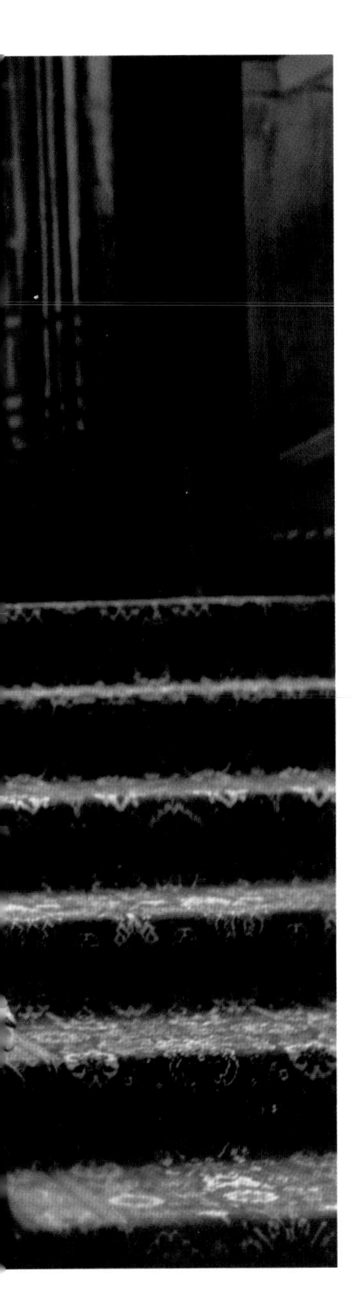

cutting off the supply of water. Gardener looks into hose-pipe, man steps off hose-pipe, gardener gets face full of water. Perhaps the first filmed slapstick gag. My favourite Lumière film from this period (1895–7) is the twenty-three-second long, accurately titled, *Demolition of a Wall.* Three men demolish a wall.

Much innovative work was also produced in Britain early in the twentieth century. One film that I've seen recently with an audience is *Blood and Bosh*, produced by Cecil Hepworth in 1909. It's a deliciously wicked parody of the worst excesses of melodrama and it got many big laughs. In France the trick films of Georges Méliès were immensely popular. Méliès, a former stage magician, was among the first to utilize the movie camera's ability to make objects materialize, disappear or turn into something else by means of stop-motion (stopping the camera, adding/removing the object to/from the shot, then starting the camera again). His novelty films were extremely popular for their outlandish special effects, such as the double exposure in *The Man with the Rubber Head* (1902), where we see Georges' disembodied head inflated by bellows operated by Georges in the guise of a scientist.

By 1908–9 film comedy had progressed from its very simple early days, but not by a great deal. Max Linder, a French stage actor, was the most popular comedian of this period. His real name was Gabriel-Maximilien Leuvielle, but he changed his name when he made his first film in 1905. This was partly because the theatrical profession looked down on the movies – as I've already mentioned, Buster Keaton's father actually turned down an opportunity to make films – and a pseudonym meant that few people need know of your involvement. These early comedies are simple affairs, often revolving around a single situation or attitude. The camera moves very little, and we are mainly watching filmed stage performances. In *Max's Hat* (1913), for example, he has trouble keeping his new hat from being damaged. Three hats are wrecked before a fourth one is bought. He visits a friend's house, places his hat on the floor and doesn't notice when a small dog pisses into it. He picks up the hat and resists as each family member tries to take it off him. The father succeeds and tries on the hat. He is soaked in what appears to be three or four pints of liquid.

These films were often no more than seven or eight minutes long and so were quick to produce. Max's character is that of a boulevardier, a 'man about town', and his usual costume is a silk hat and cutaway coat. Onscreen he has an engaging personality and a big, winning smile. He has charisma and often stands out from the other actors. However, he needs all these qualities because he doesn't have dialogue – the art of spoken comedy is denied him. In one sense, this is a severe restriction, but in another it's breathtakingly liberating. No language means no language barrier. Simply change the title-cards and a comedy film can be shown to anybody, anywhere. Max Linder's films, distributed by Pathé (the pioneering French production company with an extensive distribution network), made him known all over the world: everybody understood the joke about the dog pissing in the rich man's hat. He wasn't afraid to borrow from others, too. Fred Karno was furious when, in 1907, he saw Linder's *At the Music Hall*, which stole his own music hall sketch, *Mumming Birds*, and put it on the screen. He attempted legal action but got nowhere.

Opposite A purpose-built cinema from the early 1920s. This one is showing Buster Keaton's *Sherlock Junior*. Note the musicians seated in front of the screen.

Harold Lloyd has left us a graphic account of what it was like to see these early films, recalling in his autobiography his first encounter, at the age of ten, with cinema:

> A medicine show came to Pawnee City. Medicine shows – and there are as many today as ever – were like church socials in that it cost nothing to get in but something to get out. The entertainment ranged from a blackface banjoist on a high pitch on the street to a full-length dramatic stock company performing under a big tent where the doctor sold his herb tonic and snake-oil liniment between acts. This was about 1902 and the moving picture yet was a novelty. In many of the smaller towns one never had been seen, and it was a stroke of showmanship on the part of the med doctor to buy a worn copy of this early film. Draping a sheet from the second-story windows of a building across the street from his pitch, he would project the film on the sheet, attract his push, as a pitch man attracts his crowd, then depend on his native eloquence to do the rest.[1]

He also records visits to nickelodeons – small and inexpensive neighbourhood cinemas:

Below A nickelodeon in Pittsburgh, photographed *c.*1905. The young Harold Lloyd was one of many to become a devotee of this relatively cheap way of seeing early films.

> In Denver later, and still later in Omaha, much of my money went to nickelodeons ... If I had a quarter I went to five shows in an afternoon. Most of the films were French, comedy chases made by Pathé, a house that was to distribute my pictures long afterward. The recipe was a misunderstanding which would set the gendarmes in pursuit of the comedian over and through as many obstacles as the director could think of. Frequently the films were reversed after the first showing, defying the laws of gravitation. If it was comic to see a posse of French cops chase the funny man over a high wall, it was much funnier to see them fall up instead of down.[2]

The comedian he mentions is probably Max Linder.

Soon purpose-built cinemas of the sort that Oliver Hardy worked in were becoming very much part of people's lives as well. In January 1909 the *New York Times* reported that an estimated 45 million people went to the pictures every week – it was the beginning of film as entertainment for a mass audience. The medium was moving away from being just a popular novelty and was becoming an art form. In 1910 a film show would typically consist of several one-reelers, each lasting ten to fifteen minutes. Westerns were immensely popular, as were comedies, but there was also room for straight drama and educational subjects. Audiences were vocal and were encouraged to sing along to popular tunes as the lyrics were projected onto the screen. Entrance fees were five or ten cents, as opposed to fifty cents for a top vaudeville show.

Supporting acts

Alongside the silent comedy greats were a number of other actors who appeared in film after film and who often themselves acquired a loyal following.

Of these, Ben Turpin has to be one of the most distinctive. He appeared on the vaudeville stage before making his film debut at the newly opened Essanay studios in 1907. *Mr Flip*, a comedy from 1909, still survives and Ben is very funny as a rather dim young man attempting to flirt with women who keep hitting him. He then joined Mack Sennett in 1917. Ben was an extraordinary actor whose permanently crossed eyes were basically his one and only joke. He would often appear as a heroic figure with the eyes comically undermining his courageous stance. His last appearance was in the Laurel and Hardy film *Saps at Sea* in 1940.

Mack Sennett attracted quite a troupe of actors at his studios, but it is sometimes forgotten that he himself appeared in films. He had initially worked as a boiler maker and done some chorus work in Broadway shows. In 1908 he drifted into movies, working at the Biograph studios under D.W. Griffith. It has to be said that he was an appallingly bad actor and was only ever given one lead role – in a 1909 film called *The Curtain Pole*, a picture loosely based on Max Linder's Pathé comedies.

For a number of years, Mack conducted an affair with Mabel Normand, an actress who appeared in a number of Keystone productions,

Below **Mabel Normand and Mack Sennett.**

Below right **Mabel Normand as a maiden in distress and Ford Sterling as the mallet-wielding villain in *Barney Oldfield's Race for a Life*, released in 1913.**

and who also directed Charlie Chaplin in some of his early films. At one time, she was a major figure in Hollywood, co-starring with Charlie and Marie Dressler in *Tillie's Punctured Romance*, for example. However, after her relationship with Mack broke up, she took to drink and drugs, and in 1922 became entangled in the scandal surrounding the murder of her close friend William Desmond Taylor. Although she managed to keep working, her health broke down and she died of tuberculosis in 1930.

Another actor to make frequent film appearances was Ford Sterling, whose early experiences as a performer included working in a circus as 'Keno the Boy Clown'. He also appeared on the Broadway stage and in vaudeville. He was appearing in Biograph films when Mack Sennett – also working for the company – left and set up Keystone in 1912. Ford Sterling joined him and became one of the principal comedians. His over-the-top manic comic acting may well have been an acquired taste even in 1912; it certainly didn't impress Charlie Chaplin.

Above left The cross-eyed Ben Turpin.

Above Ford Sterling and Minta Durfee (Roscoe Arbuckle's wife) in a scene from *Dirty Work in a Laundry.*

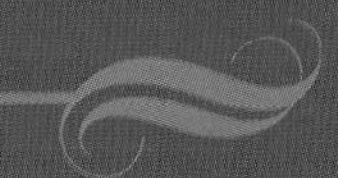

Below Mack Sennett, who set up the Keystone film studio in 1912, in a photograph taken some years later. An indifferent director and an even worse actor, he could at least spot talent in others – including Roscoe Arbuckle and Charlie Chaplin.

When it came to producing comedy films, Charlie's new employer Keystone may have been the first to devote itself exclusively to light-hearted films but it certainly wasn't the first to make them. As early as 1907 the unforgettably cross-eyed Ben Turpin was appearing in comedies for the Essanay Company in Chicago, and two titles, *Mr Flip* (1909) and *A Case of Seltzer* (1909), still exist. Production standards were pretty rudimentary, and it was thought ridiculous not to show the actors full-figure in the belief that audiences would laugh if they saw people cut off at the knees or even find it ghoulish. The camera very rarely moved, and the actors would simply enter or exit either from one side of the frame or the other.

One man who helped to change this rather rigid approach to cinema was D.W. Griffith. Originally a stage actor, Griffith appeared in a few films for the Biograph Company before finding his true vocation as a director. Between 1909 and 1913, he made a series of films for Biograph that further developed the expanding language of cinema. He didn't invent the close-up or crosscutting between two scenes, but he used them fluently to tell stories more effectively and, in 1915, directed the first-ever American feature film, *The Birth of a Nation*, about the American Civil War. In a period of just six years American cinema progressed from nine-minute films to a three-hour epic. Sadly, appalling racism against African-Americans mars this extraordinary work – any film that makes the Ku Klux Klan the heroes can't be all good – but it nevertheless showed a remarkable facility for storytelling and manipulating the emotions of the audience. Film was moving people in a way that only the theatre had previously done.

Mack Sennett, who had worked under Griffith at Biograph, set up his own company, Keystone, in July 1912 and encouraged Mabel Normand, a Biograph actress, to join him. He also poached Fred Mace and Ford Sterling from Biograph, and they were soon joined by Roscoe Arbuckle. Born in Kansas in 1887, Arbuckle was an experienced vaudevillian who had made his first film as early as 1909. At a time when obesity in the general population was not common, Roscoe was a huge man, and his professional name was 'Fatty' Arbuckle, even though he hated being called 'Fatty'.

Although Sennett admitted that 'it was those Frenchmen who invented slapstick and I imitated them … I stole my first ideas from the Pathés,'[3] there was very much a house style at Keystone. It was haphazard, relied heavily on improvisation and didn't always work! *A Muddy Romance*, made in November 1913, illustrates the problem perfectly. Mack Sennett heard that the lake in Echo Park was about to be drained, so he sent over a cameraman, camera, actors and costumes, and ordered them to shoot what they could, saying they would work out the story later. So they put some comedy policemen in one boat and Mabel Normand and a couple of actors in another, and we see them out on the water. Then Ford Sterling turns up. In 1913 Ford was one of Mack Sennett's principal comedians, and his usual comic appearance was that

In a period of just six years American cinema progressed from nine-minute films to a three-hour epic ... Film was moving people in a way that only the theatre had previously done

Above A scene from D.W. Griffith's *The Birth of a Nation* (1915), the first American feature film and the first to explore the real potential of cinema. It was probably the highest grossing film of the silent era, though its overt racism makes for uncomfortable viewing today.

of a German or Dutch character with top hat, frock coat and a small goatee beard. His comedy acting looks awfully over-the-top these days, and here he bites noses, pulls legs, throws bricks and jumps up and down on the spot.

In Ford Sterling's defence it must be acknowledged that he was being directed by Mack Sennett. Although hugely influential, Sennett was not a gifted comedy director, and he was an even worse comedy actor – his acting could be called rudimentary or non-existent. He usually plays a 'rube' (country bumpkin), and his immobile, wooden features are matched by his heavy, sullen movements. He is, by a country mile, the worst actor at Keystone and possibly anywhere in movies at that time before or since. Sometimes, he forgets to 'act' altogether and just stands there and spits. His 'comic' performances redefine the word useless. But it's his studio, so who's going to tell him?

Although Sennett admitted that 'it was those Frenchmen who invented slapstick and I imitated them …', there was very much a house style at Keystone. It was haphazard, relied heavily on improvisation and didn't always work!

In the finale to *A Muddy Romance* the water is drained from the lake, leaving a thick, muddy landscape. We see the policemen in their boat on the muddy lake bed. Then we see a couple in the other boat topple out of it for no apparent reason and succeed in getting very muddy, very quickly. This action is repeated: we see all the policemen back in the rowing boat and then see them all fall out again. Mabel and the two other actors are shown standing in their rowing boat when Mabel, who is wearing a beautiful white dress, inexplicably jumps out into the mud. This is crazy, unmotivated mayhem. This weak finale demonstrates the danger of filming sequences without a clear comic thought. It's all very well to rush off to Echo Park and film rowing boats in mud, but

where are the gags? None of the business with boats has much comic value, but producing a comedy every two or three days meant that, sometimes, bad decisions were made in a hurry.

Charlie Chaplin's first film at Keystone, *Making a Living*, was shot in three days and was released on 2 February 1914. It was directed by Henry 'Pathé' Lehrman, an Austrian who acquired his nickname after falsely telling D.W. Griffith that he had worked with the prestigious Pathé company in France. Mack Sennett had met him at Griffith's Biograph studio, and when he set up Keystone in 1912 he took Lehrman with him, putting him in charge of the second film unit, where it was his job to direct the screen newcomers. He'd directed Roscoe Arbuckle, and now it was Charlie's turn. Lehrman was not the most popular man with actors: he had a reputation for endangering their safety and having a tough, autocratic manner. Charlie appears in a similar costume to the one he was wearing in the Karno sketch, *The Football Match*: top hat, frock coat and cane. He is lively enough in this, his first film and moves well, but although he's got good comedy energy, at times his inexperience in front of the camera is obvious. He pulls faces but drops them so quickly that there is not enough time for them to register properly.

His next film, *Kid Auto Races at Venice*, released on 7 February 1914, is only a few minutes long. It's firmly in the Keystone tradition: go to a real public event that's got lots of movement and mix your actors in with it. *Kid Auto Races* features children in wooden carts rolling down a big wooden incline. Lehrman is filming the day's events with a newsreel cameraman, and Charlie consistently walks into the shot, prompting the director to encourage him forcefully to get out of the way. For the first time Charlie is wearing the Tramp costume in public. Mack Sennett had told him to find a funny outfit, so he borrowed a pair of Arbuckle's trousers and a small bowler hat from actress Minta Durfee's father. Remembering that Sennett had been surprised by his youth, he added a tiny black moustache for maturity, and a springy bamboo cane completed the look. To British audiences, the bowler hat and cane suggested middle-class origins, and this was a comic contradiction that Charlie enjoyed playing with when he created the costume.

Opposite **A fairly typical over-the-top moment from a Keystone Cops film. The actor on the extreme right is Roscoe Arbuckle. Fourth from right is Al St John.**

As well as seeing the birth of Charlie's Tramp character, admittedly in sketch form, *Kid Auto Races* is also notable for recording the antagonistic relationship between Lehrman and Charlie. Lehrman gets quite violent with Charlie, on one occasion grabbing him by the throat and pushing him forcefully down to the ground, right out of the frame. It's too quick for Charlie to turn it into a comic fall, and he gets up, clearly angry. He moves to confront Lehrman but thinks better of it, instead pulling a face at the director, but it's not comic, it's furious. Lehrman doesn't like this Englishman and lets him know it. Right at the very end of the film, Lehrman kicks Charlie in the back, once again knocking him over with some power. The hostility between these two leaps off the screen.

Charlie's third film, *Mabel's Strange Predicament*, released just two days later on 9 February 1914, confirms the breakthrough in costume. The film was initially directed by Lehrman, but Mack Sennett himself took over, presumably

Above The birth of the Tramp. Charlie Chaplin in his second film, *Kid Auto Races at Venice.*

due to more trouble between Henry and Charlie. The film opens in a hotel lobby, where Charlie, in his Tramp costume, is very drunk. Sennett had originally seen Charlie playing a drunk onstage, so this was familiar territory. As Charlie wanders about the lobby, the camera confidently remains on him. There are no cut-aways or attempts to speed up the action. He admires a pretty woman and flirts with her, waving his cane around. She walks off, giving him the cold shoulder, and his cane swings up and knocks off his hat. This is performed in a single take, in a beautiful, fluid manner. Charlie later recalled how actors from the other sets and assorted technicians gathered behind the camera and watched this, his first unhurried moments in a Keystone film. On the street car going home that evening an extra told Charlie that he'd never heard such laughter on the set before.

Later in the film Charlie gets pushed by another hotel guest, played by Harry McCoy, an old vaudevillian. Although, superficially, the push is in Lehrman's style (hand gripped around the throat), it is so gentle it's a mere butterfly's sneeze compared to Lehrman's aggressive shove in *Kid Auto Races*. McCoy pushes Charlie back into a chair, and we glimpse for a moment Charlie the real man and not the comedian. Not realizing he's still in shot after falling into the chair, Charlie stops acting drunk. He looks around, adjusts his bowler and looks, with some uncertainty, over at McCoy. Perhaps he's wondering if the fall was OK.

For the first time Charlie is wearing the Tramp costume in public. Mack Sennett had told him to find a funny outfit, so he borrowed a pair of Arbuckle's trousers and a small bowler hat from actress Minta Durfee's father

The Keystone studio made ample use of exterior locations. Parks were a regular favourite with their lush greenery, bridges and lakes, and Charlie's fourth film, *Between Showers*, released on 28 February 1914, was set in one. The film also features Ford Sterling, whose acting style was the dominant one at Keystone when Charlie arrived, and the two of them are directed by Charlie's tireless adversary, Lehrman. Ford jumps up and down manically on the spot, and even Charlie indulges in some over-the-top acting, no doubt following Lehrman's direction.

Charlie's fifth Keystone, *A Film Johnnie*, released on 2 March 1914, features him as a movie fan visiting the Keystone studio and getting in the way. Charlie's open-mouthed wanderings around the set illustrate how it must have been for him when he first arrived. The film parodies Keystone's methods of movie-making: a fire breaks out nearby, and the cast and crew are quick to rush over to film some scenes in front of the blaze. In the middle of the mayhem Charlie lights a cigarette by firing a gun at the end of it.

Charlie's next film, *Tango Tangles*, released a week later on 9 March, is directed by Mack Sennett and features the three biggest comics at the studio: Ford Sterling, Roscoe Arbuckle and Charlie himself. Unusually, all three are wearing their street clothes and avoid any comic make-up. Charlie looks about twelve years old, and we can readily understand Mack Sennett's shock at Charlie's youthful looks when he first met him out of make-up. *Tango Tangles* is set in a dance hall, and some of the footage is shot in a genuine dance hall, although no attempt is made to match it up with the material filmed back at the studio – the lack of continuity makes it quite confusing to watch. Charlie enters drunk, wearing a very smart suit with a black bow tie. He's carrying a smarter version of his usual bowler hat and cane, and I wonder if this is to identify him to the cinema audience because, without the toothbrush moustache or Arbuckle's trousers, he simply doesn't look like Charlie Chaplin. It's a real measure of how quickly he had become an audience favourite if the carrying of a hat and cane was considered enough to identify him.

Shortly into the film there is an unguarded moment that lends this Keystone a tantalizingly brief moment of documentary. Charlie enters the scene with his back to us and approaches Minta Durfee. (Minta, who was born in 1881, was married to Roscoe Arbuckle, and the two of them had been a double act in vaudeville.) Minta is playing the hat-check girl, and when Charlie says something to her she suppresses a giggle, then his drunken attempts to rest his hand on the table cause her to laugh out loud. It's very charming. Minta's warm appreciation of Charlie's antics gives us an insight into the spirit in which

Charlie pushes at a swing door, and it swings back and hits him hard in the face. He does this three more times, each with a variation and all in one continuous take

these films were made … that is, as long as Henry Lehrman wasn't directing.

Ford Sterling is the band leader, and it's no surprise to see him play the cornet in a completely over-the-top fashion. Roscoe Arbuckle is on clarinet, and his and Charlie's more realistic performances are increasingly making Ford Sterling's approach seem heavy-handed and dull. There is also a problem with Sterling's individual gags, which lack credibility in an otherwise realistic comedy landscape. At one point he stops playing to talk to Arbuckle and turns the cornet around in his hands so that when he next brings it to his lips he's surprised that it's the wrong way round. It looks silly, and you wonder why a band leader would make that mistake. Later, we see Charlie and Minta dancing together in the real dance hall, with genuine members of the public dancing away in the background. Most of them are looking straight into the camera and grinning.

Charlie's next film, *His Favourite Pastime*, released on 16 March 1914, finds him playing a drunk again. This time he's back in the tramp costume, and he's quite an unpleasant character. He kicks people violently with little hint of comedy. One masterful piece of slapstick does stand out, however. Charlie pushes at a swing door, and it swings back and hits him hard in the face. He does this three more times, each with a variation and all in one continuous take. It's difficult to get the timing right on this. He has to be hit by the door convincingly, four times in a row. No other comedian on the screen then could have done it so well. Later he creates more mayhem in the bar when he gets his foot stuck in a spittoon.

His eighth Keystone picture, *Cruel, Cruel Love*, was released on 26 March 1914. In his previous two films Charlie had been cast as a drunk, but in *Cruel, Cruel Love* he is a well-to-do gentleman who is heartbroken when his fiancée ends their engagement. A couple of moments are untypical of the Keystones. After drinking a glass of poison, which is, in fact, water, Charlie has a vision of hell. The frame dissolves into an image of two demons with pitchforks, lifting him up by the neck with gusto. This film was directed by the veteran George 'Pop' Nichols, who had been in movies for ten years but who, according to Charlie, 'had but one gag, which was to take the comedian by the neck and bounce him from one scene to another.'[4] In his vision of hell Charlie is indeed bounced up and down by the neck on the demons' pitchforks, but the scene is startling chiefly because we are seeing a vision of Charlie's imagination. We go into the realm of the interior. I'm tempted to believe that the image may have been Charlie's idea, although the execution is certainly George Nichols'.

Shortly afterwards, there's a moment that, with hindsight, seems pure Chaplin. It begins with Charlie's face in close-up. He then staggers back melodramatically towards a window at the end of a corridor. He falls backwards so completely that his legs go over his head and hook onto the window ledge. He gets stuck in this position, but there's a cut-away before the joke is properly concluded. We should see Charlie stuck in this unflattering pose for at least a couple of seconds. His position must register with us. Nichols doesn't 'see' the gag and edits it out. Charlie found this infuriating and asked Mack Sennett to let him direct his own films. Sennett refused and put Charlie into a film that Mabel Normand was starring in and directing, *Mabel at the Wheel*, which was released on 18 April 1914.

Mabel Normand wouldn't listen to Charlie's suggestions either. As always, the excuse was that there was no time to film material that wasn't immediately obvious. Everything was about the chase. In *Mabel at the Wheel* Charlie wears the same costume he wore in his first film and is directed to impersonate Ford Sterling's style of acting. Sterling and Lehrman had recently left Keystone to work for Universal on a series called Sterling Comedies, the intention being to rival the Keystone output.

Even old Ford Sterling gags are recycled. Charlie whistles, and two henchmen immediately appear. It's a direct steal from Barney Oldfield's *Race for a Life*, which had been released on 3 June 1913. During filming, a huge argument broke out between Mabel and Charlie, who refused to follow her direction. Sennett got involved, but although he listened to Charlie's complaints he had to back Mabel, who was the director and star of the film. George Nichols also complained about Charlie being difficult to work with, and Lehrman wasn't a fan either. Perhaps Mack was thinking that this talented but stubborn Englishman might be more trouble than he was worth. Roscoe Arbuckle interceded on Charlie's behalf, telling Sennett that Charlie was too good to let go and reminding him of the great material that he was coming up with. Sennett wasn't sure, but he changed his mind when he got a telegram from the New York office requesting more of the Chaplin films. A compromise was quickly reached: if Charlie co-operated on *Mabel at the Wheel*, he would be given the chance to direct his own films. He happily agreed, and filming resumed in the same old slapdash Keystone way.

His first film as director is *Twenty Minutes of Love* (although it runs for only ten), which was released on 20 April 1914. It's the usual park comedy: a couple of benches, a beautiful woman and a policeman. Chaplin recalled making the film in a single afternoon, but it demonstrated to Mack Sennett his picture-making ability.

The next film, *Caught in a Cabaret*, was co-directed with Mabel Normand

***Twenty Minutes of Love* is the usual park comedy: a couple of benches, a beautiful woman and a policeman. Chaplin recalled making the film in a single afternoon, but it demonstrated to Mack Sennett his picture-making ability**

Watching the Keystone films from this distance in time, it's sometimes hard to see what exactly is meant to be so funny about them. Looking at people jumping up and down and running from room to room can be baffling

and harmony reigned. It was filmed from a Chaplin script, although 'script' might be too grand a word for the creative process involved. Charlie found making films at Keystone an exhilarating experience. In the theatre he was used to repeating the same act, night after night – once the act was set, there was no need to invent new comic business – but films demanded new business and different variations on familiar scenes. Someone would get an idea, a vague one at first, and then people would start to chip in with their own.

Sennett, although an exceedingly clumsy actor himself, was nevertheless an enthusiastic audience for comic ideas, laughing genuinely and often. This played a large part in creating a happy atmosphere on the Keystone lot, and Charlie gained belief in his own taste and transferred that confidence to others.

In Charlie's fifteenth Keystone, *The Fatal Mallet*, released on 1 June 1914, he co-stars with Mack, who was making one of his thankfully rare appearances onscreen. At one point, Charlie hits Mack over the head with a giant mallet, and Mack falls back onto the floor, unconscious. Charlie steps on Mack's stomach as he crosses the room and Mack visibly reacts. Charlie, grinning all over his face, then re-crosses the room and treads on Mack's upper thigh as he exits. He's clearly having great fun standing on the boss's principles.

Watching the Keystone films from this distance in time, it's sometimes hard to see what exactly is meant to be so funny about them. Looking at people jumping up and down and running from room to room can be baffling, particularly if you're viewing a poor print. These films were made quickly, without much preparation, and were designed purely to entertain the audiences of their day. They weren't expected to last more than a week.

In *The Rounders*, released on 7 September 1914, Charlie teams up with Roscoe Arbuckle. This was their only film as a double act, and they play posh drunks. ('Rounder' is an old term for scoundrel or rogue.) Charlie, who had made great strides in just a few months, revives the gag that George 'Pop' Nichols didn't get in *Cruel, Cruel Love* back in March. He is arguing with his wife in their bedroom when he drunkenly staggers backwards onto the bed and ends up with his legs hooked over the top of the bed rail. He holds this position for a couple of seconds. It makes the action very funny. Will he stay like this all night? He looks comfortable enough, and he's probably too drunk to move. It's one of the big laughs this picture still gets when you show it on a big screen to a live audience.

While watching a couple of Keystones in preparation for this book, I was struck by the absence of custard pies. Instead, many of the films featured a great deal of brick-throwing. In *Mabel at the Wheel*, for example, thirty-five or more bricks are thrown in the space of fifteen seconds. It becomes amusing

Above **Charlie and Roscoe Arbuckle play a couple of posh drunks in *The Rounders*.**

because it is so relentless. A brick is a more plausible object to throw because you can just pick it up from the side of the road, while a custard pie requires advance baking. The usual wisdom is that the Keystones aren't funny any more, but I disagree. I don't think the Keystones were ever particularly funny in the first place. They were made far too quickly, but even so every so often a moment works beautifully.

In Charlie's thirty-first film at Keystone, *His Musical Career*, released on 7 November 1914, there are a couple of genuinely funny moments that still get laughs today. Charlie applies for a job at a piano workshop. Mack Swain, the other piano-mover, employs him, and they have two jobs in Prospect Street: they must deliver a new piano to 666 Prospect Street and repossess a piano from number 999. Naturally, they mix the two jobs up. There are at least two laugh-out-loud sequences. First, having manoeuvred the bulky upright piano out of the shop and onto the pavement and having trapped Mack Swain underneath it, they eventually push it towards the road. At the side of the road we see a donkey attached to a very small cart. The juxtaposition of the cart and the piano is very funny, although Mack and Charlie do get the piano onto the cart remarkably easily. When they arrive at the address, there's some very funny business as they try to manipulate the piano up a flight of stairs. The Laurel and Hardy sound short, *The Music Box* (1932), in which they deliver a piano up a huge flight of steps, has similar business. I know this will be heresy to some, but *The Music Box* is very slow when watched with a cinema audience today. It has some funny moments, but it drags and the piano goes back down the steps far too many times.

The biggest laugh in *His Musical Career* occurs after Mack has entered the first house and beckons Charlie into the living room. Charlie enters from the right side of the frame, bent double. He is carrying the piano across his shoulders with the keyboard facing us. He's about to put the piano down when the owner says he would prefer it against the wall. Charlie struggles back with the piano, but the owner's daughter wants it in the middle of the room. Eventually, the piano is lifted off Charlie just as it threatens to crush him. But now he can't straighten up. Mack Swain tries to un-bend him by placing Charlie face down on the floor with his head and feet touching but his bum sticking up in the air. Mack pushes the bum down with his foot, and Charlie becomes horizontally flattened. He is lifted to his feet by Mack, and the two of them exit. The action lasts nearly two minutes and it's the funniest scene in all of Chaplin's Keystones.

On 14 November 1914 Mack Sennett released America's very first comedy feature film, *Tillie's Punctured Romance*, which was 72 minutes. Long films of any description were still something of a novelty in 1914, and Sennett was probably inspired by D.W. Griffith's massive production, *The Birth of a Nation.* When it was released in 1915, Griffith's film, some three hours long, was a massive hit, and the exhibitors made fortunes. Mack Sennett directed *Tillie's Punctured Romance*, and he hired the Broadway actress Marie Dressler because the picture was based on her great stage success, *Tillie's Nightmare.* The film co-starred every Keystone comic employed by the studio, except for Roscoe Arbuckle, whose bulk counted against him. A big woman herself, Marie Dressler wanted to be the only big star on the screen. Charlie Chaplin and Mabel Normand played substantial supporting roles. The film was an immense hit but was regarded as a one-off, and Charlie himself thought the film was without merit. It follows the usual Keystone style (lots of jumping up and down and over-the-top mugging), and it gives the impression of lasting forever, but contemporary audiences loved it. Buster Keaton went to see it four times.

Charlie's year-long contract with Keystone was coming to an end. He was the most successful comedian at the studio and was on his way to becoming an international celebrity. His weekly wage of $150 didn't seem appropriate to that level of fame, and Charlie demanded $1,000 a week. Mack Sennett protested that even he didn't make that much.

Although Sennett couldn't meet Chaplin's wage demands, an old, established film company called Essanay, which had been founded in 1907 by George K. Spoor and G.M. 'Broncho Billy' Anderson, did. As Chaplin recalls in his autobiography:

Charlie's year-long contract with Keystone was coming to an end. He was the most successful comedian at the studio and was on his way to becoming an international celebrity

> A young man named Jess Robbins, who represented the Essanay Company, said he heard that I wanted a ten-thousand-dollar bonus before signing a contract, and twelve hundred and fifty dollars a week. This was news to me. I had never thought of a ten-thousand-dollar bonus until he mentioned it, but from that happy moment it became a fixation in my mind.[5]

The deal was signed in November 1914, the same month that *Tillie* was released. Charlie had managed to get his money up to $1,250 a week, a considerable fortune in those days, but the move to Essanay also meant a move to Chicago where their studios were based, and Charlie was aghast at the penny-pinching measures he encountered. At Essanay they screened the rushes as negatives rather than go to the expense of developing the film, making it difficult to see exactly what had been captured on camera. Charlie hated the Chicago winter and only made one film there, *His New Job.*

> The studio personnel were stuffy and went around like bank clerks, carrying requisition papers as though they were members of the Guaranty Trust Company – the business end of it was very impressive, but not their films. In the upstairs office the different departments were partitioned like tellers' grilles. It was anything but conducive to creative work. At six o'clock, no matter whether a director was in the middle of a scene or not, the lights were turned off and everybody went home.[6]

While Charlie unhappily embarked on his next five films, shot at Essanay's Californian studio in Niles, Harold Lloyd was making his first film appearance as a comedian. The film, released on 17 April 1915, was called *Just Nuts*, and Harold played a character called Willie Work. How did he get there? In the winter of 1912–13 he happened to be living in San Diego when the Edison Film Company, normally based in New York, sent a small crew to California to take advantage of the weather there. They settled in Balboa, not far from San Diego. Requiring some extras one day, they called at the Connor School.

> I enlisted, made up as a three-fourths-naked Yaqui [a native American people] and served a tray of food to the white man's party in one fleeting scene. That was my debut in pictures. The three dollars pay, however, was more significant at the moment.[7]

While he was working at Universal, Harold met a fellow extra called Hal Roach, an ambitious man and a very bad actor. He had previously found employment in Westerns chiefly because he was able to stay on a horse

To further his career, Harold moved to Los Angeles. A much bigger city than San Diego, its theatres stayed open all year round (whereas in San Diego they closed in the summer), and Harold reckoned that if stage work proved difficult to come by, there were always a few picture companies knocking about.

In 1911 Universal had been the first to open a studio in Hollywood at Sunset Boulevard and Gower Street. That's where Harold headed, looking for work as an extra. Getting past the front gate was a major obstacle, but Harold hit on the perfect plan. He simply waited until the extras returned from lunch and then joined them wearing the same make-up as everyone else. This didn't get him any immediate work, because the extra jobs were always allocated in the morning, but he was able to persuade the other extras to let him in through the dressing-room window on future mornings. He soon learned that the assistant directors were the men who had the power of casting.

While he was working at Universal, Harold met a fellow extra called Hal

Roach, an ambitious man and a very bad actor. He had previously found employment in Westerns chiefly because he was able to stay on a horse. Roach for his part was impressed by Harold's knowledge of theatrical make-up, and on the Universal production of *Samson and Delilah* Harold helped Hal to make up a mob of hairy Philistines:

> He took the gum arabic, I the crêpe hair, and we trotted the hobos past us on a conveyor-belt system later adopted by Henry Ford. He slapped on the gum with one motion, I a hank of hair with another, and where the hair landed it remained. Our aim was poor, but good enough for mobs in 1913.[8]

Harold met up again with Hal Roach when the two of them were both employed on a film based on the Wizard of Oz stories. Hal astonished Harold by announcing that he'd inherited $3,000 and wanted to set up his own studio. Hal was to be the director, and Harold would be the lead comedian at $3 a day. Harold came up with a character, 'Willie Work' (the brutal answer is, 'No he didn't'), which was a poor copy of Charlie Chaplin's tramp. The sixth and final Willie Work film, *Just Nuts*, which was well received at Pathé, featured another actor, Roy Stewart, and the leading actress was Jane Novak, while Harold played the comic relief. Pathé wanted more films with this trio. Harold was incensed, however, when he discovered that Stewart was being paid $10 a day,

Opposite **Early Hollywood – a view across the first film studio to be built, Universal. At this time, Hollywood still had a strongly rural feel to it.**

Below **Harold Lloyd's first real break came when a fellow film extra, Hal Roach, announced his plan to set up his own studio with Harold as the lead comedian. Here they are in a photograph from around 1916. Lloyd, in his Lonesome Luke guise, is sitting in the second row, fourth from left, with Hal Roach immediately behind him and the actress Bebe Daniels immediately in front.**

Right The extraordinary cross-eyed Ben Turpin and Charlie Chaplin attempt to exchange glances in *His New Job*. Chaplin was no fan of Turpin's over-the-top performances.

which was double the amount he was getting. An argument with Hal Roach led to Harold going to work for Mack Sennett at Keystone.

In his few Keystone films Harold appears mainly in the background. In the 1915 *Miss Fatty's Seaside Lovers*, for instance, he can be seen playing a rather ordinary young man. Harold did not impress Mack Sennett, who was worried about the financial state of the studio and was thinking of ways of saving money:

> In this frame of mind I was watching a new picture one night when I spotted a skinny, pale-faced young man who I thought was doing everything wrong. 'That guy a school teacher or something? He hasn't got any notion how to be funny.' Upon being told that the actor in question was getting $50 a week: 'Fifty bucks! Jumping Jehosephat, we can get comedians for that kind of money. Fire that guy first thing tomorrow morning. Don't even let him on the lot.'[9]

To be called a terrible comic by Mack Sennett would have finished off less determined men than Harold Lloyd.

In his first film for Essanay, *His New Job*, released on 1 February 1915, Charlie parodies the Keystone studio. Charlie is applying for a job at the Lodestone Film Company. He enters and waits in the reception area, where a very young Gloria Swanson tells him to speak to the man sitting behind the desk. In ten years' time this shy sixteen-year-old would be one of the reigning queens of the silver screen, but here she looks like a teenager who doesn't want to be in this film. Ben Turpin, who had been working intermittently at the Essanay studios and on the vaudeville stage, walks into the reception area with a jaunty gait, as cross-eyed as ever.

It's not a particularly inspired comedy, and there are more than a few incidents of people getting swords shoved up the rear. The Tramp is not a very sympathetic character here, and you can easily understand why he's unemployed: his tendency to attack people without warning would make him difficult to work with.

Chaplin's next film, *A Night Out*, released two weeks later, is a less successful remake of the Keystone film, *The Rounders*, in which he had co-starred with Roscoe Arbuckle. Here, Charlie is teamed up again with Ben Turpin, and they play two drunks out on the town. A long film, at thirty-four minutes, it is most notable for the first appearance of Edna Purviance (rhymes

Sometimes in these early films we see personal antagonism, thinly disguised as rough slapstick. It happens here in a park-bench scene with Ben Turpin and Charlie

An offscreen relationship with Edna has clearly developed since their first film together, and they can be seen flirting like crazy. He whispers something to Edna that makes her genuinely laugh

with reliance). Edna was born in 1895 in Paradise Valley, Nevada, where her mother, Louise, ran a hotel. As Edna entered her teens she became a popular amateur stage performer, and in 1913 she moved to San Francisco. Two years later she was recommended to Charlie as a leading lady. He interviewed her at the St Francis Hotel, liked her and hired her. In *A Night Out* Edna plays a hotel guest who finds herself in the same predicament as Mabel Normand in *Mabel's Strange Predicament* – that is, in her pyjamas and cuddling her dog under a strange man's bed. Obviously a regular occurrence in the hotels of the day.

Sometimes in these early films we see personal antagonism, thinly disguised as rough slapstick. It occurred in *Kid Auto Races at Venice*, when director Henry Lehrman forcibly kicked Charlie up the race-track. It happens here in a park-bench scene with Ben Turpin and Charlie. Ben hits Charlie with much more force than is needed in order to push him off the bench. When it's Charlie's turn to retaliate, he hits Ben over the head with a brick. Turpin goes into a spasm of twitches as if he has been given an electric shock: a style of over-the-top comic performance that Charlie hated. Charlie hits him with the brick three more times, watching Ben's convulsions with increasing dismay. The fourth blow knocks Turpin out conclusively and Charlie walks off with a satisfied air.

A Night Out is longer than it should be because, strangely, two takes of the same action are edited together. Charlie sits on the bed, unaware that Edna's underneath it. She pops her head out, he spots her and looks down drunkenly. His bowler hat falls off, he bends down to pick it up and sees Edna under the bed. The same action is then repeated, this time from a slightly different camera angle. This editing together of two separate takes is just crass incompetence by Essanay.

From now on Charlie took control. He spent longer making *The Champion*, released on 11 March 1915, than any other film up to this point in his career, but it was worth it. *The New York Dramatic Mirror* (1915) purred: 'Without doubt the funniest burlesque prize fight ever shown upon the screen.' It's hard to imagine the first title-card of *The Champion* appearing in a basic Chaplin Keystone: 'Completely broke. Meditating on the ingratitude of humanity.'

An offscreen relationship with Edna has clearly developed since their first film together, and they can be seen flirting like crazy. He whispers something to Edna that makes her genuinely laugh. It's excellent direction from Charlie because Edna had never acted onscreen before and, at times, she appears inappropriately formal. Edna's moments of laughter give her a natural, warm onscreen presence. One shot, a tight close-up of the two of them, shows their noses almost touching and their lips moments apart. Her arm is around his shoulder and his hand is around her waist. They are deeply in love.

Left Female lead in several early Chaplin comedies, Edna Purviance also developed an off-screen romance with Charlie.

Charlie's next film *In the Park* was released one week later on 18 March 1915. As with many of the Keystone comedies, the action, suggested by the title, is set in a park, but this time the humour takes a decidedly risqué turn. The Tramp talks to a policeman who is holding his truncheon at an upwardly suggestive angle. Charlie tweaks the end of it between his fingers. Charlie has fun lampooning the Keystone style of comedy, where every park film ended up in the lake. Here, Leo White in his Count mode (wearing a shiny top hat, fake beard, moustache and whiskers) decides to commit suicide and believes the best available method is to ask Charlie Chaplin, as the Tramp, to kick him up the arse and into the lake.

The next film, *A Jitney Elopement*, was released on 1 April 1915. ('Jitney' was a then current nickname for a car.) There are many lovely moments. First, Charlie shows amazing dexterity in slicing a loaf of bread diagonally and turning it into a wheaty concertina. Second, the general spirit in which the Essanays were made is demonstrated in the scene where Edna and Leo White approach a park bench. He lifts up his frock coat, revealing holes in the seat of his trousers, through which his undergarments are poking. Clearly, Edna isn't expecting this and dissolves into delightful peals of laughter. She is bent double with joy even after she has sat down. Later, she indulges in some physical slapstick with Charlie, falling off a substantial tree branch about three feet from the floor. She falls awkwardly and appears to hurt her leg. Later, more physical slapstick results in her falling off the branch again. She seems to be in some distress. This is the last time Charlie ever asks her to fall over in the name of comedy.

He lifts up his frock coat, revealing holes in the seat of his trousers, through which his undergarments are poking. Clearly, Edna isn't expecting this and dissolves into delightful peals of laughter

Chapter 3
"Charlie Centre Stage"

CHARLIE
CHAPLIN
IN
The VAGABOND

All Rights Controlled by EXPORT & IMPORT FILM CO. Inc.

Charlie Centre Stage

Charlie Chaplin became a global star in 1915. America, Europe, China, Africa ... the world – everybody understands an underdog. *The Tramp*, released on 11 April 1915, marks a huge development in Charlie's story-telling abilities, enhanced no doubt by his relationship with Edna Purviance, which seems to have encouraged him to develop a softer side to the Tramp's nature. As for Edna, her performance is much more disciplined and serious than in their previous film together, *A Jitney Elopement*. A real sense of mischief pervades *Jitney* that is entirely absent from the far more serious picture that is *The Tramp*.

Charlie first appears hobbling down a dusty road. A car comes hurtling round the bend behind him and passes perilously close to his right foot. It's a matter of two or three inches. The Tramp falls over. He has barely struggled to his feet when another car, coming in the opposite direction, misses him by the width of a shoelace. It's a stunningly well-staged scene, with just seven seconds between the first and second car. Unusually for a gentleman of the road, he carries a clothes brush with which he fastidiously brushes himself down. He sits with his back to a tree and performs a simple manicure, making sure that his hands are clean before he eats. He then sharpens his knife on the sole of his shoe.

Edna, playing a farmer's daughter, appears. She is walking through a meadow, holding a large bundle of banknotes, and it's her bad luck that a rather obvious-looking villain is lurking in a bush, in the optimistic hope that a young woman will walk by waving cash in the air. Manchester-born Leo White, who appeared in a number of Chaplin films, is cast as the villain. He attacks Edna, but she escapes with the money and runs past Charlie, who comes to her rescue. Charlie kicks the villain up the rustic setting and he runs away. Edna explains that the crook was after her money. After some deliberation, Charlie grabs the notes from her and moves to walk away, but Edna's distress pricks his conscience. As he debates with himself whether or not to return the cash, he glances a number of times directly into the camera, involving us in his dilemma. He has looked into the camera before, but never to such a degree. Here he is conveying his state of mind and encouraging a deeper level of communication with his audience.

Edna's father rewards him for rescuing his daughter by giving him a job on the farm. Charlie accepts, is handed a pitchfork and immediately creates havoc. The unfortunate Paddy McGuire plays a fellow farm labourer, who gets pitch-forked up the arse so many times you can't help feeling that Charlie doesn't like him very much. At the end of the picture he must have had a behind like a colander. We are firmly in the territory of Keystone cartoon violence. People

Right Paddy McGuire has his backside turned into a colander by Charlie in *The Tramp*.

can be continually stabbed in the rear or hit over the head with a mallet, but apart from a momentary agony, when they might go cross-eyed with the sheer trauma of it all, they get up and carry on as normal.

There's more inventive material when Charlie is given the task of milking a cow. He places the bucket under the animal, having first raised his hat and explained to the cow that the bucket needs filling. He eventually moves the cow's tail up and down in a pumping action, assuming this will produce milk.

The villain turns up at the farm with two accomplices to steal Edna's money – clearly this is a poor place to be a robber because she's the only person around here with anything worth stealing – but Charlie chases the intruders off the premises. As he attempts to clamber over a fence he is accidentally shot in the leg by Edna's father. He falls dramatically, rather than comedically. This is all in long-shot. Then we cut to a tight close-up of Charlie holding his leg, which is bleeding. The close-up brings us up short, which adds emotional impact. He is carried back to the farmhouse, and we see the nasty wound on his leg. Charlie's performance, as he lapses into unconsciousness, is beautifully underplayed and is all the more effective for it. The Tramp feels pain and has suddenly become more like a real human being.

His convalescence on the farm is interrupted by the arrival of Edna's sweetheart. Realizing there is no future between him and Edna, Charlie

Below An iconic moment in cinema history: Charlie walks away at the end of *The Tramp*.

People all over the world responded to this moment in the same way as they do now: it makes you feel good. He's not asking you to feel sorry for him, he's sharing his view of life: tomorrow's another day

composes a short note, which he leaves on the kitchen table. It reads 'i thort your kindness was love but it aint cause I seen him. XXI Goodbye.' He leaves. Edna finds the note and reads it. We see a close-up of the note, which, curiously, is now in different handwriting.

As Charlie walks away, down the same dusty road we first saw at the beginning of the film, he unwittingly creates one of the most iconic images in the history of cinema. Even people who have never seen one of his films are somehow familiar with it, and it's one of those images that has led Charlie's detractors to accuse him of overt sentimentality. It's true that as Charlie ambles down the road, he does, for a moment, look disconsolately down at his shuffling feet. If that was the final image of the film, it would indeed finish on a sad note: 'The clown with a tear in his eye.' But Charlie doesn't do that. He shrugs off his down mood, kicks up his heels and quickens his pace. He's not going to be defeated. We feel genuine uplift at this because Charlie, for a brief instant, has skilfully essayed a mood of hopelessness, which he transforms into jaunty determination. And all this with his back to the camera. That's what makes this iconic. People all over the world responded to this moment in the same way as they do now: it makes you feel good. He's not asking you to feel sorry for him, he's sharing his view of life: tomorrow's another day.

By now Charlie was world famous, and a Chaplin craze, 'Chaplinitis', started to take hold. You could buy toys, dolls, statuettes and, if you were Adolf Hitler, you could even grow your moustache like him. Such songs as 'The Moon Shines Bright on Charlie Chaplin' were big hits of the day. Comic strips featuring Charlie appeared, and even the serious-minded magazine the *Tatler* published a large picture of Charlie on its front cover on 15 March 1916, describing him as 'possibly the widest known personage in the world'.

For other would-be stars it was almost impossible to escape Chaplin's shadow, and a number, rather than seeking to originate their own styles, resorted to impersonating the great man. As already mentioned, in Harold Lloyd's first films as a solo comic we see him, not in the guise we're familiar with, but playing a Chaplinesque character called Willie Work. The comedian Billy West also did an imitation of Chaplin in his vaudeville act and then adopted the tramp costume for a series of highly lucrative films. A full-page advertisement in the *Moving Picture World* of 30 June 1917 brazenly proclaims West as the 'funniest man on earth'. In truth, however, the films were poor copies of Chaplin's, because although Billy West's physical resemblance to

Right **By 1916 a Chaplin craze was sweeping the world. This photograph from a few years later shows Charlie looking at one of the many pieces of merchandise that appeared – in this case a knee-high model doll of himself, complete with bowler hat, baggy trousers and cane.**

Chaplin was really quite convincing, his movements and gestures were wrong.

Charlie's former roommate on the Karno tour, Stan Jefferson, was another imitator. Stan had had a tough time since Charlie's departure, and without their star comic, the Karno troupe had broken up. Stan had found it difficult to get work. Had he returned to Britain he would have been conscripted to fight in the trenches of the First World War, so it made sense to stay in America, and in April 1915 we find him impersonating Chaplin onstage, the *Albany Evening Journal* reporting that 'Mr Jefferson impersonates Charlie Chaplin to the letter'. This must have been a galling time for Stan. The comic he had been rooming with just eighteen months ago was now world famous. Stan thought he was a good comic himself but, such was Chaplin's massive impact on audiences

By now Charlie was world famous, and a Chaplin craze, 'Chaplinitis', started to take hold. You could buy toys, dolls, statuettes and, if you were Adolf Hitler, you could even grow your moustache like him

in 1915, it was easier to get work impersonating him than originating something new. After December 1917 the name Stan Jefferson disappears altogether – there are no references to him at all in theatrical periodicals after this date. What happened to him?

Meanwhile, Charlie continued his relentless upward rise, and his tenth film for Essanay, *A Woman*, released on 12 July 1915, features the most astonishing transformation scene he ever filmed. Here he plays the usual Tramp, but, at one point, he disguises himself as a fashionably dressed young woman, obviously without the toothbrush moustache. In his first scene in drag, which is with Edna, he is clearly making her laugh a great deal. To call his performance 'drag', implies an over-the-top, exaggerated portrayal of womanhood for comedic effect. Instead, he plays the part completely straight and, slightly worrying for me, he looks absolutely gorgeous! There's an extraordinary close-up of Charlie flirting directly into the camera. There's more than a touch of Princess Diana about him.

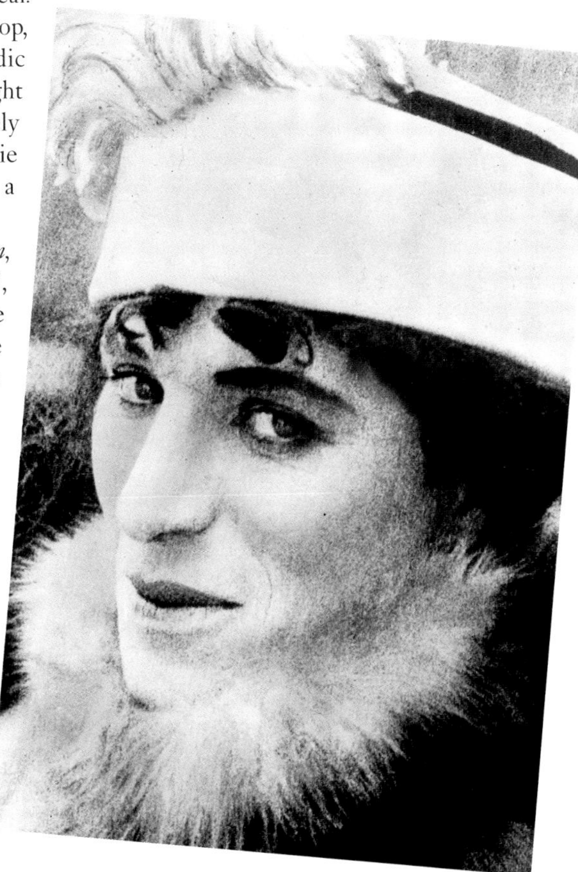

Below **Shades of Princess Diana? Charlie plays an astonishingly realistic-looking and fashionably dressed young lady in his 1915 film *A Woman*.**

After the spirit of fun in dressing up in *A Woman*, his next film, *The Bank*, released on 9 August 1915, consolidates the advances he made in *The Tramp*. The bank set feels authentic, and the storyline is simple but pleasing. Charlie plays a janitor, who opens the bank's safe early in the morning and removes his bucket and mop. Edna, a typist, leaves on her desk a tie, a birthday present for the cashier, who is also called Charles. Charlie mistakes this present as being for himself, and he writes a letter to Edna and leaves her a small bunch of flowers. Later, Charlie observes a bank customer and suggests, through subtle mime, that the customer doesn't look very well. He feels his pulse and then asks him to stick out his tongue. He moistens a postage stamp on the extended tongue, then goes over to a post-box to post his letter. It won't fit in the box so he tears it up to make it fit.

In the following scene Charlie sees Edna

He sees the cashier and Edna canoodling away. He gets rid of the flowers and wanders off with a jaunty shrug. Suddenly, we seem a long way away from the park comedies of previous months

throwing his flowers and letter into a waste bin. He sits in a corner, closes his eyes and the scene fades. The bank is robbed and Edna is held hostage, but Charlie comes to the rescue. He and Edna share a tender scene in which Edna kisses a rose and gently lays her head on Charlie's shoulder. This is a beautifully restrained piece of acting from Edna, and she benefits greatly from Charlie's direction (his method throughout his career being to act the part out for the actor). Charlie wakes up and realizes it's all been a dream: he is hugging and kissing his mop. He sees the cashier and Edna canoodling away. He gets rid of the flowers and wanders off with a jaunty shrug. Suddenly, we seem a long way away from the park comedies of previous months. This is an unsentimental ending to what is Charlie's most accomplished film so far. A contemporary review from *Variety* said:

> It is the most legitimate comedy film Chaplin has played in many a long day, perhaps since he's been in pictures. While there were no boisterous guffaws from upstairs that his slapstick would have pulled, the use of cleaner material brought more enjoyment to the entire house, also left a better impression.

Charlie's thirteenth film for Essanay, *A Night in the Show*, released on 20 November 1915, gives us a unique opportunity to see part of the Fred Karno sketch *Mumming Birds* that had first alerted Mack Sennett to Chaplin's talent as a comedian. Charlie plays two parts in this film; first, Mr Pest, the drunk toff of Karno fame and, second, Mr Rowdy, who's up in the balcony causing mayhem by pouring a bottle of beer over the head of Mr Pest below. This, I believe, is a polite variation of a joke that I remember hearing back in my schooldays. In the version I heard, a gentleman in the balcony urinates over the edge onto a man's head below. The man looks up and says 'What are you doing?' The bloke up in the balcony says, 'I'm having a piss.' And the bloke downstairs says, 'Well, spray it around a bit.' This is the action that is played out in this film, with the beer flowing from a bottle making a more genteel substitution. I feel sure that this is the joke Charlie is alluding to. Charlie, as the toff, invades the stage on several occasions and generally disrupts the action.

His last film for Essanay, *Police*, was released on 27 March 1916. At the end of the picture he echoes the ending of *The Tramp*. He walks away from the camera light-heartedly. A moment later he throws his arms in the air joyfully. Everything is rosy. Then a policeman enters the scene, and Charlie reverses his direction, walking back towards us with a quick glance into the camera that seems to say, 'Aye, aye, I'm off.'

Charlie had now fulfilled his contract at Essanay, and George K. Spoor, co-owner of the company, offered $350,000 for twelve two-reelers. Charlie, whose business interests were now being represented by his half-brother, Sydney, wanted a bonus of $150,000. Spoor refused, so Syd started negotiations with the Mutual Film Corporation and eventually secured the extraordinary sum of $670,000. Charlie was to be paid $10,000 a week plus a bonus of $150,000 on signing the contract. At this time, the US president earned $75,000 a year. Newsreel footage of Charlie signing the contract shows him blinking his eyes in astonishment at the astronomical sum he is being offered.

> What this contract means is that I am left free to be just as funny as I dare, to do the best work that is in me, and to spend my energies on the thing that the people want. I felt for a long time that this would be my big year, and this contract gives me my opportunity. There is inspiration in it. I am like an author with a big publisher to give him circulation.[1]

A studio, named the Lone Star Studio, was built in Los Angeles exclusively for his use.

Charlie's first film with Mutual was *The Floorwalker*, released on 15 May 1916, a mere two months after his last film for Essanay. In Kevin Brownlow's and David Gill's masterly documentary series *Unknown Chaplin* the first programme is full of out-takes from the Mutual series, which demonstrate how Charlie went about making his movies. Incredibly, he rehearsed on film, shooting sequences many times in order to improve them or to incorporate new comedy business as it occurred to him. For this, his first Mutual film, he builds an escalator in the middle of a department store. When Mack Sennett saw it he commented, 'Why the hell didn't we think of using a moving stairway?' There's a subtle reference to the size of his Mutual contract when Charlie looks into a bag full of money and flutters his eyelids in exactly the same way he did in the promotional newsreel.

Edna Purviance, as usual, plays the female lead. One of the villains is played by Eric Campbell, making his first appearance in a Chaplin film, and his astonishing forest of facial hair (eyebrows and beard shooting in all directions) and his glowering presence greatly enhance Chaplin's slapstick. An ex-Karno performer, he was spotted by Charlie and Syd when he was appearing in the New York show *Pom Pom*. He was immediately signed up for the entire Mutual series. *The Floorwalker* also contains a version of the famous mirror routine, a great music hall favourite: one character would exactly mimic the actions of

Syd started negotiations with the Mutual Film Corporation and eventually secured the extraordinary sum of $670,000. Charlie was to be paid $10,000 a week plus a bonus of $150,000 on signing the contract

Above The giant, bewhiskered Eric Campbell plays a round of golf with Charlie – a still from an uncompleted Chaplin short (the golf routine idea was later used in *The Idle Class*). A stalwart of a number of Chaplin films, Eric was invariably cast in the role of the villain. Offscreen, he and Charlie formed a close friendship.

another in order to convince them that they were a reflection. The routine later turns up in the Marx Brothers film *Duck Soup* (1933).

The Fireman, released on 12 June 1916, again features Eric Campbell, this time as Charlie's corrupt boss. In one scene Eric repeatedly thumps Charlie, who falls to the floor, badly hurt. Here he is reprising the moment in *The Tramp* when he was shot and in pain. He plays both scenes straight, the only difference being that in *The Fireman* Charlie reveals he is acting by suddenly jumping up and kicking Eric into a barrel full of water. There's a hint of self-mockery here.

The finale finds Charlie climbing over 20 feet up the outside of a burning building to rescue Edna. It's an extraordinary stunt, filmed in a single continuous take. I presume nobody from Mutual was in the studio that day, watching their big investment pulling off this stunt without the benefit of a double or a safety net. Here he's introducing a new element into his comedy: the thrill factor. Another new feature is the use of camera trickery. Charlie reverses the film so it looks as if he is leading two horses backwards, into a position where they can be harnessed up to the fire truck. The technique is more obvious a moment later when we see Charlie driving the horse-drawn fire truck backwards, at speed. Charlie was always looking out for fresh ways of putting his jokes across.

His next film, *The Vagabond*, was released on 10 July 1916. Deliberately echoing the title of *The Tramp*, Charlie is signalling his intention to make a serious dramatic film with comic interludes. In the opening shot we see a pair of saloon doors under which appear, shuffling towards us, the most recognizable feet in the world. Such was Chaplin's fame at this time that he could be identified by his shoes alone. Although it's a comic opening, there's a certain sadness about it: he seems weary and forlorn. He's a busker, who finds a position outside the saloon. He starts to play his violin, but a rival band of buskers also set up outside, and, when Charlie goes inside to pass the hat round, the customers assume he's with the brass band. Then Charlie sees Leo White, who appears as an exaggerated Jewish stereotype, surreptitiously helping himself to slices of ham (strictly non-kosher). He is playing a stereotype to make it clear what the gag is: Charlie takes the 'fresh ham' sign out of the joint, replaces it with one reading 'roast beef' and indicates to Leo that the ham is now labelled 'roast beef' and therefore doesn't ostensibly break any dietary laws. This is Charlie trying to help. Had this been a Keystone film, he would have kicked everybody up the arse, bashed someone over the head with a beer bottle and run off with the 'beef'. Although the scene ends with a chase, it's a far more restrained affair.

The next scene is played purely for drama. It is set in a beautifully furnished drawing room, where a wealthy woman is sewing. A title-card

Below **Charlie serenades his real-life sweetheart Edna Purviance in *The Vagabond*.**

This is very typical of Charlie's approach. Yes, he wants to touch our hearts, but he never forgets that he is a comedian first and foremost. In his films a tender moment is almost always undercut by slapstick

identifies her as 'The mother'. She lifts the photograph of a child from her sewing-box, looks into the middle distance and places her left hand against her brow. It's such a simple gesture, but it clearly indicates her loss. There is no histrionic acting; its strength lies in the quiet stillness of the performance. Charlie's direction here is superb. The actress, Charlotte Mineau, had worked with Charlie at Essanay, and she plays the scene with beautiful understatement. This is the first time in a Chaplin film that another actor has been entrusted to carry a dramatic scene on their own. Then a caption, 'The Gypsy Drudge', introduces us to Edna.

The dramatic tone is continued as we see Edna bullied and harassed by an old woman who pushes her into working harder. Eric Campbell, appearing in his most unsympathetic role so far, threatens to whip Edna with a crop. Charlie comes into view, ambling along a country lane and clutching his violin. Seeing Edna bent over a washboard and bucket, he decides this will be an ideal place to busk. His soulful playing of the violin lifts Edna's spirits and, moved by the music, she looks up at Charlie. His sudden increase in tempo causes Edna to speed up in tandem with the music. This is very typical of Charlie's approach. Yes, he wants to touch our hearts, but he never forgets that he is a comedian first and foremost. In his films a tender moment is almost always undercut by slapstick.

Eric Campbell is genuinely menacing – this is no comic role – and Charlie rescues Edna from a beating, the two of them making their escape in a horse-drawn caravan. They set up home by the side of the road, and Charlie sets about grooming Edna (scrubbing her face and brushing her hair). She goes off to fetch some milk from a nearby farm and meets an artist who is setting up his canvas on an easel. He had been lacking inspiration until Edna appeared. The artist is played by Lloyd Bacon, who had played Edna's sweetheart in *The Tramp*, thus further linking the two films. He notices a shamrock-shaped birthmark on Edna's arm and decides to paint her. Edna invites him to meet Charlie, who has prepared a meal back at the caravan. We have seen the delightful care and attention, imagination and artistry with which Charlie sets the 'table' (an upturned bucket): he substitutes his shirt for a tablecloth and skilfully rolls up its sleeves, sculpting them into napkins as if it were the most exclusive restaurant. This is ingenuity, elegance and humour in the face of poverty. But Edna seems not to notice the efforts he has gone to. She is transfixed by the artist. Charlie sees that she can't take her eyes off his rival, and he wanders away, feeling sorry for himself, and then sits on a hot stove, jolting us back to the comic. However, the mood is one of a love that is not to be.

Charlie studies Edna's devoted gaze as the artist leaves. He knows he has lost her. It's a beautifully understated scene: there are no looks to camera, just the occasional wistful glance at Edna. A title-card appears: 'LATER "The Living Shamrock".' This ushers in the biggest continuity blunder in all of Charlie's movies. The mother visits the art gallery and faints when she recognizes Edna's shamrock-shaped birthmark in the portrait: 'That birthmark! My child!' The odd thing is, it isn't a painting but a photograph of Edna that she's looking at. Perhaps a painting had been done and it didn't look anything like her or maybe there simply wasn't enough time to paint a life-like portrait (after all, Charlie was making a new film every month). Either way, we have an artist who paints photographs.

The artist leads the mother to the caravan where Charlie and Edna are living. When he hears that Edna has now been reunited with her mother, Charlie undercuts the sentiment by dropping fresh eggs on the artist's shoes. As he watches Edna, with her new mother and the artist, disappear over the horizon in a chauffeur-driven car, Charlie slumps against the caravan. He is profoundly alone. With his back to the camera, he raises his arm to wave goodbye, but then turns the gesture into one of stroking the back of his head. It's moving and effective. He turns to face us. He attempts to lift his spirits by rubbing his hands together and kicking up his heels, but this time the depth of his loneliness defeats him.

A title-card announces: 'The awakening of the real love.' Inside the car Edna is seen glancing out of the back window. She becomes distraught and urges the driver to turn the car around. Charlie is sitting on the steps of the caravan when the car returns. Edna bundles Charlie into it, urging him, 'You come too.' The car heads off towards the horizon, and we have a wonderfully happy ending. These last moments of *The Vagabond* are as moving now as they were in 1916.

Released only fifteen months after *The Tramp*, *The Vagabond* clearly demonstrates the strides that Charlie had made as a filmmaker. Unlike his first two films for Mutual, his character in *The Vagabond* is a fully rounded, somewhat endearing human being, someone with whom we're invited to identify. Three films in, and Charlie's Mutual period is shaping up to be something special. Not only was he the most famous comedian in the world, but he was also the most highly respected. He was striving to make better films by improving and building on past achievements, and in so doing he was leaving his comic contemporaries a long way behind. Roscoe Arbuckle and the other Mack Sennett comics must have looked at these films with a mixture of awe and admiration. Charlie was raising the standard, and the best of the other comedians would be inspired to reach for the same heights themselves.

Not only was he the most famous comedian in the world, but he was also the most highly respected. He was striving to make better films by improving and building on past achievements

At this time Roscoe Arbuckle was second only to Chaplin in worldwide popularity. In a world where few people were obese, Arbuckle stood out like a big sore thumb. 'Nobody loves a fat man' was a popular saying of the time, and in several interviews with Arbuckle in the 1910s the phrase is often quoted, only for the journalist to point out that Roscoe was the exception: Roscoe was very popular, especially with children.

In the early Keystone films Roscoe had been as guilty of over-the-top gestures as everybody else, but by 1915 working methods were improving. The acting was certainly subtler, and the use of scenarios and scripts becoming more widespread, making it more likely that a good comedy would be made: it's generally much better to have some idea why you are filming some action rather than, for example, filming people falling in and out of rowing boats, marooned in a lake of mud, and then hoping somehow to create a film around it. Those days were gone, and improvements in acting, directing and story-telling were happening all the time.

Roscoe had remained friends with Charlie after he left Keystone and moved to Essanay. The magazine *Pictures and the Picturegoer* reported that, on 26 June 1915, the pair were spotted sharing a box at a Los Angeles theatre. According to the report, when they were seen by the audience they were obliged to perform a forty-minute routine onstage. Imagine being the next act waiting to go on.

Throughout 1915 Roscoe's films steadily improve. In *Fatty's Faithful Fido*, released on 20 March 1915 (one month before *The Tramp*), we see the familiar Keystone mixture: there is still lots of brick-throwing, but there are also some other better thought-out pieces of business. Clearly, more time is being spent in rehearsal and in the staging of scenes. The imprint Charlie made at Keystone was immense; and Roscoe borrows a classic piece of Chaplin business with the use of a boxing-dummy mounted on a tippy-turvy base. Imagine a 6 feet high Subbuteo player with no arms, and you have a giant prop that bounces back at you. Charlie had built a lovely routine around this same prop in *Mabel's Married Life*, released on 20 June 1914. *Fatty's Faithful Fido* also showcases Roscoe's lightness of step on the dance floor. For such a big man, he was extraordinarily agile and was much admired for his ability to throw himself about. Here his comedy partner is Al St John, a real-life nephew, who had first impressed Mack Sennett with his trick-cycling skills.

Fatty's Plucky Pup, released on 18 June 1915, begins with a clearly defined comedy routine. Roscoe's favourite pastime is smoking in bed, and he accidentally sets fire to the bed. Taking his time, he wanders into the kitchen to fetch a single tea-cup of water. He throws it over the burning bed, to little effect, and goes back into the kitchen to refill the cup. Distracted by his appearance in the mirror, he spends some time combing his hair. He then takes the cup of water back to the burning bed, drinks

Opposite Roscoe Arbuckle and a perilously placed Mabel Normand on the grand staircase in *He Did and He Didn't*.

Below At one time, second only to Chaplin in popularity: Roscoe 'Fatty' Arbuckle.

most of it and throws the rest over the bed. After wiping his finger around the cup, he flicks it towards the flames. His wife rushes in with a bucket of water, which goes all over Roscoe. Eventually, the fire is extinguished.

The above sequence lasts for just over two minutes and shows Arbuckle following Chaplin's lead in adopting a less frantic approach. Roscoe is directing his own films now, and the slower pace allows the comedy to develop and character to start to come through. There's still plenty of watery slapstick with hose-pipes and some fierce attempts at dog-catching, with Roscoe coming to the rescue.

Six films later, the growth in Arbuckle's storytelling ability is immense. *He Did and He Didn't*, released on 30 January 1916 and co-starring Mabel Normand, is a little gem of a comedy. The film opens with Roscoe and Mabel as a married couple getting ready for an evening's entertaining. They live in a big house, and the sets are impressive, particularly the large hallway with its imposing staircase. Once you employ the method of writing scenarios before anything is filmed, you can plan ahead and build the sets you need. On occasion, Roscoe looks directly into the camera for several seconds. It's quite charming and might have been the result of Chaplin's influence. A childhood

Below A very drunk Roscoe Arbuckle takes a nap in *A Reckless Romeo.*

friend of Mabel's arrives at the house, and Mabel takes him into the living room. Time has obviously been taken to light the scene well, and the set is beautifully lit, with a fierce glow coming from the fireplace.

Later, Roscoe, Mabel and the friend sit down to a lobster dinner. Again, the lighting is subtle and atmospheric, and they sit around a table that is pooled with light, while Mabel is fully lit and the other two, shown in profile, are in half-shadow. An intruder then makes his way into the house and is seated in the vast hallway when he suddenly notices a fierce-looking lion-skin rug on the floor, the gaping mouth exposing two sharp fangs. The robber jumps out of his skin, falling backwards off the chair. I reckon this gag was remembered by Charlie Chaplin, who later expanded on it to great effect in his one-man Mutual comedy, *One A.M.* Of course, I am speculating, but it is known that the major comics of the day did watch each others' pictures, and on the odd occasion when Charlie borrowed a gag, he inevitably put his own stamp on it.

After the lobsters have been consumed by the trio, they retire to their bedrooms and have vivid nightmares. The end of the film features Roscoe looking straight into the camera as he retires backwards into the bedroom, giving a huge, warm, friendly grin at us.

Left **A very drunk Charlie Chaplin takes a nap in *One A.M.***

Charlie is let loose on the strangest set he ever conceived ... there's a stuffed bear, two grand staircases and a giant pendulum, which swings menacingly in front of the bedroom door

Roscoe released *A Reckless Romeo* in July 1916. Long considered to be a lost picture, a print was finally discovered as late as 1998 in the Norwegian Film Institute. It begins with a title-card, '3 A.M.', and a very drunken Roscoe attempts to get back into the house without disturbing his wife and mother-in-law. Roscoe's wife discovers him in the living-room and he claims it's really midnight (despite the cuckoo clock on the mantelpiece showing three o'clock). When the clock strikes three, he cuckoos nine more times in the dark to convince his wife that it really is midnight. When he gets to his bedroom he struggles to get undressed. He is spooked by his own braces dangling behind him and tries to club them to death with his shoe. His butler enters, explains the mistake and runs his master's bath.

Once the bath is filled, Roscoe jumps in, fully clothed, and goes to sleep, underwater. Still in the same position, he's woken up next morning by the butler. At the breakfast table he gets a frosty reception from his wife and mother-in-law. He looks at them, he looks at us, and the picture dissolves into a view of the Statue of Liberty. It then dissolves back to Roscoe: here is a man who feels he has no such thing as liberty. He goes down on his hands and knees and pleads for forgiveness from his wife, who quickly capitulates and embraces him. Roscoe delivers a broad wink directly into the camera.

Later, there's more familiar material in a park. Roscoe flirts with some young women and, to be perfectly fair, they flirt right back. Then Al St John turns up, and the two men start fighting, unaware they are being filmed by a film crew looking for newsreel material. Roscoe gets a black eye but later tells his wife he was injured while he was protecting a blind man from being robbed. He goes to the cinema with his wife and mother-in-law, and they are astonished to see newsreel footage of Roscoe flirting with the young women and then fighting Al St John. Al happens to be in the cinema audience, and he and Roscoe start another fight in the auditorium while, onscreen, their fight continues. It's a lovely double image. Once outside the cinema, Roscoe is told by the two women, 'Just wait until we get home.' He picks up a brick and throws it through a shop window. He is arrested but is gleeful at the prospect of spending a night in a police cell rather than under his own roof.

Both Roscoe in this film and Charlie in his next Mutual, *One A.M.*, portray wealthy men who own huge houses. It has to be remembered that Chaplin didn't always play a tramp, and Roscoe also varied his character. However, when Charlie is playing a rich man, he's inevitably a drunk: a drunkenly incapable tramp is not a richly comic idea. We laugh more readily at a rich man's inebriated attempts at dignity.

Above **In *One A.M.* Charlie's lavish house even has its own suit of armour. Note the well-padded staircase, which allowed Charlie to tumble down it unscathed.**

One A.M., Charlie's fourth film for Mutual, was released on 7 August 1916. In it Charlie shares the opening scene with Albert Austin, who plays a taxi-driver delivering the drunken Charlie back home. Charlie takes a long time to find the handle on the taxi-door, and this scene immediately presents a problem: a man trying to do something simple and constantly failing is a recipe for tedium. To help it along Charlie inserts a rare verbal gag in the form of a title-card: 'They should build these handles nearer the door.' For the most part, however, boredom is kept at bay by a string of inventive visual gags. Once inside the house, Charlie is let loose on the strangest set he ever conceived. It's surreal before the term 'surrealism' was coined: there's a stuffed bear, two grand staircases and a giant pendulum, which swings menacingly in front of the bedroom door, braining anybody who dares to enter.

There is no film record of Charlie's onstage performances, but *One A.M.* gives us an excellent idea of what he would have been like. His physical agility is superb in this film. The many tumbles down the stairs are beautifully executed, although if you look closely, you will notice that the stairs are very heavily padded and that Charlie's feet sink deeply into the steps. His antics on top of a revolving table while he is trying to light a cigarette from a lightbulb are Charlie at his acrobatic best. The film revels in bizarre images: one of my favourites is Charlie tossing a top hat onto the head of a stuffed ostrich.

Albert Austin enters, wanting to pawn his alarm clock … Charlie examines the clock, initially by giving it a good shake. He produces a stethoscope and listens to the clock's 'heart'. Then he takes its pulse

Once he gets past the pendulum and into the bedroom, he encounters a very stubborn bed that falls out of the wall and flips up and down at random. Here the film slips into tedium, and the comedy business with the bed becomes irritating. All the bed gags are inventive but, because it has taken Charlie so long to get into the bedroom, we just want him to go to sleep. Charlie reflected upon this rare moment of failure when he said of *One A.M.*, 'one more like that and it's goodbye Charlie'.[2] This is over-harsh, for there are many wonderful things in *One A.M.*, but Charlie's opinion indicates his quest for perfection, and the sheer number of gags he performed must have made his contemporaries despair. In *One A.M.*, apart from the brief opening scene with Albert Austin, Charlie is onscreen alone for the entire picture. It was unheard of in 1916 to make a solo film, but once again Charlie pushed the boundaries of what comedy could do.

After *One A.M.* Charlie made *The Count*, released on 4 September 1916, and like all the Mutuals, it abounds in rich, comic material. The out-takes show that Charlie filmed the kitchen scene (with its Keystone-style gags about stinky cheese) first. The rest of the film is much stronger. A great deal of silent comedy revolves around smells, but there is even a sound gag in *The Count.* Charlie gestures to Eric Campbell to stop slurping his soup so that he can hear what Edna is saying to him. One especially memorable moment at the dinner table shows Charlie tucking into a giant slice of watermelon and having to clean his ears out with a napkin.

The Count has a lovely opening sequence. Charlie is a tailor's assistant, shyly attempting to measure a rather buxom woman. At one point, he measures her waist but doesn't realize that he's also looped the tape measure around a tailor's dummy behind her. We see Charlie's eccentric list of measurements. It reads:

Neck 12
Ear 1½
Mouth 2
Waist 5 feet
Finger 1

Charlie's next film, *The Pawnshop*, which was released on 2 October 1916, contains more individual gags than any other Mutual picture. There are far too many to describe fully here, so, pausing only to note the wondrous sight of Charlie with his head stuck in a cello, I shall concentrate on just one gag sequence. Albert Austin enters, wanting to pawn his alarm clock. That's all he wants to do. Charlie examines the clock, initially by giving it a good shake. He produces a stethoscope and listens to the clock's 'heart'. Then he takes its pulse. He tests the bell by flicking it with his finger. Something worries him about the inside of the clock. He hits the exterior with a hammer, listens again and decides he needs to operate. He produces a big hand drill to make the initial incision, then he takes the back off with the aid of a traditional tin-opener. He sniffs the contents as if he's sniffing dodgy sardines. He then removes the mouthpiece from a candlestick telephone and places it in his eye, like a jeweller's magnifying eye-glass. Still not entirely happy with the clock, he removes pieces of it, bit by bit, pulling out the main spring in the manner of a draper measuring out yards of ribbon (not a common sight these days). Much to Albert Austin's astonishment, Charlie empties the clock of all its contents onto his counter. He plays with his hammer, bringing it crashing down on Austin's hand. Then he winds the empty clock and, to the amazement of both men, the contents on the counter start moving about. Charlie tries to hammer the clock works into submission. When that doesn't work he squirts oil all over them. Thus subdued, the bits of clock are scraped back into the clock and then poured into Albert's hat. Charlie looks at Austin, looks into the hat and then looks back at Austin. He shakes his head as if to say: 'You can't pawn this pile of junk.' This moment gets as big a laugh now as it did over ninety years ago. At the Edinburgh Fringe Festival 2006 I showed this routine from *The Pawnshop* every day for two weeks, and it always got a huge response. The entire sequence

Below Charlie checks the health of Albert Austin's alarm clock in *The Pawnshop*, destroying it in the process.

Improving the gags: *One A.M.* and *Easy Street*

Charlie Chaplin's increasing mastery of gags and comic timing can be seen in two of his early films, *One A.M.* and *Easy Street. One A.M.* is full of brilliant ideas, and surviving out-takes show how carefully Charlie worked on the film, but one sequence goes on too long and overrides the story. The drunken Charlie, having spent a long time getting to the bedroom, encounters a stubborn bed that falls out of the wall and flips up and down at random. The comic action drags on so much that the routine starts to become annoying – it's the one scene in the film that would have benefited from further editing.

In the slightly later *Easy Street*, on the other hand, Charlie doesn't put a foot wrong. In one of the most cleverly constructed sequences, the giant Eric Campbell bends a street lamp in two to show his strength. Charlie seizes his opportunity and manoeuvres the lamp over Eric's head, delivering gas rather like a dentist.

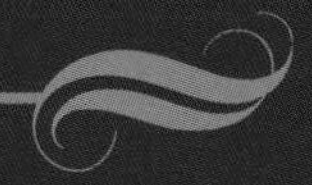

Opposite page **Charlie deals with an awkward bed in *One A.M.***

Left **The fearsome Eric Campbell is about to demonstrate his skill at lamp-bending in *Easy Street*.**

Below **Charlie manages to fit the lamp over Eric's head.**

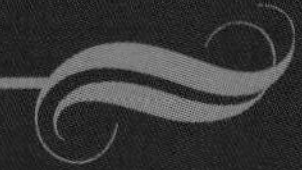

In *Behind the Screen* Chaplin has a gentle dig at the old Keystone style of comedy. A title-card reads: 'The comedy department rehearsing a new idea.' This new idea turns out to be the throwing of custard pies into people's faces

is over four minutes long, and no other film comedian of the day could generate so much material from a single, simple prop. *The Pawnshop* remains a terrific comedy.

Charlie's next film in the Mutual series, *Behind the Screen*, was released on 13 November 1916. It is set in a film studio and has a few valuable shots of the technical equipment of the day. The camera is a large box with a very basic lens at the front, mounted on a simple tripod. The handle to crank the film through the camera is located on the side. This method of hand-cranking relies on the camera operator being able to maintain a steady speed throughout the course of a scene, but it also offers the opportunity for some really stunning special effects.

In the documentary *Unknown Chaplin* a series of out-takes from *Behind the Screen* shows Charlie making numerous attempts at a particularly hazardous stunt. A dramatic scene set in a prison is being rehearsed in the film studio, and a masked axe-man is trying a few practice swings. Charlie enters and walks towards the man who suddenly brings his axe crashing to the floor, narrowly missing Charlie's feet. We can see how sharp the axe is because it's embedded in the floor. This apparently dangerous piece of business was filmed over and over again with few variations. How was it done? The camera operator simply hand-cranked backwards, and Charlie staged all the action backwards. Thus, he walks backwards towards the axe which, at this point, is stuck in the floor. He steps over the axe and continues walking backwards as the axe-man now lifts the axe and waves it in the air. Projected onto a screen, the action appears natural and there's no hint of camera trickery: Charlie walks in, the axe is plunged into the ground, and Charlie smoothly steps over it. Despite all this hard work, the sequence was never used. Perhaps it was considered too gimmicky. Other comics of the day marvelled at such behaviour and extravagance – spending all that time on a gag and then not using it!

In *Behind the Screen* Chaplin has a gentle dig at the old Keystone style of comedy. A title-card reads: 'The comedy department rehearsing a new idea.' This new idea turns out to be the throwing of custard pies into people's faces. After being splattered several times, one actor storms off declaring, 'I don't like this highbrow stuff.' Parodying this sort of comedy also enables Charlie to indulge in it; he impressively hits Eric Campbell twice in the face with a pie, thrown from a distance of 7 feet. Charlie parodies his old Keystone boss, Mack Sennett: Albert Austin lunching on raw onions and Eric Campbell's habit of spitting everywhere reflect two of Sennett's less appealing characteristics.

Like *Behind the Screen*, his eighth Mutual film, *The Rink*, released on 4

December 1916, has its high spots without being particularly ground-breaking. *The Rink* is partly based on an old Karno sketch, *Skating*, that Syd Chaplin had starred in. There are two separate visits to the skating rink, which feels repetitious, but this is nitpicking because the quality of the individual gags outside the skating sequences is very high.

We first see Charlie as a waiter at the back of a restaurant. He ambles forward to Eric Campbell's table, which is in the foreground. Eric is waiting for the bill. Charlie checks what Eric has eaten by examining the stains on the front of his shirt, and he then reprises the watermelon gag from *The Count* by looking into Eric's ear and writing 'melon' on the bill. A female customer orders a cocktail. 'Yes sir,' says Charlie. For some reason the cocktail bar is located in a corner of the kitchen. The camera moves in closer as Charlie speedily and ambidextrously removes two corks from two bottles, pours some of the contents into a cocktail shaker and replaces the corks in the bottles. This trick would be beyond Ben Turpin. Charlie cracks an egg into the shaker, then throws in the shell. He sniffs the contents and judges them to be a bit off, so he adds a flower to sweeten the aroma. He has his own way of shaking a cocktail: he holds the cocktail shaker completely still while he furiously flaps his elbows. It's a lovely gag and all the better for being filmed in close-up.

Henry Bergman, who had made his debut in *The Pawnshop*, appears in two roles in this, his third film with Chaplin. Henry initially crops up in *The Rink* as an irate diner, and for the first time working with Chaplin he has been allowed to play with the make-up box. His facial hair is appallingly over the top. The eyebrows, as wide as your average trouser-belt, are bad enough, but the moustache and beard are so luxuriant that Henry looks as if he has run head first into a very hairy, sticky wall.

Chaplin's next film, *Easy Street*, released on 22 January 1917, strikes a deeper note of realism. For the first time we see Charlie as a true down-and-out, huddling against a wall for warmth. His spirits are lifted by the sound of music wafting towards him. It is coming from the Hope Mission, where Edna is singing a hymn. She is beautifully lit, and her hair takes on the appearance of a halo. This is a moment tinged with autobiography, recalling as it does the young Charlie's experience of sitting out in the street late at night unable to get into the house and feeling miserable until the tune 'The Honeysuckle and the Bee' came to his ears.

Charlie walks into the Mission and takes his place in the congregation, but not before eyeing up the collection box. He is handed a baby to hold, but doesn't realize he is also holding the baby's bottle upside down. The contents

Chaplin's next film, *Easy Street*, strikes a deeper note of realism. For the first time we see Charlie as a true down-and-out, huddling against a wall for warmth

quickly soak his lap. Charlie looks at the baby with astonishment, assuming it's responsible for the impressive cascade. Later, through talking to Edna and Albert Austin, Charlie is lifted from his gloom and resolves to make a new start in life. To prove his commitment, he removes the collection box from inside his trousers and hands it back. Out on the street he passes the police station and, after some deliberation, decides to join the force. Eric Campbell, cast as 'The Bully', is meanwhile single-handedly beating up a crowd of people in the middle of Easy Street.

Charlie gets into uniform and times his entrance into Easy Street just as Eric is patrolling his victorious battlefield. The camera moves in slowly as the terrifying Campbell, wearing a police helmet as a trophy, stalks Charlie across the street. The mood of comical menace is beautifully sustained throughout. Charlie hits Eric across the head with his truncheon, but Eric barely notices. He offers his head to Charlie a couple of times, and he whacks it to no effect. To further demonstrate his strength, Eric gleefully bends a lamppost in half. This enables Charlie to clamber up Eric's back and lower the lamppost over his head. This being 1917, it is a gas lamppost and Charlie administers the gas to Eric in the manner of an anaesthetist, knocking the villain out. It takes half a dozen policemen to carry him back to the police station.

Many other commentators before me have noted that the main set of *Easy*

Street resembles the streets of Charlie's youth (being so close in name to East Street, where he was born). It certainly doesn't look like Hollywood, California. One street sign reads 'Marie Antoinette Alley', perhaps as a satirical allusion to her attitude towards the poor and starving, perhaps Chaplin is saying that 'Easy Street' isn't meant to represent South London specifically: it could be any ghetto. Later, we see portraits of Tsar Nicholas and Tsarina Alexandra on the wall, possibly to further the notion that this is a universal setting.

While he is on the beat Charlie discovers the bully's wife, a very poor, run-down woman, hiding a sack of produce she has just stolen from a greengrocer's stall. A copper with a social conscience, he himself shoplifts from the stall and fills her arms with stolen vegetables. As he tells her not to cry, his own sympathetic sobbing is both comical and touching, but avoids sentimentality. The charitable tone is undercut when the bully's wife drops a flowerpot on Charlie from an upper floor window.

Back at the police station Eric wakens from his gas-induced sleep and is not a happy man. A squad of police officers, raining truncheons down on his head, has no visible impact on him, and he breaks out of the station and makes his way back to Easy Street. Once home, he beats his wife, and Charlie, who is on the other side of the street, hears the commotion and rushes over and up the stairs, to investigate. His astonishment on facing Eric Campbell again quickly

Opposite Although filmed in Hollywood, Chaplin's *Easy Street* has a strongly autobiographical element to it and recalls the streets of Charlie's childhood.

Above A street scene from Edwardian South London.

Edna, meanwhile, is kidnapped by a mob and dumped in a cellar, where a desperate-looking man injects himself with a hypodermic needle. This is social realism at its rawest

turns to panic. A chase round the room ensues, and then around the street, and then around the block. The chase is genuinely involving because a strong mood of menace has already been established. If Eric catches Charlie, he will kill him. Having cornered Charlie in his bedroom, Eric locks the door and swallows the key. Eventually, Charlie evades the thug and then manages to knock him out by lobbing a stove out of an upper window onto him.

Edna, meanwhile, is kidnapped by a mob and dumped in a cellar, where a desperate-looking man injects himself with a hypodermic needle. This is social realism at its rawest. The addict attacks Edna, who fights him off until Charlie suddenly appears, having been dropped through a hole into the cellar by the previously mentioned crazed mob. Charlie lands on the syringe and has a sudden spasm of energy. He overpowers the druggy assailant and fights off the local mob with super-human strength. Then an inter-title card appears:

Easy Street is transformed, and there are boxes overflowing with greenery. Charlie is a respected police officer now, and the local citizens bow or shake his hand. Eric and his wife emerge. He is much better dressed and is far more subdued, and he even shows his newfound chivalry by swapping positions with his wife, so that he walks nearer to the kerb. (In an age when roads were frequently muddy, splashes from passing traffic were a major hazard.) Charlie is shown waiting for someone, and as Edna appears his face lights up with genuine pleasure, the openness of his acting as fresh today as it was then. The two of them walk arm in arm towards the Mission, and the scene fades to black.

Easy Street was immediately recognized as a classic by contemporary critics and audiences, a status it has never lost in the intervening ninety years. It is also the most autobiographical of all his films from the Mutual period. His mother's movement into religious circles following the collapse of her stage career, for example, is evident in Edna's character. She clearly is a true believer, and when she first comes into view Charlie bathes her in a heavenly light. The scenes of domestic abuse are played dramatically and were most likely drawn from Charlie's own experiences as a boy when he saw his drunken father hurling an ashtray at Louise's head and knocking her unconscious.

In 2005 I was pleased to be invited to an open-air screening of *Easy Street* in the grounds of the Imperial War Museum in London. Like many others, I was enormously looking forward to the event: seeing a Chaplin film on the big screen in the neighbourhood in which he lived as a child was a rare treat. Unfortunately, somebody had made an idiotic decision somewhere along the line, and the film was projected with the most disastrous musical accompaniment imaginable: very loud, throbbing drum 'n' bass. Immediately, the film was ruined. The music must support the film sympathetically and not dominate it. I screamed over the top of the throbbing din to the operator, who was sitting in a van with two huge speakers on top of it, to turn the sound off. After much shouting, the wrong, wrong music was stopped, and the film immediately picked up as it played to the ambient sounds of modern Kennington. Pleasingly, as Charlie the policeman first waddled down Easy Street, a police siren started wailing in the distance.

***Easy Street* was immediately recognized as a classic by contemporary critics and audiences, a status it has never lost in the intervening ninety years. It is also the most autobiographical of all his films from the Mutual period**

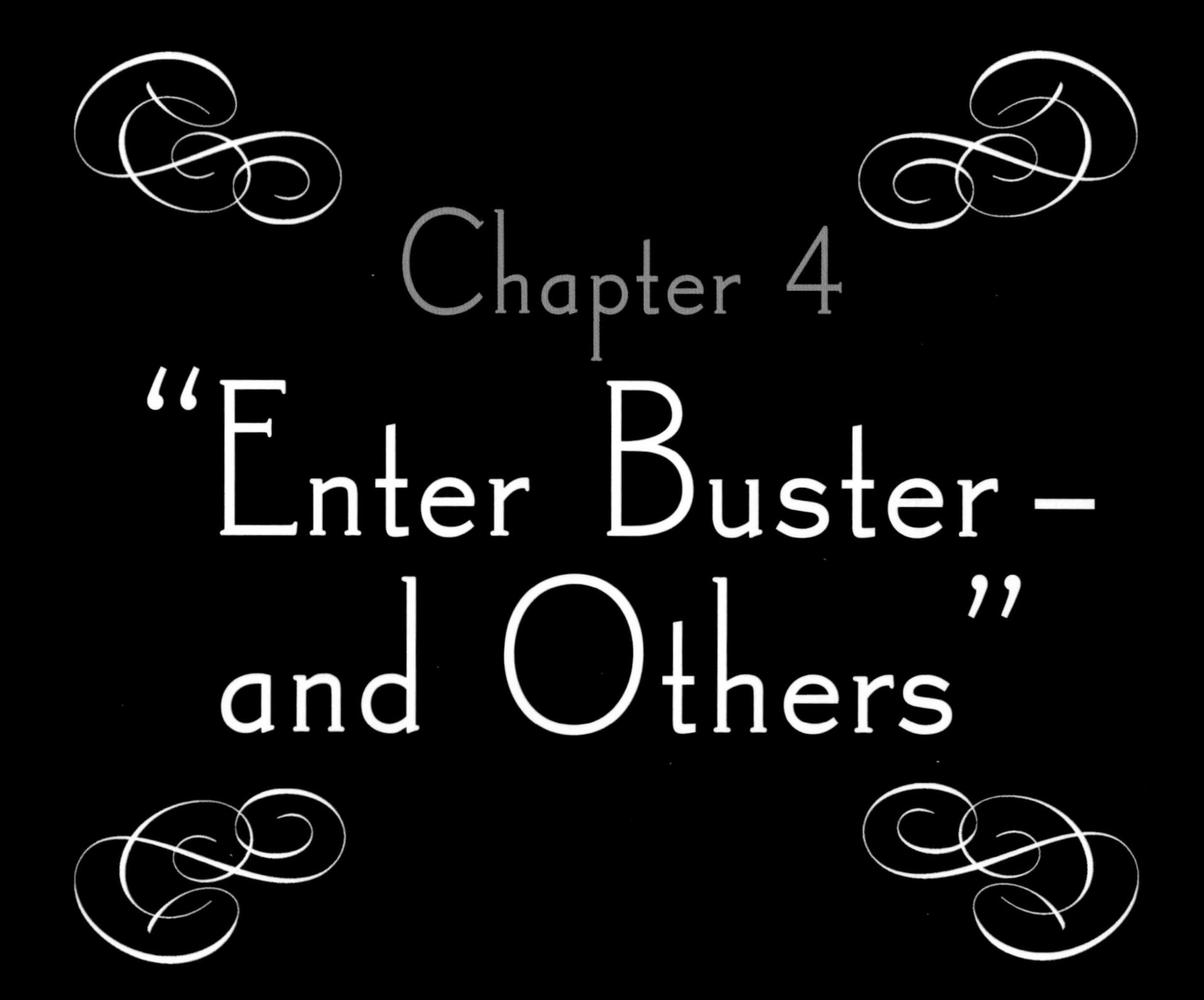

Chapter 4
"Enter Buster – and Others"

Charlie Chaplin

His Signature

In his First Million Dollar Picture

"A DOG'S LIFE"

A "First National"  Attraction

Enter Buster – and Others

Shortly after *Easy Street* was released to huge acclaim in January 1917, Buster Keaton decided it was time to break up the family act, the Three Keatons. His father, Joe, had been drinking heavily for some time and had made a few powerful enemies. He had, for example, threatened Martin Beck, an important impresario, with physical violence, which had led to a drop in the quality of the act's bookings. By this point Buster, although only twenty-one, was a veteran of the stage, and he knew it was not the time for him to go backwards, so in February 1917 the Three Keatons were disbanded, and Buster immediately signed up for the *Passing Show of 1917*, a stage production at the Winter Garden Theater, New York, for $250 a week. This was an opportunity for him to branch out into other areas of show business, and he began to work up an act.

One morning he was walking the streets of New York when he bumped into an old vaudeville acquaintance, Lou Anger. Lou had appeared with the Three Keatons on numerous occasions but had now retired from the stage and was working as studio manager at the Colony Studio on 48th Street. Lou introduced his companion, Roscoe Arbuckle, who asked Buster if he had ever been in a film studio. Buster admitted that he hadn't, so the next morning Roscoe showed him around. He was totally bowled over by what he saw:

> The Colony Studios were housed in a big loft building on East 48th Street. When I got there the whole place was humming with activity. Besides the Arbuckle Company, Norma [Buster's future sister-in-law] Talmadge's own company, her sister Constance's and a couple of others were making romantic dramas in other parts of the studio. This seemed wonderful to me. It was like being in a great entertainment factory where different shows were being manufactured at the same time.[1]

Buster was especially fascinated by the camera:

> Roscoe – none of us who knew him personally ever called him Fatty – took the camera apart for me so I would understand how it worked and what it could do. He showed me how film was developed, cut and then spliced together. But the greatest thing to me about picture making was the way it automatically did away with the physical limitations of the theatre ... The camera has no such limitations. The whole world was its stage. If you wanted cities, schools, deserts, the Atlantic Ocean ... for your scenery and background, you merely took your camera to them.[2]

Below **Buster Keaton makes his screen debut – a scene from the 1917 short *The Butcher Boy*, starring Roscoe Arbuckle. Buster is on the extreme right.**

Roscoe asked Buster to play a small part in the next scene he was shooting for his new comedy, *The Butcher Boy.* The set was a large grocery store with a butcher's counter in one corner. Thrilled with this new environment of filmmaking, Buster readily agreed.

Before Buster's appearance in the film, Roscoe takes a couple of moments to demonstrate his uncanny ability with deadly knives. He throws them up in the air, and they land impressively, blade down, embedded in the wooden counter. It's hard to imagine a comedian today endeavouring to get laughs from such sharp knife play. Buster enters as a customer, and his attention is caught by a barrel of molasses. He approaches Roscoe, puts his big, empty tin on the counter and places the money to pay for the molasses inside the tin. Roscoe fills the tin and demands payment. Buster tells him the money's in the tin and wanders off to look around the shop, leaving his hat upturned on the counter. To get at the money, Roscoe pours the molasses out of the tin and into the hat. He retrieves the coin, licks it, puts it in his pocket and cheerfully pours the molasses back into the tin. Buster returns to the counter, picks up the tin and puts his hat back on his head. Roscoe bids him good day by raising his hat, but when Buster attempts to reciprocate, his hat remains mysteriously stuck to his head. He drops the tin of molasses on the floor and seeks Roscoe's help in getting his hat off. The hat is successfully removed, but Buster now finds one foot firmly stuck in the spilt molasses. Roscoe has an idea. He lifts a boiling kettle off the hot stove, meanwhile spilling a pint or so over the head of a bald man who is playing draughts, then pours the hot water over Buster's foot. This loosens Buster sufficiently to allow Roscoe to boot him out of the shop.

The 'gag' with the hot water over the bald man's head is hardly a gag at all. It provokes a shock reaction from an audience today precisely as it must have done among the more sensitive audience members when it was first shown. It's a visual equivalent of a four-letter word dropped into a comic's act to boost the potential laughter. The act of swearing can be funny, but the almost compulsive use of f***, sometimes to hide poor-quality material, can become monotonous. The temptation is enormous because an audience often laughs at f*** because of the shock value. Pouring apparently boiling water over a bald head strikes me as the same kind of laugh.

Buster was always proud that his first scene in motion pictures was captured in only one take, and it's a remarkably assured debut. Rather like Charlie's Tramp, which emerged in only his second film, Buster establishes his comic persona from the very start with the deadpan face and porkpie hat. If Buster hadn't got his foot firmly stuck to the floor, I'd say he'd hit the ground running.

The 'gag' with the hot water over the bald man's head is hardly a gag at all. It provokes a shock reaction from an audience today precisely as it must have done among the more sensitive audience members when it was first shown

Rather like Charlie's Tramp, which emerged in only his second film, Buster establishes his comic persona from the very start with the deadpan face and porkpie hat

Back to the action. Al St John arrives on a bicycle, cycling right up to the steps of the store. He runs in, quickly demonstrating the differences between him and Buster Keaton as comedians. Buster had a routine, whereas Al has a couple of kicks at Roscoe's behind before venturing a couple of jabs at his stomach. Arbuckle uses his tummy to bounce Al across the store and then throws large bags of flour at him. The comedy has dropped several, considerable, notches since Buster's business with the coin and molasses.

Buster recounts how Roscoe explained the next scene, in which Buster was to return to the store, looking for his hat:

> As you come in the store ... I will be throwing some of these bags at St John. He will duck, and you will get one right in the face ... Now it is awfully hard not to flinch when you are expecting to get hit with something like that. So as you come in the door, look back. When I say 'Turn!' you turn, and it will be there.[3]

It was! Arbuckle, who weighed 280 pounds, threw custard pies with a considerable deal of force. As Buster later recalled in his autobiography:

> I found out that day that he also could put his whole heart and every ounce of his weight into throwing a flour bag with devastating accuracy. There was enough in that thing to upend me completely. It put my feet where my head had been, and with no co-operation from me whatever. Enough flour went up my nostrils and into my mouth to make one of mother's old-fashioned cakes.[4]

This sort of rough horseplay was meat and drink to Buster – it was reminiscent of his stage experiences with his father, Joe. For the remainder of the film Buster merely becomes an adjunct to Al St John. He throws a custard pie at Al. Al throws one back. Buster ducks, and it hits another customer. Buster laughs and runs away.

Then the film abruptly changes locale. We leave the store far behind, and the scene shifts to a girls' boarding school, to which Roscoe's sweetheart has returned. To gain entry, Roscoe turns up at the school gates dressed in a voluminous velvet coat and sporting a long wig, full of ringlets tied with a giant bow. Once inside the school, he grabs the earliest opportunity to prance around, exposing a pair of oversized drawers. Al St John, Roscoe's rival in love, also dons drag, wearing a frightful wig and horn-rimmed glasses. They all sit around the dinner table, and Al 'borrows' Charlie's noisy soup gag from *The Count*, filmed six months earlier. Roscoe stops Al's slurping with the plea: 'Softer

Chaplin's contemporaries were always amazed at the care and effort he expended on each film. Nobody had ever shot so much footage for a two-reel comedy, but then, nobody else had the power that Charlie had in 1917

with the soup, please.' Buster does very little else and the film soon peters out.

Over the years film historians have debated why Buster doesn't stick to his trademark frozen face in this and the other Arbuckle pictures that follow. There is often talk of his not yet having discovered his mature style, but my belief is that it's simply how he's being directed. His reactions are there to serve the material. After nearly twenty years onstage, he would indeed be an indecisive man if he hadn't managed to find his true performing persona. In his first appearance with the molasses he is authentically deadpan throughout. No smile cracks his lips. This is chiefly his material, and he shows how comfortable he is with the style. Later, when he joins in the custard-pie throwing, he laughs when the other customer is hit because it provides the motive for the following chase, but in the molasses, hat and coin sequence Buster shows that his mature style is already in place.

The Butcher Boy was released on 23 April 1917, just one week after *The Cure*, Charlie Chaplin's latest comedy for the Mutual Film Corporation. *The Cure* is set in a sanatorium for alcoholics, but the creative process was anything but restful, and as the plentiful out-takes shown in the documentary series *Unknown Chaplin* demonstrate, *The Cure* was not instant. Initially, Charlie cast himself as a porter, pushing Eric Campbell around in a wheelchair. The out-takes reveal that he spent hours attempting to perfect a routine that was set in the lobby of the sanatorium. As one of the uniformed attendants, Charlie brings order to the chaos caused by patients milling around the lobby by directing them in the manner of a traffic cop: some wheelchairs are halted while others are waved through. He tries the routine several different ways, but none is to his satisfaction. He then introduces a new character, a resident drunk, played by John Rand, and realizes that this character has more potential than the attendant and so simply swaps roles. As a patient, Charlie makes a less likely traffic cop, and although he tries the idea again, this time in his new guise, he eventually rejects it, and it does not appear in the finished film. Although the idea didn't reach the screen in Charlie's films, Harold Lloyd later appropriated it.

Charlie's next film, *The Immigrant*, which was released on 17 June 1917, was a landmark even by his own high standards. It has been reported that he eventually shot 90,000 feet of film, as much film as D.W. Griffith used for his three-hour epic, *Intolerance*. He then spent four days and nights, without sleep, editing it down to the required 2,000 feet. *The Immigrant* is splendidly represented in the *Unknown Chaplin* documentary by a plethora of out-takes.

The Immigrant's story is a simple one. Charlie meets Edna and her mother onboard a ship bound for New York. Later, after the death of Edna's mother, she and Charlie are reunited when they bump into each other in a restaurant. Eric Campbell is, again, in great menacing form, this time as a head waiter. Several times he batters a customer, played by John Rand, to the ground for being 5 cents short on his bill. In his autobiography, Charlie maintained that:

> No member of my cast was injured in any of our pictures. Violence was carefully rehearsed and treated like choreography. A slap on the face was always tricked. No matter how much of a skirmish, everyone knew what he was doing, everything was timed.[5]

When it's Charlie's turn to pay the bill his coin arouses Eric's suspicions, and he bends it double between his teeth. Henry Bergman plays a fellow diner, an artist, who is captivated by Edna's beauty and offers to paint her portrait. The artist pays his bill, and Charlie is finally able to pay his own bill with the generous tip left by the artist. Getting an advance on the modelling fees, Charlie grabs Edna, and the two of them disappear into a registry office.

The out-takes show that the restaurant scenes, which constitute the second half of the film, were shot first and were the result of much painstaking effort. Initially, Henry Bergman was cast as the aggressive waiter. He was bulky but roughly the same height as Chaplin, and as Charlie's business with the coin developed, it became apparent that Eric's impressive glowering and potent air of menace would be perfect for the waiter's part. Bergman's scenes were reshot, with Eric stepping in to much greater effect. Chaplin's contemporaries were always amazed at the care and effort he expended on each film. Nobody had ever shot so much footage for a two-reel comedy, but then, nobody else had the power that Charlie had in 1917. Mutual tolerated his methods because his films were making them a fortune.

In the earlier part of the film the shipboard scenes depend on the perceived comedy of people feeling desperately seasick. We first see Charlie bent double over the ship's rail. He has his back to us, and we assume that his convulsions are provoked by the motion of the ocean. When he turns to face the camera, however, we see instead that he has landed a large fish. The boat rocks significantly from left to right and then back again; unfortunately, so does the horizon. This effect was achieved by placing a pendulum under the camera, which then moved from side to side. Charlie walks up and down on deck, indicating the slope by sticking out one leg and shuffling sideways with the other.

A dinner bell is rung, and the immigrants rush to the dining room, which is set on rockers to mimic the swell of a violent sea. One female immigrant (played by Henry Bergman in drag) runs in and slides backwards and forwards along the heavily polished floor. Charlie joins the woman as the two of them battle against the slippery surface. Once he gets to the dining table the gag is extended: Charlie and a fellow traveller share a bowl of soup as it slides back and forth across the table, one taking a quick spoonful before it slithers back to the other. Edna appears at the door, and Charlie gallantly offers her his seat.

Later, Charlie gets involved in some onboard gambling. In one tantalizing out-take from *Unknown Chaplin* he becomes suspicious of another card-player's shuffle and dons a pair of glasses to help him detect fraud more easily. The spectacles have big, round frames, and they look like the ones that Harold Lloyd would soon adopt as he attempted to shake off the obviously Chaplinesque character he was playing at the time, Lonesome Luke. Is this a coincidence? Charlie never used the glasses gag in the final version of *The Immigrant*, so if Harold was inspired to use them for himself, he would have needed somebody on the set to relate the information back to him. It is possible. After all, Harold certainly had insider knowledge of *The Cure,* Chaplin's previous film. Ultimately, though, the suggestion can't be proved or disproved.

One of the more controversial moments in *The Immigrant* is introduced by an inter-title card indicating the ship's arrival in New York: 'The arrival in the Land of Liberty.' An excited passenger points to something out on the horizon, and the other immigrants eagerly jump up to see the view. It is the Statue of Liberty, and we cut to a shot of Charlie, Edna, her sick mother and half a dozen immigrants looking at the statue with awe and reverence. The ship's crew immediately cordon in the immigrants with a thick rope, hastily and roughly pushing them into a corner. Charlie examines the rope's thickness across his

Below **A controversial moment in Chaplin's *The Immigrant*. Charlie, Edna Purviance and Kitty Bradbury gaze longingly at the Statue of Liberty just before the ship's crew manhandle them.**

It's just possible that seeing an Englishman having a go at the United States was what prompted Roscoe Arbuckle to have a go at Chaplin in his next film, *The Rough House*

chest and then scans the horizon to make sure he has just seen the Statue of Liberty. His wry look into the camera tells us what he's thinking. This was a remarkably satirical comment for its day and has a very modern feel. The idea that the United States might not be the idealized land of liberty is one that we can readily accept today, but in those days it would have been considered highly controversial, even un-American.

It's just possible that seeing an Englishman having a go at the United States was what prompted Roscoe Arbuckle to have a go at Chaplin in his next film, *The Rough House*, which was released on 25 June 1917, just a week after *The Immigrant. The Rough House* features a joke at Charlie's expense, and this was at a time when he was revered by his contemporaries as the greatest screen comic of them all. In an early scene Roscoe spears two bread rolls with a couple of forks and uses the rolls to imitate Chaplin's feet shuffling along, with his characteristic manner of turning a corner while hopping on one foot. Roscoe's expression, as he performs this manoeuvre, suggests that he considers this piece of comic business to be old hat and predictable. He is showing off to the maid, who laughs at his antics, but there is a certain disdain in Roscoe's performance.

Obviously, this is impossible to prove one way or the other, but the scene has also received attention over the decades for another reason: years later Chaplin featured a Dance of the Rolls in his film *The Gold Rush*, and some people have suggested that he took the idea from Arbuckle. Others have speculated that Chaplin himself might have originated the gag back in his shared Keystone days with Arbuckle. Perhaps, over lunch one day, Charlie demonstrated his gag with the French loaf (as seen in *A Jitney Elopement*), cutting it to create a concertina. Maybe he then speared a couple of other loaves and demonstrated his comic walk.

The rest of *The Rough House* is typical of Arbuckle films of this period. It begins with Roscoe lighting a cigarette while he's in bed but then falling asleep and dropping the cigarette onto some newspapers beside the bed. Waking to a healthy flame licking up the bedside cabinet, he gets up and looks at the fire with some curiosity. After a while he decides to do something about it and casually exits the bedroom, saunters through the dining room and into the kitchen. He pours some water into a small tea-cup, retraces his steps and throws the water over the blazing bed but to no avail. Realizing that he needs another cup, he goes back into the kitchen but, on his return to the dining room, he stops to take a bite out of an apple. He then absentmindedly drinks the water

Above **Inspired by Arbuckle? Charlie Chaplin's famous Dance of the Rolls in his 1925 film *The Gold Rush* may have been inspired by a Chaplin-teasing scene in Roscoe Arbuckle's *The Rough House.***

from the cup. He goes back to the kitchen, refills the cup, throws it on the bed, then goes back to the dining room, where his wife asks him what's going on. It's a reworking of the routine from 1915's *Fatty's Plucky Pup.* He tells her that the bed is on fire. She reacts with horror, and eventually the gardener's hose-pipe is used to extinguish the fire and soak everybody through.

This action has the feeling of a vaudeville routine. The staging would be simple, and the setting could be a hotel lobby. A character enters from the wings in a nightshirt and asks the host for a glass of water. The character exits and then quickly re-emerges, seeking a second glass of water. Perhaps on the third entrance he is asked 'Are you thirsty?' to which the reply must be, 'No, my bed's on fire.' It certainly has the feeling and pace of an established routine. Buster Keaton could plausibly have helped with the staging. An experienced comedy eye, behind the camera, would be invaluable when the main star was acting in a scene because the action could be viewed for the first time only on the following day (today it can be viewed the instant it's shot), so somebody with authority to give the action the thumbs up would be a boon.

The next scene is set at the breakfast table. Here we see the little dig at Charlie Chaplin with the routine with the bread rolls. An inter-title card reads: 'The grocer's boy makes a delivery.' A cyclist appears in the distance, and as he approaches the camera, we see it's Buster Keaton, his head held high, and moving rapidly through the landscape. This is what he loved about cinema: the freedom from the physical limitations of the theatre. He cycles into a washing line, which hits him neck-high, knocking him off his bike. The fall is shot from behind, which lessens its impact, but this is still the early days of Buster's film career – it is only his second Arbuckle film.

Buster enters the kitchen and quickly indulges in some horseplay with the always hard-working Al St John. Part of the Three Keatons stage act is revived when Al swings a broomstick above his head towards Buster, who ducks every time it swings his way. The action is filmed with the camera operator under-cranking so that, when the picture is projected at normal speed, the action is all the faster. This was probably Buster's idea. He was new to filmmaking, and this sort of simple camera trick would have appealed to him because, again, it would have been impossible onstage.

A few moments later Buster throws a knife towards Al, who is crouched behind the piano. The knife, or at least the very tip of it, lands directly in Al's mouth. Jokes with knives were an Arbuckle trait, but this may have been another Keaton gag because, again, it relies on a simple camera trick. The camera is cranked backwards and the action is staged backwards (much as Chaplin did in his out-take from *Behind the Screen*). Al St John stands behind the piano with a knife in his mouth, which is then pulled out on a thin piece of wire. Once the film is projected, the knife terrifyingly appears to land right in his mouth.

Roscoe falls onto a circular table, which revolves, just like the one in Charlie's solo comedy, *One A.M.* Roscoe is pushed round and round on the table by Buster and Al, and he claps with excitement like a kid on a carousel. The fighting carries on outside the house. Roscoe throws a bucket of white goo over Al, who notices Buster roaring with laughter. Keaton is again breaking his deadpan approach because the action demands it. His laughter motivates Al to throw something at him, and this knocks him over backwards. Buster gets up and splutters, but he has the most endearing grin on his face. This isn't acting: he's having the time of his life. He seems to be admiring the accuracy and power of the shot, supplied by an offscreen Roscoe who, as we've seen, was renowned for his object-throwing expertise. Later in the film Al and Buster join the police force, and this is the nearest we ever get to seeing Keaton as a Keystone Cop. He has tremendous fun tumbling over hills, somersaulting off dunes and getting stuck on top of fences.

Roscoe's next film, *His Wedding Night*, was released on 20 August 1917. Initially, the setting closely resembles the opening sequence in *The Butcher Boy*. Roscoe is serving behind a counter, but this time the scene is a drug store. A

Buster gets up and splutters, but he has the most endearing grin on his face. This isn't acting: he's having the time of his life. He seems to be admiring the accuracy and power of the shot

'Unquestionably the horse is superior to man. One hundred thousand men will go to see a horse race, but I bet not a single horse would go to see one hundred thousand men running' – inter-title card from *Oh Doctor*

customer orders a milkshake, and Roscoe demonstrates his amazing dexterity by throwing a glass over his shoulder and catching it behind his back. He mixes the concoction in a style that was obviously influenced by Charlie's cocktail shaking in *The Rink*, but Roscoe merely shakes himself, ignoring any subtlety the business might offer.

A large bottle of perfume is on display, with a sign encouraging customers to try a free sample. Roscoe is outraged by the amount people are using, and he quickly puts up a sign that reads '4 dollars an ounce'. A large African-American woman enters the store and leans against the sign. When she walks away we see that the lettering on the sign is now imprinted on the back of her dress (on her behind, which is even worse). In crude terms, this appalling joke places a monetary value on the woman and conjures up images of slavery. The joke is also poor because it breaks the logic of the situation: the words should appear on the woman in reverse, not as they do. Al St John appears and immediately recycles Chaplin's gag from *The Count*: he eats a watermelon then cleans his ears out with a napkin. Inevitably, Al starts a fight and is eventually thrown out of the store. Several kicks up the arse later and he's hobbling down the road, away from the camera, very much in the style of Charlie's end sequence in *The Tramp*.

As in his previous Arbuckle film, Buster makes a fantastic entrance on a bike. We see him cycling down the road with a big box on his head. He cycles directly into a bicycle rack and is deposited right outside the drug store. The camera is nearer to the action than in the previous film when he cycled into a washing line, and so the gag makes a greater impression. Apart from this, Buster has very little to do in this film. He delivers a wedding dress, which, for some unfathomable reason, he decides to model for the prospective bride. The reason he does this, of course, is so that Al St John can kidnap him in the mistaken belief that he is the bride. A sack over the head helps the misunderstanding.

Later in the film Roscoe amply demonstrates the lengths to which some comedians will go to get a laugh. The racism re-emerges as Roscoe holds a mule while it repeatedly kicks an African-American. He then sticks his own head between the mule's hind legs and it ends up sitting on him.

Roscoe Arbuckle's next film, *Oh Doctor*, was released on 20 September, and by now there was a new name in the creative team, Jean Havez. He is credited as writing *Oh Doctor*, although that mainly meant composing the inter-title cards, and he certainly earned his money. One card reads: 'Unquestionably the horse is superior to man. One hundred thousand men will go to see a horse race, but I bet not a single horse would go to see one hundred thousand men running.' This kind of joke is unusual in Arbuckle films, and although it's not hilariously funny, the 'high class' humour, sounding rather like Oscar Wilde on a bad afternoon, is intended to lift the comic tone.

In *Oh Doctor* Buster plays Roscoe's prepubescent son, who spends a lot of time either being annoying or crying. His performance is very funny – the only really funny thing in the film. Again, he's following the dictates of the storyline and Arbuckle's direction: he laughs, he cries. Al St John's Chaplin fixation continues, but this time he's carrying a cane and wearing a bowler hat. It's enough to remind you of Charlie and to show how lacking Al St John is in comparison. Towards the end of the film Roscoe disguises himself as a policeman, and we're straight back to the Keystone days when he picks up a brick and throws it at somebody.

Meanwhile, Chaplin hadn't exactly been idle, and, on 22 October, four months after *The Immigrant* was first publicly screened, his last Mutual comedy, *The Adventurer*, was released. *The Adventurer* begins and ends with a chase. Dressed as a convict, Charlie is chased up and down hills, always eluding his pursuers. Later in the film he finds himself as a guest at a big country house. In one scene he's eating ice cream on a balcony when he drops a large dollop of it down the front of his trousers. His discomfort is somewhat relieved when he shakes the offending dessert out of his trouser leg. It drops through the grating of the balcony and onto the bare back of a rather posh and dignified woman. As she recoils from the freezing sweet, she stands upright and it falls further down her back. Eric Campbell reaches for the pesky pudding and gets a firm slap for his trouble. As Charlie is chased through the house, he saves one of his greatest gags from the Mutual period until last. He becomes a lampstand

Left **In a scene from *The Adventurer* that didn't make the final cut Edna Purviance and Charlie listen in some horror to Eric Campbell's piano playing. Eric's unusually subdued appearance here bears witness to the trauma he was suffering in his personal life.**

As Charlie is chased through the house, he saves one of his greatest gags from the Mutual period until last. He becomes a lampstand by placing a large lampshade over his head and standing very still

Opposite Charlie in prison garb attempts to avoid capture in *The Adventurer.*

by placing a large lampshade over his head and standing very still. His pursuers rush past him, none the wiser. He kicks Eric in the stomach and runs off.

Eric Campbell was by now a well-established fixture of Chaplin films, his imposing physical presence adding an essential dimension to the comedy. He was also now globally recognized, and he and Charlie had become firm friends. In *The Adventurer*, though, he seems subdued, and given what was happening in his private life this is scarcely surprising. In the course of the summer and autumn of 1917 he was hit by a series of personal tragedies. On 9 July his wife, Gertrude, died of a heart attack while they were dining out in Santa Monica. Two weeks later his daughter, Oona, was hit by a car and badly injured while she was shopping for mourning clothes. Clearly traumatized, Eric then met and quickly married a woman named Pearl Gilman, who filed for divorce only two months later, citing drunkenness and cruelty on Eric's part.

But if things were going badly for Charlie's friend, they were going very well for Charlie himself, for having now left Mutual, he accepted a magnificent contract with First National. Remember, in 1914 he was paid $150 a week, rising to $1,250 a week a year later. Then came the extraordinary Mutual deal: $10,000 a week plus a bonus of $150,000. Having fully justified the money by making twelve comedies that were streets ahead of his nearest competitor in terms of the sheer number of gags, subtle characterizations and coherent storylines, Charlie was in a fantastic position to negotiate. After all, such was his enormous worldwide popularity that the Mutual Film Corporation had made back their investment in him on his very first release, *The Floorwalker.*

The deal with First National, skilfully negotiated by his brother Sydney, obliged Charlie to deliver eight two-reelers in sixteen months. For their part, First National would pay $1 million plus a $75,000 bonus and would facilitate the building of Charlie's own studio. Also, after a few years, the rights to the films would become exclusively Charlie's.

As for Eric, after his second marriage fell apart, he moved to the Los Angeles Athletic Club, in rooms next door to Charlie's own. As it would be a couple of months before Charlie would be filming again – the new studio was being built for him – he suggested to Mary Pickford that she should use Eric in her new film, *Amarilly of Clothes-Line Alley.* She readily agreed. Eric would be better off working, rather than having lots of spare time to brood. On 20 December, three days into the filming, Eric attended a party. He drank excessively and attempted to drive home, crashing his car at 60 mph on the wrong side of the road. He was killed instantly.

A forgotten star

Larry Semon is an example of a comedian who was massively successful at the time but who is virtually forgotten today. He was born in West Point, Mississippi, on 16 July 1889 and was working as a newspaper cartoonist in New York when the film company Vitagraph approached him to write and direct comedies for them.

Larry's father was a stage magician called Zera the Great, and in his youth he had gained a great deal of stage experience. When he was on his deathbed, Zera asked Larry to promise that he would abandon the stage in favour of pursuing his talent as an artist, and this he did, but now that Vitagraph had offered him a chance to get into pictures, Larry grabbed the opportunity with both hands. He started by directing films, but within three months he was starring in them. His comedy philosophy was simple: the gag is king. In a world before sophisticated animated cartoons, Larry was using sophisticated cartoon humour. In *Risk and Roughnecks* the emphasis is entirely on continuous manic action. The film is expertly directed by Semon, and the comic effects are pulled off with aplomb. He films the action in reverse in one sequence where he is seen eating spaghetti, making it twirl in magical ways. Later he smashes each of the villains over the head, causing them to somersault down the street until they ultimately roll straight into prison.

Below Larry as the Scarecrow, Dorothy Dwan (Larry's wife) as Dorothy in a 1925 silent version of *The Wizard of Oz*. The large actor playing the Tin Woodman is Oliver Hardy. Stan Laurel also featured in some Semon films.

In an inspired piece of marketing the main title-card for *Plagues and Puppy Love*, which was released on 1 October 1917, shows Larry Semon's face five times. The title also reflects the decision to give each of the Semon comedies an alliterative title. In *Plagues and Puppy Love* the gags come thick and fast. Larry inflates his chest outrageously and then blows a policeman backwards across a park. A small dog is attached to numerous balloons and floats away.

Although not Chaplinesque, Larry Semon still borrows heavily from the iconic comic. In his first appearance we see Larry ambling along a dirty road. He pulls out his pockets to show he has no money. He then comes across a horseshoe, which he picks up for luck. He is immediately knocked off his feet by a car

Left Larry Semon *c.*1920 when he was one of the top comedians of silent film.

Below Larry in *Spuds*, made the year before his death.

passing perilously close to him (or, rather, passing perilously close to one of his stuntmen). He's hit in the rear by another car, which propels him 30 feet up in the air. Reversing the film reveals how this was done. A stuntman is flown on a wire into the path of a stationary car. Once he lands on the ground, the car is quickly reversed away from him. When the action is played backwards it looks exactly as if the car has rocketed him upwards. We also get Larry's version of the Keystone Cops: fast-moving, bumbling policeman falling in and out of crazily steered motor cars. Action is everything. Larry isn't interested in developing an emotional, well-rounded character.

By 1926 Larry's popularity was waning. In March 1928 the man who had once earned a million dollars a year filed for bankruptcy. A few months later he was dead.

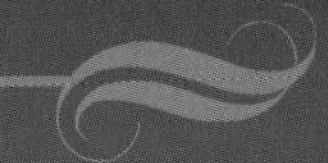

Charlie was deeply upset by Eric's death. So, too, was Stan Jefferson, the young comedian who had roomed with Chaplin on the Karno tours. As he later recalled:

> Eric was such a wonderful guy. People used to say he had a heart as big as himself, and Eric was a mountain of a man ... He had a beautiful big voice, again just like himself. The odd thing though was that he was really a very shy man, like Charlie in that respect.[6]

As I've already mentioned, the name Stan Jefferson disappeared from the vaudeville circuit at some point in 1917, and you would be forgiven for thinking that the man faded into obscurity. The last time we hear of Jefferson he's touring in a double act with an Australian woman called Charlotte Mae Dahlberg. Perhaps in an attempt to change his luck (he had noticed that Stan Jefferson contained thirteen letters) he decided to alter it, and Stan Jefferson disappeared. Stan Laurel took his place.

Remarkably, he got the chance to make a film within two months of changing his name. Stanley Comedies was formed in June 1917 when an ex-general manager at Universal Studios, Isadore Bernstein, announced his plans to form two comedy units. Adolph Ramish, the owner of the Los Angeles Hippodrome, is said to have introduced Stan to Bernstein, and the resulting film was called *Nuts in May*. Only tiny fragments, in very poor condition, remain of the film, however. The 'nuts' in the title refer to the patients in an insane asylum, and there are a few camera tricks showing a speeded-up steam-roller cracking open some nuts. But through the fog, Stan looks like a very young Stan Laurel.

The film wasn't released, and Stan returned to the stage, but Carl Laemmle, head of Universal Pictures, saw the film and liked it enough to offer him a four-film contract. None of these films, *Phoney Photos*, *Hickory Hiram*, *Whose Zoo?* and, in a return to a familiar theme, *O, It's Great to be Crazy*, all made between September and October 1917, exists any more, but in the fourth, we know that Stan plays a character, Sam Squirrel, who works in an insane asylum. And, if there isn't a joke about squirrels and their nuts in there somewhere, then certify me now.

Stan returned to the stage and the double act with Charlotte, but he got lucky again when a major new comedy film producer suddenly lost the services of his star comic, the circus clown Toto. Stan had been seen onstage by the experienced comedy director Alf Goulding, who recommended him to the producer Hal Roach.

Meanwhile, Stan's future partner had made his way into films, too. Oliver Hardy got his break with the Lubin film company. His first film, *Outwitting Dad*, was released in April 1914, and he went on to make another thirty-eight films that year. On the credits he's listed as Babe Hardy, a nickname apparently bestowed by a cheerful barber. As Simon Louvish points out in his joint biography of Laurel and Hardy, the adoption of the nickname Babe stopped people calling him Fatty.

Left The imposing figure of Oliver Hardy looms over his colleagues. The figure on the right is not Charlie Chaplin, but Billy West, who made a lucrative film career out of a passable imitation of the Tramp.

Oliver and his wife of two years, Madelyn Saloshin, a talented pianist, moved to Jacksonville, Florida, where several film studios were based, and his career continued to flourish. In 1916 he made forty-seven films. Then he teamed up with another comedian, Billy Ruge, a much smaller man, and they made a series of comedies for the Vim Film Company under the double act name of Plump and Runt. In one of them, *One Too Many*, Oliver plays a young man who wakes up one morning to find a letter from his uncle. The letter ends: 'Will arrive about two. Am just dying to see your wife and baby. Your Uncle John.' For some reason, Oliver has told his uncle that he has a wife and baby, when he has neither. He asks Billy Ruge, who is playing a janitor, to help him: 'Here's $50. Get me a baby.' The rather unpromising subject of child-snatching is explored for whatever comic potential it might have. Billy Ruge approaches women in a park, who are quite happy to part with their children in exchange for a few dollars, and at one point he runs away from the camera in a parody of Chaplin's walk, another reminder that, at this time, Charlie was so popular that other comics would look for laughs by impersonating aspects of him.

In an era of imitators, 1917 saw Harold Lloyd trying to break free from the shackles of Charlie Chaplin. His character Willie Work had given way in 1915 to Lonesome Luke, but even this persona clearly still owed a debt to Charlie's Tramp. Fifty-three Lonesome Luke films appeared between June 1915 and December 1917, and audiences loved them. In April 1917 the *New York Dramatic Mirror* wrote:

> To have become in less than eighteen months a comedian so popular as to be ranked with the leaders in that line and one who is an advertised attraction in many theatres, is the story of Harold Lloyd's achievements in the Pathé Lonesome Luke comedies.

Andrew L. Stone, the owner of a San Francisco theatre, said: 'Of all the shows I ran, the Lonesome Lukes with Harold Lloyd seemed to be the most popular, even more popular than Chaplin.'[7] But any joy that Harold felt at Lonesome Luke's success was surely tempered by the nagging question of how much this popularity was down to the close resemblance to Charlie's Tramp.

In the event, Harold eventually persuaded Roach to introduce someone new to the screen: instead of a shabby tramp, the new character would look and dress like an ordinary man. Harold realized that Lonesome Luke didn't work in romantic situations, and he also wanted to be able to employ a wider range of

Below left He may look like Charlie Chaplin here, but this is actually Harold Lloyd as the Chaplin-inspired Lonesome Luke. He is talking to Bebe Daniels, with Snub Pollard behind.

Below right The transformation. With added glasses, Harold Lloyd becomes recognisably Harold Lloyd.

The 'glasses character', as he was called, was in some respects little different from Harold in real life: he was energetic, resourceful, courageous, quick-witted and charming

acting skills. A more rounded character was still some way ahead, but the new look was immediately popular. Harold adopted a pair of horn-rimmed spectacles, and these came to define the nature of the character. The 'glasses character', as he was called, was in some respects little different from Harold in real life: he was energetic, resourceful, courageous, quick-witted and charming. The spectacles never actually had any glass in them because it would have reflected the studio lights, and they had the advantage that without them Harold Lloyd could walk down any street in the world and not be recognized.

In *All Aboard*, released on 25 November 1917, the character is, at this early stage of his development, fairly unlikeable. He kicks people in the stomach without provocation, and he resorts to violence at the drop of a hat. But, at times, he does have great charm. Although Harold has left the Chaplin look behind, he is still clearly influenced by his material. One scene features the cast in a ship's dining room. The room rocks from side to side, as did the dining room in *The Immigrant*, but Harold extends the gag by hiding in a large trunk, which slides between the passengers' berths. It's worth noting that it is the trunk that's funny in this scene, not Harold. He has some funny business in his fight with the villain, in collaboration with Harry 'Snub' Pollard, an Australian comic who is more obviously the clown in the film. His upside down Kaiser Wilhelm moustache and baggy pants are a marked contrast to Harold's 'straight' look. The glasses character was an immediate hit and was so successful that Lonesome Luke was retired at the end of 1917. Harold had swapped certain box office success for a chance to find his own comic personality.

Meanwhile, Arbuckle and Keaton continued their relentless pace of filmmaking, and the next film, *Coney Island*, was released on 11 October 1917. The film, which is shot in a real amusement park, contains some superb footage of the rides of the day, not to mention the stunning opening shots of Luna Park lit up at night. Roscoe's wife's entrance to the park is witnessed by a genuine park employee, who is featured at the extreme right of the frame. Unnoticed at the time of filming, like all onlookers glimpsed in silent comedies he remains utterly unamused.

When Buster reaches Luna Park his sweetheart is stolen by Al, who's able to pay her entrance fee. In a beautifully timed piece of business he then has a go at one of the 'test your strength' machines, swinging the mallet behind him just as Roscoe is walking by, sending his hat flying and knocking him over. Having seen what he's accidentally done, Buster sits down and laughs gleefully.

Above A contemporary postcard of Luna Park, the setting for Arbuckle and Keaton's *Coney Island*.

Opposite Buster swings the mallet, Roscoe Arbuckle takes the blow in *Coney Island*.

Roscoe retaliates by picking up the mallet and hitting Buster over the head with it, registering a hit on the bell, which, in turn, wins him a cigar.

One capsized boat-ride later, a soaked Roscoe decides to get out of his wet clothes by hiring a bathing suit. There is none in his size, and he is told to 'hire a tent'. Roscoe then spies a woman, roughly his size, and he steals her costume. Never needing much excuse to climb into women's clothes, Roscoe steals the costume, parasol and all, and spends the second half of the film in drag.

Eventually, he reaches a truce with Al St John and they resolve 'that women were the cause of all our trouble. From now on we cut them out. We stand one for all and all for one.' Then a pretty woman wanders past, and Al, without hesitation, goes after her. Roscoe then spies another woman and skips towards her, not for a moment worrying that his chances might be scuppered by the woman's bathing costume that he's still wearing.

Buster's father Joe Keaton makes his first appearance in the pictures in *Out West*, which was released on 20 January 1918. He plays a railway employee who chases Roscoe across the top of a train. Roscoe jumps off, casually rolls a cigarette in one hand and then lights a match on the train as it passes behind him. With perfect timing, he then leaps back onto the train. He is later booted off the train and finds himself in a desert. An inter-title card reads: 'Exhausted, hungry and half-dead, Fatty wanders through the wilderness.' He is so thirsty that we see him literally spitting cotton. Then he sees a mirage: a clever double-exposure transforms the left-hand side of the frame into a seascape. He finally finds a genuine water hole and impressively drains the contents in three or four

3000 GOOD

Al shoots the bartender, who collapses onto the counter and then onto the floor. He is clearly dead. Without skipping a beat, Buster flips up a sign reading, 'Bartender Wanted'

gulps. Three Native Americans ('Red Indians' in the language of the day) spot Roscoe at the water hole, his huge backside pointing towards them. This prompts the remark, 'Look! Big fat paleface!' The Native Americans, who are armed with bows and arrows, wouldn't be human if they didn't immediately take aim at the vastly unsuspecting posterior. Three arrows hit the mark, causing Roscoe great pain until he pulls them out, one by one. Incidentally, this joke beautifully illustrates W.C. Fields's definition of comedy. A great clown himself, Fields once argued that comedy was far more truthful than drama because, in all the dramatic Westerns ever made, not once does a cowboy get an arrow in the arse. Yet it must have happened at some point in real life.

An inter-title card brings Al St John into the action: 'Wild Bill Hiccup plans a raid on the saloon.' On entering the saloon, Al orders everyone to put up their hands. They all obey, including the clock, which moves its hands up to five to one. Al shoots the bartender, who collapses onto the counter and then onto the floor. He is clearly dead. Without skipping a beat, Buster flips up a sign reading, 'Bartender Wanted'.

Roscoe comes tumbling into town and bursts through the swing doors of the saloon. Al's guns end up in Roscoe's hands. After an orgy of shooting, Roscoe flicks his hat into the air with his foot and then keeps it airborne by shooting at it. Having succeeded in doing this, he catches the hat on his head and then flicks it onto Buster's head. Roscoe indicates to Buster that he'll take the bartender's job, and they shake hands on it.

It's a pity that what happens next in the film shames them both. An African-American man, played by Ernie Morrison, is tormented by the cowboys. They fire guns at his feet, forcing him to dance and act in the stereotypical 'Comedy Negro' fashion that was standard at the time: shaking his hands, palms outwards, in exaggerated fear. With a wink to Buster, Roscoe joins in with the gun firing. The man is terrified out of his wits as he runs up and down the length of the saloon, while a storm of bullets are fired at his feet. Buster joins in the general 'fun' by shooting his guns, too. A woman from the Salvation Army (played by Alice Lake) enters the saloon and stops the 'entertainment', declaring that they should all be ashamed of themselves. Ernie Morrison is now on his knees at her feet, with tears streaming down his face, reduced to a child-like status. The cowboys melt away to the corners of the saloon, and Ernie nods his grateful thanks and exits. It could be argued that Roscoe undergoes a change of heart under the influence of the woman from the Salvation Army and that the racism is exposed for what it is. Nevertheless, it's still a disturbing sequence.

Arbuckle's next film, *The Bell Boy*, which was released on 18 March 1918, has a couple of wonderful gags right at the beginning. First, Roscoe, dressed in a bell boy's uniform, exits from the lift. A cigarette emerges from inside his mouth, and it is, miraculously, still lit. He takes a couple of puffs before discarding it. A little later we find Buster standing inside a telephone booth polishing the glass with a cloth. At one point he sticks his head through the 'glass' to polish the other side of it. There is no glass at all, but, through Buster's subtle mime, we have been fooled into thinking there is.

There follows a curious sequence involving a 'tall, dark stranger'. He is dressed in black and sports a black top hat, a huge black beard and ferocious eyebrows. Roscoe and Buster react with fright when they first catch sight of him, and they both hide behind the hotel counter. The stranger suddenly adopts the stereotypical pose of a caricature of a gay man: his left hand goes to his hip, while his right hand hangs limply from the wrist. He minces over to the counter, and Roscoe concludes he has no need to fear this overtly effeminate man and starts to play pat-a-cake with him.

The bearded man asks for a shave, so Roscoe directs him to the barber's suite. In a parody of the man's mincing, Roscoe skips lightly up and down in front of Buster, who is clearly amused by his co-star's antics. Roscoe straps the man into the barber's chair so that his arms are tied down, and he sets about his beard with scissors and gusto. After a few moments, the hairy customer is revealed to the audience in his new guise as 'General Grant, hero of the Union Army'. Roscoe salutes him, but then swings him round in the chair and attacks the beard again. This time he is made to look like Abraham Lincoln. Roscoe gives him a stove-pipe hat, and the image is complete. Up pops an inter-title card: 'Abraham Lincoln, who freed the slaves.' The heavily bewhiskered patron is once again pushed down into the barber's chair as Roscoe refashions his beard, this time to resemble Kaiser Wilhelm II. Roscoe immediately starts hitting him with soapsuds. America had by now entered the First World War, so this patriotic soaping would have been lapped up by a domestic audience. (Later in the film we see a sign that reads 'FRENCH AND GERMAN COOKING' with the words 'AND GERMAN' crossed out.)

The Bell Boy features a tantalizing glimpse of Joe and Buster Keaton working together. Joe, who had long been an opponent of the movies, had obviously changed his mind, and he throws himself into the action by immediately kicking his own son up the hotel lobby. The picture also contains a hilarious slapstick sequence involving a horse-drawn elevator, a plank of wood and an elk's head.

***The Bell Boy* features a tantalizing glimpse of Joe and Buster Keaton working together. Joe, who had long been an opponent of the movies, had obviously changed his mind**

A month after *The Bell Boy* was released Charlie Chaplin released his first film for First National. *A Dog's Life*, at just over thirty-two minutes, was Charlie's longest film to date. I discount *Tillie's Punctured Romance* because, although it was a feature, Charlie merely co-starred and did not write or direct it. Released on 14 April 1918, *A Dog's Life* is a giant leap in his career, showing once again that he is leagues ahead of his contemporaries.

> My first picture in my new studio was *A Dog's Life*. The story had an element of satire, parallelling [*sic*] the life of a dog with that of a tramp ... I was beginning to think of comedy in a structural sense, and to become conscious of its architectural form. Each sequence implied the next sequence, all of them relating to the whole ... If a gag interfered with the logic of events, no matter how funny it was, I would not use it.[8]

His confidence was sky-high. A new studio had been built for him at La Brea Avenue, and for the first time Sydney was to appear onscreen with him. Their closeness is amply illustrated in the scene where Charlie is trying to steal food from Syd's lunch wagon. Every time Syd turns his back, Charlie crams more food into his mouth but immediately stops chewing the moment Syd swings round to look at him. The brothers' performances dovetail into each other beautifully. This is one of several notable sequences in the movie. In another the tramp is passing an employment office just as a job in a brewery is being advertised. He rushes in and manoeuvres himself to the front of the queue. A clerk appears behind the counter, and Charlie steps forward but is beaten to the window. Another clerk opens a second window, and Charlie

Right Charlie poses with his two co-stars in *A Dog's Life*.

Opposite The rewards of success. Charlie and his half-brother-cum-business manager, Sydney, start work on Charlie's new studio.

LA BREA AVE.
De LONGPRE AVE.

Edna tries to flirt with Charlie but is hopeless at it. She gives a very funny performance as she winks in a curiously stilted way. He thinks she's got something in her eye

waddles over but, again, is beaten to it. He then dashes from one window to the other in an increasingly frantic fashion, missing out every time. His mistiming is perfectly timed!

Edna Purviance is, naturally, the love interest, and this is by far her best role to date. She works at the Green Lantern Dance Hall but is totally unsuited to her job. Her singing leaves the audience weeping, wailing and sobbing in a wonderful medley of mime. The bartender is so moved that he puts the money he has stolen back into the till.

Once Edna gets offstage, the manager tells her she must make more effort to get on with the customers: 'If you smile and wink, they'll buy a drink.' This is the old music hall tradition with which Charlie's family had grown up, and indeed, one wonders if there's something of Charlie's mother in Edna's failed attempt to win over her audience with her singing. Edna tries to flirt with Charlie but is hopeless at it. She gives a very funny performance as she winks in a curiously stilted way. He thinks she's got something in her eye. She then rolls her eyes and twitches, as if attempting to say, 'Do you want to come upstairs?' Charlie is puzzled. 'I'm flirting,' Edna explains. Finally understanding, Charlie looks her up and down and smiles. He fixes her with a look and the mood relaxes. They then dance crazily across the dance floor, with Charlie dragging a dog behind him on a lead. The dog's name is Scraps.

On Charlie's first visit to the Green Lantern he discovers that no dogs are allowed, so he sticks Scraps down the back of his trousers. Unfortunately, the dog's tail sticks out of a hole in the trousers and, when Charlie ties his shoelace, the protruding tail thumps merrily away at a bass drum, much to the puzzlement of the drummer, who is played by an old vaudevillian called Chuck Riesner. Riesner's timing here is immaculate as he looks in bemusement at the drum and then into the camera.

Charlie is intent on retrieving a wallet that is in the possession of two crooks who are drinking in a private booth. The crooks are played by Albert Austin and Bud Jamieson, Jamieson taking the role that would have gone to Eric Campbell. Bud was 6 feet tall and a versatile actor, and he had last worked with Charlie in the Essanay days, appearing, among other things, as a crook in *The Tramp* and as his boxing opponent in *The Champion*, but he was no Eric Campbell. Charlie no doubt realized that trying to replace Eric was impossible, and Bud made no further films with him. Hiding behind a curtain in the private booth, Charlie knocks Albert Austin unconscious. He then threads his arms through Austin's coat and miraculously convinces the other crook that these (somewhat foreshortened) arms are Albert's. By hand gestures alone, he conveys the message that Albert wants his share of the wallet. The juxtaposition of Albert's motionless face with Charlie's frantic gesturing is hilarious. Charlie then hits Bud over the head with a bottle and grabs the rest of the wallet's contents.

The salvation that the displaced wallet brings to the desperately impoverished Charlie and Edna quite likely had a biographical source. One day, when he was a child, Charlie later recalled:

> Sydney came bursting into the darkened room ... exclaiming: 'I've found a purse!' He handed it to Mother ... When Mother recovered, she emptied its contents on the bed. But the purse was still heavy. There was a middle pocket! Mother opened it and saw seven golden sovereigns. Our joy was hysterical. The purse contained no address, thank God.[9]

Arbuckle and Keaton's next film, *Moonshine*, released on 13 May 1918, sends up the notion of making a film with jokey inter-title cards. After shooting a cowboy who falls off a cliff, one character remarks: 'That was a beautiful fall. He sure earned his pay cheque.' At another point Roscoe rescues Alice Lake from being attacked by her father, but then blames her and throws her into a lake. She immediately gets out and rushes to Roscoe with the words, 'I love you.' Her father is, understandably, baffled: 'This is crazy! You beat up my daughter and she jumps into your arms.' Roscoe replies, 'Look, this is only a two-reeler. We don't have time to build up to love scenes.' The father replies, 'In that case, go ahead. It's your movie. I wash my hands of both of you.' The

Left **Roscoe Arbuckle frequently donned female clothing in his films, as here in *Goodnight Nurse*. Buster Keaton holds his hand.**

reference to two-reelers might be a gentle nod to *A Dog's Life*, which had been released the month before as a three-reeler.

Roscoe's next picture, *Goodnight Nurse*, which was released on 8 July 1918, again features Roscoe putting on women's clothing and then flirting with Buster in the most comical and outrageous fashion. He sucks one of his own fingers while looking suggestively into the camera. Let's just say that the gag is very near the knuckle.

Buster's last film with Roscoe in 1918 was *The Cook*, released 15 September, and it is most notable for lifting the entire ice-cream-going-down-a-posh-woman's-back gag from Chaplin's *The Adventurer*. In other places Roscoe does his old trick of flipping a pancake up in the air and catching it in the pan behind his back. Short of inspiration, he does it too many times.

Buster now turned away from filmmaking for a while. In June 1918 he was called up by the US Army and assigned to the infantry. He was shipped to France where, fortunately, he didn't get involved in any heavy fighting, emerging from the war unscathed.

While Buster was rushing off to fight in the First World War, Charlie Chaplin busied himself promoting war bonds. He made several public appearances alongside Mary Pickford and Douglas Fairbanks, and thousands of people flocked to see the stars in the flesh as they exhorted the public to support the war by buying bonds that would enable industry to manufacture weapons for US soldiers in France.

In terms of filmmaking Chaplin now surpassed himself, giving the comedy short film a stature it could never have dreamed of with the release of *Shoulder Arms* on 20 October 1918, while the war was still in progress. The subject matter was radical for a comedy – Charlie plays a soldier in the First World War – and his contemporaries marvelled at his daring in creating comedy from current tragedy. It's an astonishing comedy to make at that time, but it was his biggest hit to date and was particularly popular with soldiers who had experienced war at first hand. Chaplin's films were shown on bed sheets stuck to walls in many military hospitals where they raised the injured men's morale.

Shoulder Arms opens with an inter-title card that introduces us to 'the awkward squad'. At the end of the day's training, during which we've been treated to Charlie's wonderfully maladroit attempts to stay in line, Charlie returns to his tent exhausted, curls up in bed and falls asleep. A tracking shot explores the trench where Charlie is posted. It's raining heavily, and packages

In terms of filmmaking Chaplin now surpassed himself, giving the comedy short film a stature it could never have dreamed of with the release of *Shoulder Arms* on 20 October 1918, while the war was still in progress

Above Douglas Fairbanks holds Charlie Chaplin aloft, as the pair of them promote war bonds in New York in 1918. The US had entered the First World War the year before.

and letters from home are being distributed to the men. There is nothing for Charlie. He wanders out into the trench and stands behind another soldier who is reading a letter from home. Charlie's facial expressions exactly mirror those of the soldier in front of him. At first they are both anxious, but then they relax into smiles. Their faces register anxiety again before melting into relief. The other soldier resents the invasion of his privacy and wanders back down the sodden trench. It turns out there is a package for Charlie after all. He opens it and discovers a huge, smelly Limburger cheese. He immediately pulls on his gas mask, then finally lobs the cheese over the top, like a hand grenade, where it disintegrates directly in the face of a German officer, played by the diminutive Lloyd Underwood.

The next morning, after a night of heavy rain, Charlie wakes up and finds he is up to his waist in water. He reaches for his right foot and taps it hard to get the circulation going. He then repeats the procedure with his left foot and

Audiences were astonished by *Shoulder Arms*: Chaplin had seemingly done the impossible and made war funny. The sheer artistic courage of the man was extraordinary

Below A daring subject for comedy. For the first but not the last time in his career Charlie tackles contemporary events. A scene from *Shoulder Arms* released barely a month before the end of the First World War. The realism on display here is very striking.

is rather alarmed at his lack of feeling. We then see that it's actually Syd's foot (his right one at that), but under the water the illusion is perfect.

We later see Charlie and Syd enjoying beer and cake in the trench. An inter-title card reads: 'Two of a kind.' Charlie opens a bottle of beer by nonchalantly holding it above his head, allowing a sniper's bullet to knock the top off. He lights a cigarette in the same way. The sniper is clearly an excellent shot!

Beyond enemy lines, Charlie comes across a bombed-out house and, despite the lack of a front wall, he enters via the front door, taking the trouble to lock it behind him. He climbs the stairs into a bedroom with no roof and only two walls. Nevertheless, he pulls down a blind to block out the light from the window. Edna Purviance arrives back at the house and is surprised to find Charlie asleep on her bed. His German pursuers enter the house and Charlie escapes, but Edna is arrested for collaborating with the Allies.

Charlie finally rescues Edna by bluntly shoving a red hot poker up her leering German assailant. After Edna's rescue, Kaiser Wilhelm II (rather improbably, you might think) walks into the room, accompanied by two officers. He is played completely straight by Charlie's brother, Syd. The Kaiser and his men are lured into a car driven by Edna, who is now disguised as a man. The car is taken across the Allied line, and Charlie is hailed as a hero for having captured the Kaiser. He gives the Kaiser one final kick up the arse before an inter-title card appears: 'Peace on earth – good will to all mankind.' We cut back to Charlie in his tent back at camp, curled up in bed, and realize it's all been a dream.

Audiences were astonished by *Shoulder Arms*: Chaplin had seemingly done the impossible and made war funny. The sheer artistic courage of the man was extraordinary, and he comedically rarely took the easy option. He shot far more material than he ever used, including earlier domestic scenes with a huge, but unseen, wife – we gauge her size by the enormous bloomers that we see Charlie hanging up – who motivates his desire to join the army. We also see Charlie's army medical via a silhouette projected onto a window-blind: a long-handled spoon disappears completely down his throat, only to pop up again as the doctor taps his chest.

All this material was cut because at one point Charlie was considering the possibility of making *Shoulder Arms* a feature-length film. Apart from *Tillie's Punctured Romance*, no slapstick comedy feature had been made, and Tillie was seen as something of a one-off that worked because it was pumped full of comedians. Could a slapstick comedy be sustained over six reels? If Charlie couldn't do it, who could?

Chapter 5

"Comedy at Length"

Charlie Chaplin
(His Signature)

In his Third
Million Dollar Comedy

"Sunnyside"

A "First National
Attraction"

"Farm life as it should be"

Comedy at Length

On 23 October 1918, three days after *Shoulder Arms* was released, Charlie astonished his friends by announcing that he was going to get married. He had known seventeen-year-old Mildred Harris on and off for the best part of the year and had made her pregnant. They got married, but it swiftly became apparent that not only was the pregnancy a false alarm but that the couple were not at all suited to each other. Charlie and his new wife had completely different interests. As Charlie later recalled:

> My emotions were mixed. I felt I had been caught in the mesh of a foolish circumstance ... a union that had no vital basis. Yet I had always wanted a wife, and Mildred was young and pretty ... perhaps it would work out all right.[1]

Charlie felt that his marriage had a ruinous effect on his work and that making his next film, *Sunnyside*, which was released on 15 June 1919, was like 'pulling teeth'. Certainly, compared with the two masterpieces that had preceded it, *Sunnyside* is a desperately uneven affair. After a quick glimpse of the village church in Sunnyside, we see a sign hanging on a wall that reads, 'Love Thy Neighbour.' The camera pans down to show a burly man, played by Tom Wilson, asleep in bed. The alarm clock wakes him, and we see that it's half past three in the morning. He picks up a boot, goes into the neighbouring room and sits on the bed where Charlie is sleeping. He puts the boot on his right foot, stands up and kicks Charlie up the arse. This wakes Charlie.

Charlie goes downstairs to prepare breakfast. The burly man comes down to breakfast and immediately kicks Charlie up the arse. It's Sunday and, while the other inhabitants of Sunnyside dutifully attend church, Charlie, as 'the unwilling sinner', has to herd the cows. An inter-title card reads: 'His church, the sky – his altar, the landscape.' The camera follows him along a country road, the cows walking in front of him. He is reading a prayer book and doesn't notice that the cattle have taken a left turn while he carries on regardless. He looks up – the cows have gone.

We see the big frame of Henry Bergman dressed in rough rustic attire walking towards us down a country lane with some lovely hills in the background. Charlie races past Henry and then stops. He checks Henry's face, first one side then the other. No, he's not a cow, so he runs off. It's the best joke in the picture. Charlie finds the cows running amok in Sunnyside. He goes into the church to investigate and comes shooting straight out again on the back of a cow. Or, rather, a stuntman dressed as Charlie emerges on the panicked heifer. The stuntman/Charlie is thrown off the cow and lies injured under a bridge.

Right **A rather bashful-looking Charlie Chaplin poses with his wife-to-be Mildred Harris on the set of *Shoulder Arms.* The First World War lasted longer than their marriage.**

LOVERS

Above Contemporary critics loved the nymph sequence from Chaplin's *Sunnyside*.

Four nymphs appear wearing flimsy white dresses. Charlie is unconscious, so this is clearly a dream. They all dance around the bushes and trees. Charlie sits on a cactus, but this does not disturb his rural prancing. Eventually he falls back under the bridge and is awakened from his dreams by brutal reality – his neighbours are prodding him in the rear. The nymph sequence was much admired by contemporary critics, who loved the poetry and romanticism. Charlie's boss kicks his arse relentlessly (thirteen times) as they make their way home.

A strange inter-title card then appears: 'And now, the "romance".' For Charlie to put romance in quotation marks suggests a degree of cynicism unusual for him, and it could partly be that the film is a cynical reaction to having been lured into marriage with Mildred. It's interesting to note that the opening credits show the film title itself in quotation marks. The only other First National film title to have quotation marks is Charlie's next picture, *A Day's Pleasure*, and their use suggests that Charlie is giving these titles an ironic meaning. *Sunnyside* has lots of dark humour, and *A Day's Pleasure* was a chore that had to be made quickly to satisfy First National's demand for a new picture.

The following scene is very untypical of Chaplin. He pays a call on his sweetheart, Edna, but his simple-minded brother, Willie, is already there, or, rather, he's not at all there, because Willie is clearly 'the village idiot'. Charlie sits down with Edna but so does Willie. To get rid of him, Charlie suggests a

In a gag better suited to the callous Keystones, he stumbles out onto the road where he's narrowly missed by a car. One minute we're prancing with woodland spirits, the next we're watching a blindfolded half-wit stumbling into traffic

game of blind man's buff. A blindfold is tied around Willie's eyes, and he's kicked out of the house. In a gag better suited to the callous Keystones, he stumbles out onto the road where he's narrowly missed by a car. One minute we're prancing with woodland spirits, the next we're watching a blindfolded half-wit stumbling into traffic.

A 'City Chap' arrives with his sophisticated ways (and superior cane) and quickly wins Edna's heart. Charlie is distraught and attempts suicide by crouching in front of an oncoming car. Just before impact, he wakes up, and it turns out that Edna's romance was all a dream. Is there something of Mildred in Edna's character during this dream sequence? She is unusually girly and child-like, wearing an enormous bow in her hair, and this is not a million miles from Charlie's description of Mildred in his autobiography:

> Although I had grown fond of Mildred, we were irreconcilably mismated. Her character was not mean, but exasperatingly feline. I could never reach her mind. It was cluttered with pink-ribboned foolishness. She seemed in a dither, looking always for other horizons.[2]

At three reels, *Sunnyside* is too long. His two previous three-reelers justified their length, but this film is, at times, a struggle. Realizing he had to do better, Charlie embarked on his next film, which was provisionally titled 'Charlie's Picnic'. Again, inspiration was lacking. Mildred was genuinely pregnant this time and needed looking after. Then tragedy hit the couple, for on 7 July 1919 Mildred gave birth to a severely disabled baby boy who survived for only three days. This terrible event did not bring the couple closer together.

Not long after this, Charlie was at the Orpheum Theater one night when one of the acts caught his eye. John and Jackie Coogan were a father and son double act. John was an experienced 'eccentric dancer', while his son, Jackie, only four years old, specialized in the new fashionable dance, the Shimmy. Charlie was taken with the young Jackie but thought no more about it until a few days later, when he heard that Roscoe Arbuckle had signed up the talented youngster. Charlie was furious with himself. He suddenly thought of all the bits of comic business he and Jackie could have performed together: a father and son relationship onscreen. Then Charlie heard that Roscoe hadn't signed up Jackie Coogan at all; he had signed up John Coogan, the father. This news spurred Charlie into activity. 'Charlie's Picnic' was abandoned, and Jackie Coogan was contracted to star in a new project. The precise nature of the project was still vague at this point.

John Coogan made his debut with the Arbuckle company in *Back Stage*, which was released on 7 September 1919. *Back Stage* also marks the return of Buster Keaton from the First World War and his welcome back into the Arbuckle camp. The film begins with a good idea that is badly executed. We catch a glimpse of the interior of a bedroom, which is then immediately dismantled to show that it is, in fact, a theatrical set. The illusion doesn't work because the bedroom is dismantled the moment we see it, and there is no time to establish the feel of a real bedroom. It could well be that there is some missing footage at the start of the film, but every print I've seen has an identical beginning.

The next scene works much better. Armed with a bucket of paste and a brush, Roscoe is trying to put up a poster advertising a forthcoming attraction. A young boy keeps getting in the way. Using a big brush, Roscoe pastes the back of the boy's trousers and then sticks him up on the poster. The boy calls him over and hits Roscoe on the head. In retaliation, Roscoe smears the boy's face with paste, which the boy then starts to eat. At first Roscoe is astonished, but, tasting the paste for himself, he realizes it's delicious. Eventually, the boy is sent packing, and we can see the poster that Roscoe has been busy sticking up:

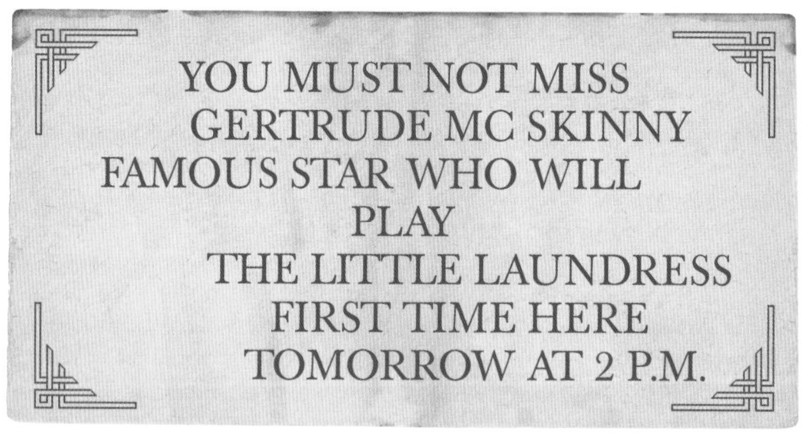

Roscoe pushes back the stage door, which partially obscures the poster. It now reads:

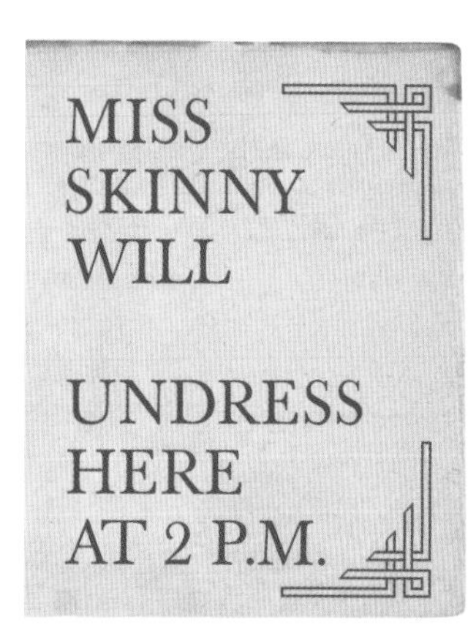

Above **The wheels fall off in Roscoe Arbuckle's and Buster Keaton's *The Garage*.**

An old man walks by, consults his watch and scampers off in anticipation. John Coogan then appears as Clarence Marmalade, the eccentric dancer. He runs through his act, his legs going all over the place.

The second half of the film to some degree resembles Chaplin's *A Night in the Show*. Buster and Roscoe have upset the acts, who consequently walk out. It's up to the two of them to put on the show, while John Coogan sits in a box at the side of the stage attempting to disrupt proceedings. At one point Roscoe is serenading his lady love with a ukulele, while backstage Buster accidentally knocks over some supports that are holding up the set. The façade of a house falls on top of Roscoe onstage, but he miraculously survives as the upper window frames him perfectly. Buster would revisit this gag in later films, improving it every time.

Buster and Roscoe's last film together, *The Garage*, was released on 11 January 1920. It was also Roscoe's last two-reeler, and it consists of the usual mayhem. A fast-moving giant turntable, used to rotate a car so that Roscoe can hurriedly hose it down, stands out as the chief comic prop.

There are some great individual gags in this picture. Having lost his trousers to a mad dog, Buster wanders in front of a huge billboard advertising the Scottish entertainer Sir Harry Lauder. A woman appears on the scene, spots him in his underwear and accuses him of exposing himself. While she marches off to find a policeman, Buster takes out his penknife and scores around the Scotsman's kilt and hat. By the time the woman returns with a policeman in tow, Buster is nicely kitted out with a kilt, sporran and hat and performs a little Scottish jig to complete the scene.

Harry McCoy, a Keystone regular, is back for this, Arbuckle's farewell to the comedy short, and a charming little in-joke sees Roscoe kiss a photograph of Mabel Normand, which is pinned up on the wall.

Roscoe was moving into features, so producer Joe Schenck handed Buster Keaton the Arbuckle unit. He also bought the studio that Charlie had used for all of his Mutual films and renamed it the Keaton Studio. It's a bold statement of intent, and in fact, in Buster's first film there, he briefly features a drunk with a big, thick moustache and a suggestion of Charlie Chaplin's characteristic walk who may be serving as a short homage to Charlie now that Buster is in his old studio. It's beyond proof, but it's a nice thought.

This first film for Schenck, *The High Sign*, proved that Buster was no ordinary comedian, and the film is no ordinary comedy. It has surreal gags

Above A publicity shot of Keaton, showing his love of trick photography, and also revealing how, although he used white make-up extensively on his face, he did not apply it to his hands.

Opposite A production still from Buster's *The High Sign*. This scene does not appear in the final film.

coming out of its ears. Early on, for example, Buster steals a newspaper from a man riding a merry-go-round. As he attempts to unfold the newspaper, it becomes quickly apparent that it's over 12 feet square. Its sheer size envelopes him like a paper duvet. Oddness abounds. In another scene, Buster steals a revolver from a policeman's holster and replaces it with a banana. There's also room for verbal puns. One miserly character is called August Nickelnurser, solely, one suspects, to pave the way for a threatening letter he receives, warning him that, unless he comes up with some money that very day, 'the first of September will be the last of August'.

Hoping to get a job in a shooting gallery, Buster practises his sharp shooting skills on the beach. His attempts to shoot bottles off a wall are a failure. Whichever bottle he aims at, he smashes another one instead. This bizarre phenomenon puzzles an onlooker, Al St John, who makes his one and only appearance in a Keaton comedy. Speeded-up motion sees him running out of the film at a thousand miles an hour. His kind of slapstick was old style. Buster would rarely resort to speeded-up motion for his future laughs.

Buster eventually manages to get the job at the shooting gallery by impressing the owner, who, it turns out, is heavily involved in a secret mafia-type society called the Blinking Buzzards. Buster discovers they have a special sign to identify one another (both hands are placed in front of the face with each thumb pressed to either side of the nose). Later, when he walks around a corner towards a banana peel on the pavement he doesn't slip on the peel but, instead, does the secret sign outwards to us, the audience. Buster is saying, 'You didn't think I was going to do that old gag, did you? I'm a better comic than that.'

That, at least, was the intention. However, when Buster attended a 'sneak' preview of *The High Sign* (he always attended previews of his films and would

In all the years they worked together, the only disagreement Buster had with Roscoe was over Roscoe's assertion that the average mental age of an audience was twelve

then expand or sometimes delete sequences depending on the audience reaction), he was mortified by the response to the banana skin gag. He realised now that it looked as though he was thumbing his nose at the audience.

The finale of *The High Sign* sees Buster chased by the Blinking Buzzards around Nickelnurser's house (a fantastic set constructed of trapdoors and false walls). The plot is similarly all over the place, and Buster was disappointed with the finished result. He showed it to Roscoe, who loved it. If anything, this confirmed to Buster that he had made a mistake. As much as he liked Roscoe, he was trying to get away from unmotivated slapstick. In all the years they worked together, the only disagreement Buster had with Roscoe was over Roscoe's assertion that the average mental age of an audience was twelve and that you should pitch your comedy at that level. There's no doubt that Buster's first film as a director/star contains plenty of intelligent gags and his performance style is immediately set: his face is frozen, his pan is dead. Now that he's directing himself, the facial gymnastics we saw in the Arbuckle films are things of the past. Nevertheless he was convinced that the film was a turkey and he persuaded Joe Schenck to shelve it. Earlier, I admired Chaplin for filming sequences and then dropping them if the gags didn't fit in with the story, but here's Buster Keaton dropping an entire film. For him, it was not a good enough debut. He was always a harsh judge of his own work, and *The High Sign* is a much better film than he gives it credit for.

Buster's next two-reeler, *One Week*, was released on 7 September 1920. It was immediately received as a classic, *Motion Picture World* describing it as 'the comedy sensation of the year'.

It opens with Buster and a new leading actress, Sybil Sealey, descending the steps of a church where they have just got married. Buster has a love rival, Handy Hank, who is still angry that he has lost out. The newly-weds have been given a vacant lot and a new house in basic kit form. It's best not to think too hard about the logic at this point. How a house can be contained within a few boxes is perhaps a mystery that will never be solved, but as long as we buy into this conceit, it's joy the rest of the way. The instructions are simple: 'To give this house a snappy appearance put it up according to the numbers on the boxes.' However, Handy Hank changes the numbers on the boxes, and when the house is revealed in all its splendour on day one, it's a curiously misshapen and lopsided affair. The roof is on halfway round, there's one very crooked window and the front door is halfway up the wall.

Each new day is revealed by a calendar page being torn away. This simple structure lends great coherence to the storytelling, and Buster can open and

Opposite **The dangers of self-assembly. Buster gets the house-building instructions slightly wrong in *One Week*.**

Right Buster on the set of *One Week*, playing dice with Roscoe Arbuckle and Sybil Sealey.

close each segment with a gag. One day finishes with Buster walking away from the beginnings of a wall, which falls towards him, neatly framing him in the open window. At times his agility and sheer bravery are stunning. He walks out of the second-storey door and lands on his back some 15 feet below. This resulted in his elbow swelling up alarmingly, but Buster just treated it with ice packs. It's a measure of his commitment that if he thought the laugh worth it, he was prepared to risk serious injury.

The house is ready for its housewarming by the Friday – the 13th – and, despite appallingly bad weather, many people have come to the party. It's raining and windy, but Buster goes outside to check the weather. The house slowly starts to spin on its foundations, and as the house picks up speed, spinning like a merry-go-round, he finds it difficult to get back inside. He keeps running at the front door as it flashes past him, but he hits the wall every time. The house, a magnificent prop, was built on a turntable that was no doubt inspired by the use of the same device in the final Arbuckle–Keaton film, *The Garage*. In *One Week* the prop is used to much better effect.

Saturday morning arrives, and the house is in a terrible state: it almost couldn't be any worse. Almost. The couple discover that they've built their house on the wrong lot. They should have built it on the other side of the railway tracks. This being Buster Keaton, he decides to move it, so he sticks some barrels under it and uses his car to tow it along, but it gets stuck on the railway tracks. We see a train approaching. Buster and Sybil avert their eyes but the train passes safely by: it was on another track. A moment later, a train from the opposite direction ploughs straight into the house. Buster hasn't shown us this second train approaching. It's much funnier for it to be suddenly there.

All the qualities that made Buster different are in this picture: stupendously dangerous stunts, elaborate visual gags and a stoical calmness at the centre of it all. In *One Week* we find him inhabiting Keaton Land

Buster picks up a 'For Sale' sign and places it by the wreckage, and he and Sybil wander off to an uncertain future.

In this first, official two-reeler Buster became a supreme silent film comedian. He had learned the rudiments of movie-making from Roscoe Arbuckle, but the pupil far exceeded the capabilities of the teacher. All the qualities that made Buster different are in this picture: stupendously dangerous stunts, elaborate visual gags and a stoical calmness at the centre of it all. In *One Week* we find him inhabiting Keaton Land. His seemingly never-changing facial expression marks him out as totally different from every other screen comedian of the time. In one sense, it's an outrageous imposition to place on yourself: it's hard enough to get laughs in silent film because there's no funny dialogue, but to restrict yourself further by freezing your face! However, I mustn't over-emphasize Buster's 'Great Stone Face', as he was once memorably dubbed. You always know what he is thinking. His eyes tell you the whole story: panic, love and everything in between.

The Saphead, a feature Buster had been filming for Metro, was released on 18 October 1920. Although he did not direct the picture, he certainly had a hand staging his individual scenes. He plays a rich twit called Bertie Van Alstyne, who has no idea about life. Despite this, his innocence and selflessness make him a likeable character. Buster's acting in this film is beautifully restrained and even poignant at times. His wedding is cancelled at the last

Left **Buster as rich twit Bertie Van Alstyne in *The Saphead*. Buster felt that the film proved he was ready to embark on feature-length films. His producer wasn't so sure.**

Hollywood lives

In the 1920s the top stars in Hollywood were making fortunes and living a lifestyle that would have seemed unimaginable at the turn of the century. Their houses were often palatial. Harold Lloyd's, for example, set in 22 acres of grounds, had a nine-hole golf course in the back garden and – like every other top star's residence – its own swimming pool and projection room. Buster Keaton's house was similarly grand, though it has to be said that it was his wife Natalie's desire to live in such golden splendour rather than his.

At the centre of Hollywood society stood Douglas Fairbanks and Mary Pickford, often dubbed Hollywood's king and queen. Friends to many of the silent starts, notably Charlie Chaplin, they combined successful careers with active social lives, and hosted numerous parties at their house Pickfair. But Hollywood also soon became associated with the excesses of wealth, and between 1921 and 1922 was rocked by a series of scandals, including the murder of Paramount director William Desmond Taylor, the revelation that Paramount star and heart-throb Wallace Reid was being treated for drug addiction – and the death of aspiring actress Virginia Rappé that led to false accusations being made against Roscoe Arbuckle.

Right 'Movie stars take to the air as new fad,' reads the original caption to this photograph. Shown from left to right are Douglas Fairbanks, Marjorie Daw, Mary Pickford, Charlie Chaplin's first wife Mildred and Charlie himself. Fairbanks starred in various popular costume dramas in the 1920s, including *The Mask of Zorro* and *Robin Hood*. His wife, Mary Pickford, was one of the first stars of the screen and a very shrewd businesswoman: she was one of the co-founders of United Artists.

Above Buster Keaton's lavish mansion.

Left The 50-foot-long sunken living room in Harold Lloyd's house, Greenacres. The room had film projection equipment and a ceiling decorated with gold-leaf.

minute, and he returns home to be greeted by showers of confetti hurled by his unsuspecting staff. He plays the scene with a simple dignity. Critics were surprised by his acting abilities, and if you'd only ever seen him in an Arbuckle film you would be astonished by the difference. *The Saphead* is not a bad film at all, and when Buster is onscreen it is very watchable. Buster enjoyed the experience and attempted to persuade the producer, Joe Schenck, to let him move into feature films, but Joe felt it was safer – and more profitable – to make two-reelers. If you made a feature and it was a flop, you could be in trouble, but if a two-reeler failed there would be another one along in a month.

Buster's next short, *Convict 13*, was released on 27 October. Sadly, the surviving print quality is poor, and there are so many blemishes that it's difficult to see what's happening. It's worth persevering with, though, because there are gems inside. Echoing entrances that he made on bicycles in earlier Arbuckle films, Buster arrives driving a motorbike and sidecar across a golf course. He starts to play golf and putts the ball towards a hole, but a small dog runs in and dashes off with the ball. Because we haven't seen the dog earlier, its surprise appearance is all the funnier. Another director at the time might well have shown the dog eyeing up the golf ball, but its sudden arrival, like that of the train in *One Week*, is much cleverer. There's a fabulous golf shot from Buster, which is easily missed simply because the print quality is so poor. He strikes a golf ball towards a wall, and it bounces straight back into his forehead, knocking him out. Buster matched Chaplin's obsession with getting things right. How many times, I wonder, did he have to film that one gag before he got what he wanted?

While Buster lies unconscious, an escaped convict swaps clothes with him. Hot on the heels of the runaway convict, the prison guards stumble upon Buster and immediately assume they've got their man. He is taken to the prison where he learns he is to be hanged that day.

The other prisoners are sitting in a mini-grandstand to watch the hanging. Buster's girlfriend, played by Sybil Sealey, exchanges the hangman's rope for a long piece of elastic. Once the trapdoor beneath Buster is released, he simply bounces endlessly up and down, his facial expression never changing. This adds greatly to the comedy. The warder is apologetic to the disappointed spectators: 'Sorry boys. We'll fix it and tomorrow we'll hang two of you to make up for this.'

Joe Roberts, whom Buster had known from their days together in vaudeville, makes his second appearance in a Keaton film, but for the first time he's playing the heavy. A tall, big man, he would become Buster's Eric Campbell, and he's certainly menacing enough as the convicts' ringleader, stalking around

Buster matched Chaplin's obsession with getting things right. How many times, I wonder, did he have to film that one gag before he got what he wanted?

Left Gallows humour with Buster Keaton as he prepares to be hanged in *Convict 13*. The black comedy to be found in much of his work sometimes counted against him with 1920s audiences, but greatly appeals to those of today.

the prison yard. Joe Keaton, Buster's dad, also has a part in *Convict 13*. Buster quells a prisoners' riot by swinging a basketball attached to a long piece of rope over his head and knocking the convicts down, one by one in a gag that harks back to one of the Three Keatons' routines: Dad is shaving himself with a cut-throat razor while Buster swings a basketball ever closer.

Buster's next two-reeler, released on 22 December, was *The Scarecrow*. It starts off brilliantly in a room full of contraptions. Buster and Joe Roberts sit down to breakfast amid a variety of strings hanging from the ceiling. One string swings the salt and pepper pots between them, while another magically lifts beer bottles out of the ice box. Everything doubles up as something else. The gramophone is turned over to become a cooker; the bath is flipped over to become a sofa; and the bed is rotated to become a piano. In this film Joe Roberts is playing an Arbuckle type, prancing around in Roscoe's usual style, but the experiment was not repeated. There is an extraordinary sequence as Luke the dog and Buster chase each other round and round the narrow walls of a derelict building. Although the action has been speeded up, it still looks like a very dangerous and difficult stunt for both man and beast. The film's finale, which involves an impromptu marriage ceremony performed at high speed on the back of a motorbike, is fast and funny.

Buster's next picture, *Neighbors*, released on 3 January 1921, features a wonderful set with two tall tenement buildings on either side of a dividing fence. This set was built in exactly the same spot as the *Easy Street* set a few years earlier. An opening title-card reads: 'The flower of Love could find no more romantic spot in which to blossom than in this poet's Dream Garden.' We

It's bravado movie-making, and sometimes with Keaton you want to laugh at the sheer audacity of it. It's all there in one take. There are no cutaways: it is filmed as it happens

cut to a lovely opening shot of Buster and his sweetheart, who is played by Virginia Fox, on either side of the fence, languorously swinging their feet. Their symmetry shows us immediately that they're in love with each other. She confirms this with a note, which is passed through a hole in the fence. It is a fairly rough-looking neighbourhood, and the sweethearts belong to neighbouring families who don't get on.

Could the flowery loveliness of the title-card, with its reference to a 'poet's Dream Garden', be a cheeky nod to Charlie's last couple of films? The dance with the nymphs in *Sunnyside* might well have set Buster's teeth on edge, and another comic might have felt that it was all a bit airy-fairy. This is all conjecture, and I haven't lost sight of the fact that the title-card is there to get a laugh at the dusty set's squalid appearance. Buster and Virginia are ordered to stay apart, but, determined to see her, Buster effortlessly climbs the outside of her building in one long, continuous take. He was always proud that he never used a stuntman. Larry Semon's films are chockfull of stuntmen all pretending to be him, but it was Buster's belief that stuntmen didn't fall in a comical way.

Joe Keaton makes another appearance, this time in a role for which he was uniquely qualified: he plays Buster's father. At one point Buster is stuck head-first in the mud, while his dad twists him backwards and forwards. Joe Roberts shouts out, 'I know a better way than that to break his neck.' The other Joe shouts back, 'He's my son and I'll break his neck any way I please.' Amid some great material, there is an uneasy racial gag when Buster leaps into a laundry basket being pulled along by an African-American woman. As he emerges from the laundry, he has a sheet over his head, giving him the appearance of a comedy ghost. The woman's family takes fright and runs away in stereotypical fashion.

Part of Buster's method was to make sure that his films finished on a big laugh or a memorable piece of action. In *One Week* it's a train crash. In the shelved *The High Sign* it's an incredible chase through a house of trapdoors and false walls. In *Neighbors* Buster is atop a three-man human tower. He is standing on the shoulders of a man who is standing on the shoulders of another man who is standing on the ground. The three of them approach the tenement block and each jumps into the open window directly in front of him. Adding Virginia Fox to their summit, they re-emerge from their respective windows, and the four of them make off in haste down the street as one long, wobbling column. It's bravado movie-making, and sometimes with Keaton you want to laugh at the sheer audacity of it. It's all there in one take. There are no cutaways: it is filmed as it happens.

Opposite Buster serenades his sweetheart with a broom in *Neighbors*.

While Buster was firing on all cylinders, it must have seemed to many that Chaplin was struggling. First National were desperate for more films – they were expecting eight two-reelers in sixteen months – but Charlie wanted to focus on a project with Jackie Coogan and to spend all the time on it he felt it deserved. When First National discovered what he was up to, they pressurized him into temporarily stopping work on his new picture and returning to the previously abandoned 'Charlie's Picnic'. He resumed work on 7 October and completed it a mere twelve days later.

By the time it was released on 7 December 1919 the film had been renamed *A Day's Pleasure*, and it has to be said that it's not very good. It's clearly rushed and made without much of Charlie's usual high quality of creativity. Set aboard a pleasure boat, the whole film has clearly been made to give First National something for Christmas. To the outside world, Charlie's career was faltering: only two films released in 1919, neither of which was up to his own admittedly very high standards. Was the Chaplin bubble about to burst?

Harold Lloyd also had a mixed 1919. On 16 March he released *Look Out Below*, his first 'thrill' picture. A cleverly placed camera filmed Harold and his leading actress, Bebe Daniels, sitting on a girder several hundred feet up in the air. In reality, however, they were on top of the Hill Street Tunnel with solid ground just a few feet beneath them. This was not a new technique, and the false impression of height had already been used for dramatic purposes by the popular serials of the day. Larry Semon employed the illusion in his 1918 film *Dunces and Dangers*, but Harold Lloyd was destined to excel at it.

Harold's last film of 1919, *From Hand to Mouth*, was released on 28 December and has several points of interest. The early parts of the film are Chaplinesque. In his horn-rimmed glasses and good clothes, Harold makes an unlikely tramp, but in this film he has no money and is starving. He looks into the window of a café at others stuffing their faces and reaches into his coat pocket for a rather

Right It looks like a daring stunt on the part of Harold Lloyd and his co-star Bebe Daniels. In reality, the girder in *Look Out Below* was only a few feet above ground.

Left **The crooks are holding Mildred Davis captive. Fortunately, Harold is holding the gun in *From Hand to Mouth*.**

meatless bone. He befriends a dog with a limp and a young girl who is about five years old. An audience of today might be dubious about his friendship with the young girl, although it must be said that Harold's wholesome appeal and genuine naturalness with her do much to lessen any feelings of unease.

At the end of *From Hand to Mouth* Harold is desperately trying, but failing, to attract the interest of a rather uninterested police force. He realizes he'll only get their attention by causing a string of offences. There's a great sequence as he finds a variety of ways to provoke dozens of cops into chasing him into the villains' den, where Mildred Davis is being held captive. This is eighteen-year-old Mildred's first film with Harold, his previous leading actress, Bebe Daniels, having been signed by Cecil B. de Mille to star in dramatic feature films. I wonder if it's only a coincidence that Mildred Davis shares her first name with Charlie Chaplin's new bride. Perhaps Harold considered it a good omen and thus favoured Mildred (who had been spotted in a film entitled *All Wrong*) over other candidates. Certainly Harold Lloyd was highly superstitious and acted accordingly – for example, he had one particular way of driving to the studios in the morning, and he followed that route exactly, both there and back.

Harold's career was going fabulously well. Sheer hard work (he'd made eighty films in two years) had established him as a firm favourite with audiences. Pathé had at last agreed to a substantial rise in the rental fees they were paying for his comedies, increasing the fee from $300 to $3,000 per picture. The studio wanted some fresh photographs of Harold to illustrate a new publicity campaign, and on 24 August 1919 a photographic session was booked at Witzel Studio, Los Angeles. He was photographed with a comedy bomb made of papier mâché; it was round and painted black with a pretend fuse sticking out of it – the kind of comedy bomb you still see in strip cartoons. Here, in Harold's own words, is what happened next:

> I put a cigarette in my mouth, struck a sassy attitude and held the bomb in my right hand, the fuse to the cigarette. The smoke blew across my face so clouding my expression that the photographer ... delayed ... As he continued to wait and the fuse grew shorter and shorter, I raised the bomb nearer and nearer to my face until, the fuse all but gone, I dropped the hand and was saying that we must insert a new fuse, when the thing exploded. Had I not lowered my hand at that instant I should have been killed instantly, my head probably blown off.[3]

Inexplicably, the prop bomb contained real explosive. His injuries were extensive: he lost the first finger and thumb of his right hand, and he was blinded. He was driven to hospital and immediately given ether as an anaesthetic.

> The pain was considerable for days but trivial beside my mental state. In a few weeks my salary was to have been raised to $1,000 a week ... with one-fourth interest in the pictures – a total of not less than $1,500 a week ... At twenty-six, after six years of incessant hard work and little money, I had stood on the threshold of, to me, breathless possibilities, only to be cut down in a moment.[4]

Harold started making fresh plans for himself. He reasoned that he could become a director. 'Direction, come to think of it in a hospital bed, was the great new art of pictures. A real director overshadowed the players; it was he really who wove the pattern of the picture.'[5] As he had these thoughts, Harold didn't know that the doctors were concerned about what they would find under the bandages: would he be permanently blind? Harold's left eye proved to be sound, and, despite fears that he might have to lose his right eye, it, too, eventually recovered. As Harold himself put it:

> In August 1919 my acting days were done and I was lucky, perhaps unlucky, to be alive. In November 1919 I walked down Broadway on my second visit to New York and saw 'Harold Lloyd' in lights over two theaters. In March 1920 I was back before the camera, taking up the fifth two-reeler picture, *Haunted Spooks*, where the explosion had halted it eight months before. First my sight was found to be intact. Then the face, that had been a frightful, hopeless thing, healed gradually without a scar.[6]

Harold's incredible recovery is entirely characteristic of the man. His unstoppable optimism and courage saw him through these most difficult times. While he was convalescing, rival producers offered him the staggering sum of $500,000 for a five-year contract. Harold contacted Hal Roach and asked if he could better the offer. Hal offered Harold a fifty-fifty partnership and a fifty per cent interest in the films themselves. Harold accepted.

'I raised the bomb nearer and nearer to my face until, the fuse all but gone, I dropped the hand and was saying that we must insert a new fuse, when the thing exploded' – Harold Lloyd

And what of Chaplin? He had devoted a year to his pet project, *The Kid*, starting work in July 1919 only ten days after his son Norman had died. Searching for perfection, he would film take after take, his shooting ratio being fifty-three to one (the enormous number of takes perhaps helping him deal with his grief). His private life intruded into the film in other ways, too. Faced with a messy divorce, he found out that Mildred's aggressive lawyers were threatening to grab footage of *The Kid* as part of the settlement. He smuggled the film out of Hollywood and, incredibly, edited it in a hotel room in Utah – all 500 rolls. Legal challenges delayed the film's release until January 1921.

When it was shown, however, *The Kid* succeeded beyond anybody's wildest expectations. It is universal, fluent, superbly funny and profoundly sad. It makes a huge leap into a deep autobiographical reservoir and reshapes personal tragedy into art. *The Kid* raised the status of film comedy, and its mixture of intertwined sentiment and laughs is still potent nearly ninety years after its creation. It is the first enduring comedy feature of the silent era. Charlie created a market and a taste for full-length comedies. He proved it could be done.

In his autobiography Charlie writes of a discussion with the short-story writer Gouverneur Morris about the structure of *The Kid*:

> When I told him about *The Kid* and the form it was taking, keying slapstick with sentiment, he said: 'It won't work. The form must be pure, either slapstick or drama; you cannot mix them, otherwise one element of your story will fail.' ... I said that the transition from slapstick to sentiment was a matter of feeling and discretion in arranging sequences. I argued that form happened after one had created it, that if the artist thought of a world and sincerely believed in it, no matter what the admixture was, it would be convincing. Of course, I had no grounds for this theory other than intuition. There had been satire, farce, realism, naturalism, melodrama and fantasy, but raw slapstick and sentiment, the premise of *The Kid*, was something of an innovation.[7]

The Kid starts as a drama. Edna Purviance plays an unmarried mother, who is billed simply as 'The Woman', perhaps suggesting a universality to her situation and thereby addressing the plight of women in general. We see Edna, with a baby in her arms, being released from the 'charity hospital' via a locked, barred gate. Is this a psychiatric hospital perhaps? In appearance it resembles the workhouse to which Charlie and his mother were taken all those years ago. The father is an artist, and we see him and another man admiring a painting in his studio. Edna's photograph falls from the mantelpiece and into the fire. The artist picks it up but then drops it back into the flames. Edna stops outside a church to watch a wedded couple leave. The unhappy-looking bride links arms with the much older groom. As Edna stands in front of the church window and sees them depart, the lights come on in the church behind her so that her head is encircled in a halo of light. Edna wanders on, passing an expensive-looking car parked outside a very grand house. She places the baby on the back seat, but after she has left crooks steal the car, unaware of the baby inside. They later pull up in a derelict district. On discovering the baby, they leave it in an alleyway.

We are five minutes into the film and the dramatic storyline has unfolded gracefully. It's only now that Charlie makes his first entrance. He's taking his morning constitutional in the very place where the baby has been left. As he walks along, dodging the rubbish thrown out of upper-storey windows, he discovers the baby. He automatically looks up to see where it might have been thrown from. He approaches a woman pushing a baby in a pram large enough for two and says, 'Pardon me, you dropped something.' She wants nothing to do with it. After numerous comical attempts to discard the infant, Charlie finds a note tucked in the blanket: 'Please love and care for this orphan child.' He softens and decides to take the child home.

The scene cuts to Edna, who is looking over a bridge in despair. An infant waddles over to wrap its arms around her. It's a heart-rending moment. She rushes back to reclaim her own child, but the car has gone. Meanwhile, Charlie returns to the single attic room in which he lives. The roof slopes in sharply at one end, just like the room in which Charlie lived when he was a child. He feeds milk to the baby from a kettle with a teat on its spout.

Five years pass, and Jackie Coogan makes his first appearance as the kid. He has been well cared for by Charlie, who scrubs the boy's neck and cleans out his nostrils. Jackie was a superb mimic, and Charlie found him an absolute joy to work with. In this, his most autobiographical of pictures, Charlie borrows an idea from somebody else's childhood. Fred Karno often recalled a ruse by which one of the gang would deliberately break windows while an accomplice was around the corner carrying panes of glass for sale. This is how Charlie and Jackie make a living.

'The Woman' has, in the intervening years, become a big theatrical star, and we see her receiving tributes and flowers to celebrate another fantastic opening night. A page boy brings in a luxurious display of bouquets. He is thrilled with the tip that Edna gives him, and he leaves with a cheeky smile. The young boy is African-American but he exists as a character and not a stereotype. There are no rolling eyes or sudden alarm at the sight of sheets emerging from laundry baskets. Then comes a scene that hasn't lost any of its power over the course of nearly ninety years. Edna visits the slum, handing out toys to the impoverished youngsters. A mother offers her a baby to hold. She sits on a doorstep and looks at the baby in her arms, then looks away. She is thinking of the child she gave up. Jackie opens the door and sits on the step near to her. It's a heart breaking moment, beautifully staged and directed. The two look at each other and smile. Edna hands Jackie a toy dog and an apple. Alone, she walks sadly away. Jackie waves after her.

Opposite Five-year-old Jackie Coogan turns in an astonishingly accomplished performance in a Chaplin masterpiece, *The Kid*. Here Charlie reckons he's thrown the police off the scent.

Right The mixture of comedy and pathos in *The Kid* has sometimes been criticized over the years by those who find Chaplin too sentimental. In fact, it's beautifully judged.

Later, another, larger boy steals Jackie's toy dog and apple and a fight breaks out between the two of them. Charlie attempts to stop the brawl, but, when he realizes that Jackie is holding his own, he applauds him and starts offering boxing tips. The other boy is in tears when his beefy big brother, played by Chuck Riesner, arrives. The brother threatens Charlie, 'If your kid beats my brother, then I'm going to beat you.' The problem is, Jackie's actually doing really rather well. The bully chases Charlie around the slum. At one point a lamppost is bent double as a gentle nod to *Easy Street*'s memorable comic business with the gas lamp.

Jackie falls ill, and a doctor is called. Charlie shows the doctor the note that had been attached to the baby's blanket. The doctor declares, 'This child needs proper care and attention,' and a few days later a wagon from the County Orphan Asylum pulls up outside their home. An orphanage official and a uniformed attendant enter Charlie's room. The official is so puffed up with self-importance that he will talk to Charlie only through the attendant. Was this a detail that Charlie remembered from his own childhood experiences with orphanage officials? Charlie resists the removal of the child until a policeman is called, and Jackie is forcefully taken. Charlie's heroic efforts to fight them off are extremely moving. He gives it everything he's got. Jackie is lowered onto an open platform in the back of the wagon, and he breaks down, sobbing for his daddy as Charlie must surely have wept for his mother when he was separated from her at a similarly early age. The scene cuts back and forth between Jackie and Charlie, accentuating their bond. Charlie is held down by the officials as he hears the child's cries. His performance is so real it's harrowing.

Charlie escapes out of the window and chases the wagon by scampering across the rooftops. It's a thrilling chase that carries an emotional punch that is completely lacking in the gratuitous and formulaic Keystone chases of old. Also, in a reversal of the norm, it's the authorities who are in the wrong, and it's Charlie who is chasing them. He jumps from roof to roof and then into the back of the wagon. He pushes the official out onto the road, and Charlie and Jackie embrace with tears in their eyes. It's an emotionally charged moment played with total conviction. Perhaps we are even beyond acting.

Edna calls at Charlie's home and meets the doctor, who shows her the note that she had written all those years before. Meanwhile, Charlie has managed to smuggle the boy into a doss house. The doss house owner settles down to read his newspaper and spots an advertisement offering a $1,000 reward for the lost child. He recognizes Charlie from his description as 'a little man with large flat feet and small moustache'. As Charlie slumbers, the owner removes the sleeping child and takes him to the police station where Edna reclaims him. Charlie awakens and frantically spends the night searching for Jackie. He reaches home exhausted, sits down on the steps outside his front door and falls asleep. David Robinson, Chaplin's biographer, noted that these steps look similar to the steps in Methney Street where the Chaplins once lived.

Charlie dreams of 'Dreamland'. The street on which he lives is filled with his neighbours, each now an angel sporting an impressive pair of feathery wings. Even a dog flies in and out of shot on wings. It's an idyllic scene until demons creep in and lust rears its head. A young girl is urged to 'vamp' Charlie. This is the one detail in the picture that needs an explanation for a modern audience. 'Vamp' means to flirt heavily, and Lita Grey, who was twelve at the time, was cast to flash Charlie her ankle before flying off round the corner. She represents temptation, and perhaps this is Charlie reflecting on his mistake in marrying Mildred Harris. When the girl's sweetheart comes on the scene, feathers fly. Charlie is shot down in angelic flight and lies dead across his doorstep. He is awakened by a policeman shaking him. He is finally reunited with Jackie at Edna's house, and the three of them disappear inside.

On its release on 6 February 1921 audiences and critics were united in their enthusiasm for this tragicomic masterpiece. *The Kid*'s huge popularity opened up the market for full-length slapstick comedies.

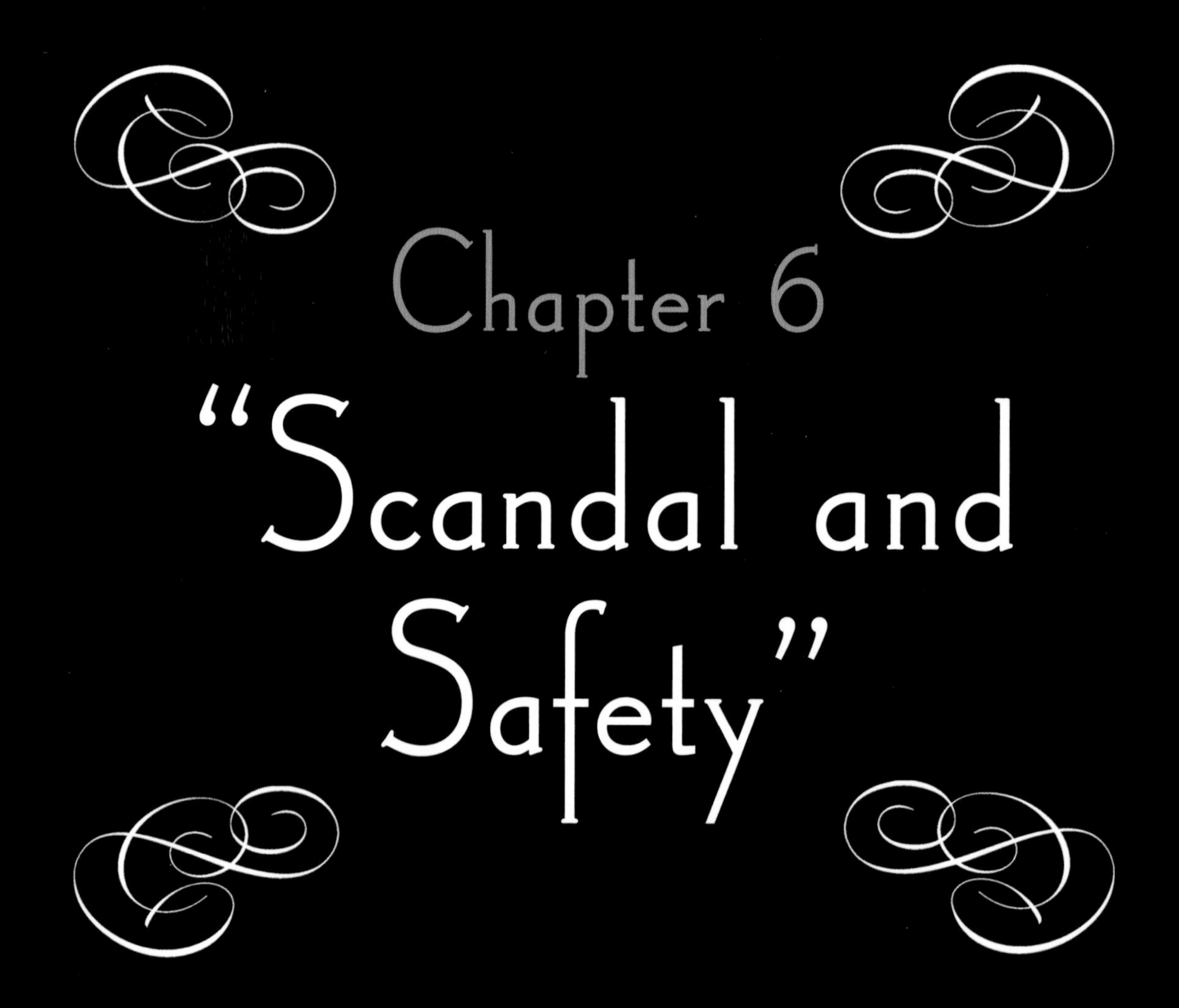

Chapter 6
“Scandal and Safety”

IN THE WEST
MAJESTIC
MAJESTIC
Pathécomedy
"Harold! Where are you?"
HAROLD LLOYD
IN
"SAFETY LAST"

Scandal and Safety

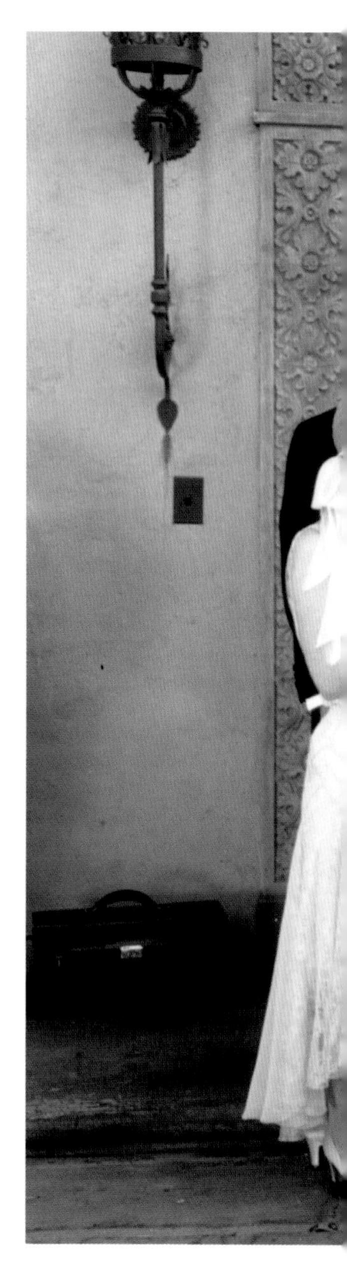

The Kid made real a world of possibility for feature-length comedy, and Chaplin must have been an object of some envy to Buster Keaton, who was desperate to start producing features as Chaplin was doing but who was forced to continue with two-reelers. His next short, *The Haunted House*, released just four days after *The Kid*, is far from being one of his best.

He plays a bank clerk, who upsets a pot of glue everywhere, causing all the money to stick together. Another clerk falls over onto the glue and can't get up. Buster's solution to his colleague's unfortunate situation is to get a kettle full of steaming hot water and pour it over the poor man's lap. When he resists, Buster knocks him out with a hammer. It's pretty desperate stuff. The difficulty of maintaining a schedule of a new two-reel comedy every month could tax even as inventive a comedian as Buster Keaton. The bank is clearly not a fruitful venue for comedy, so the action moves to a supposedly haunted house.

Counterfeiters, led by Joe Roberts, are using the house as a hide-out and are keeping people away by having a couple of gang members roam the corridors with sheets over their heads. Somewhere along the line, a theatrical company staging *Faust* is chased into the house by a disgruntled audience. There is some fun to be had with a staircase that, at the flick of a switch, becomes a slippery slope.

The end is the best bit. Buster dies and ascends the stairs to Heaven, raising his hat as he passes a couple of angels playing harps. When he gets to the Pearly Gates he's told he's come to the wrong place, and the stairs flip over to become a slippery slope all the way down to a chute that leads straight to Hell. He falls to the ground and devils immediately begin prodding him with flaming tridents.

Buster must have known that Charlie was filming a dream sequence in Heaven for *The Kid.* So many people were involved in the production and Hollywood was such a small town, that word would have spread quickly. Some comics may well have looked askance at Charlie's dancing with nymphs in *Sunnyside*, so a scene with angels in Heaven would not have passed unremarked. Did that heavenly sequence inspire Buster's comic view of the afterlife? We will never know.

Buster's next two-reeler, *Hard Luck*, released on 11 March 1921, was a lost film for many decades. This was particularly frustrating because the last gag in *Hard Luck* was one of Buster's favourites, and he often talked about it being his biggest laugh in pictures. The gag starts with Buster standing on a diving board above a country club swimming pool:

> I do a swan dive but miss the swimming pool completely and crash through the adjoining cement walk, making a big hole as I disappear. After the fade-out

Above Buster with his in-laws at a family wedding in 1927. If he looks less than happy, that's a reflection on his view of his in-laws – and his wife Natalie whom he married in 1921.

> a subtitle reading 'Years later' is flashed on the screen. Again the pool at the country club is seen, but the whole place is now a deserted ruin. There is no water in the swimming pool. In a moment I clamber up out of the hole in the cement walk. I am in Chinese costume, complete with pig-tail and help my Chinese wife and kids up out of the hole. In pantomime I point to the high-diving board, then to the hole I made.[1]

A print of the film was rediscovered in the 1980s, but it ended abruptly just as Buster stood on the diving board. The celebrated gag was still missing. A couple of publicity shots taken of Buster and his Chinese family were all that remained. Then, miraculously, Serge Bromberg at Lobster Films located the joke. Segments of individual frames were still missing, but Serge was able to reconstruct the sequence. Although the picture quality is pretty poor, you can see Buster and family emerge from the hole. The gag has finally been restored to its rightful place.

Hard Luck is a definite improvement over *The Haunted House.* The plot is perhaps over complicated, but the gags come tumbling towards you. Buster plays a character trying to commit suicide after having lost both his job and his sweetheart. He jumps in front of a street car, but it stops before it hits him and then reverses. Next, he tries to hang himself from a tree but is chased away by the police. He waits until nightfall before running in front of a speeding car. As the vehicle approaches, its twin headlights shining brightly, we see it's not a car but two motorcycles running parallel to each other. They pass harmlessly by on either side of him. He ends up getting accidentally drunk by drinking whisky that is in a bottle erroneously labelled 'poison'.

In his inebriated state, he gatecrashes a meeting of zoo officials as an unlikely title-card announces: 'Gentlemen, in our zoo we have every kind of animal but an armadillo.' Buster volunteers to capture one, and everybody agrees to entrust the task to this drunken stranger. He assures them: 'I was attached to a branch of the zoo' (omitting to mention that he was attempting to hang himself at the time).

His next two-reeler, *The Goat,* released on 18 May, is among his very best. Buster is passing a police station when he stops to peer in through the barred window to watch a murderer, Dead Shot Dan, have his photograph taken for the Rogues' Gallery. Dead Shot Dan spots Buster and cleverly makes sure that Buster's face is photographed instead of his own. Newspapers later circulate the photo of Buster looking through bars, with the headline, 'Dead Shot Dan Escapes'. Consequently everybody runs away from him and, initially, he can't figure out why.

The plot line is uncomplicated. Joe Roberts plays a policeman who, mistaking Buster for Dead Shot Dan, chases him around town. Buster shakes him off and later bumps into Virginia Fox, who invites him to dinner at her family apartment. At the dining table Buster plays with a little dog, which has the effect of keeping his back to the front door. Virginia's father enters, and it turns out he's none other than Joe Roberts. When he spots Buster, Joe eyeballs him across the table. The more he glowers, the more Buster cowers. Joe locks

Buster disappears from view as he sinks down inside the booth just as if he were going down in the elevator. Joe is completely bamboozled by this and runs down the stairs in mistaken pursuit

the front door and bends the key between his fingers. The moment is reminiscent of Eric Campbell swallowing the key in Chaplin's *Easy Street.* Joe and Buster face each other across the dining table. Buster jumps up onto the table, leaps onto Joe's shoulders and dives head-first through the transom window above the door. In an absolute rage, Joe smashes through the front door and finds Buster across the hallway in a phone booth next to the elevator. Buster disappears from view as he sinks down inside the booth just as if he were going down in the elevator. Joe is completely bamboozled by this and runs down the stairs in mistaken pursuit. Such a clever joke made me sit up and take notice when I first saw it. It's a joke that assumes a level of intelligence in its audience, and it still works really well today. The whole sequence culminates in a hilarious shot of the lift hurtling through the roof. *The Goat* is my favourite Keaton two-reeler.

Buster began work on his next short, *The Electric House*, but broke his ankle in an accident on the second day of filming when one of his shoes got caught in the mechanism of an escalator and he was thrown 10 feet into the air. The doctor advised him to avoid heavy work for five months and said that the plaster cast would be on for at least seven weeks. This was a perfect opportunity to put out *The High Sign*, which Buster had shelved in 1920, so it was released on 12 April 1921. *The Goat*, already in the can, was released on 18 May.

Now that Buster wasn't busy working the whole time, he was able to give a bit more attention to his personal life and, in particular, his relationship with Natalie Talmadge, the sister-in-law of his producer, Joe Schenck. Buster trusted Joe, who had given his parents a weekly allowance when he was away in the army, and as a producer, Joe never interfered, letting Buster and his gag writers get on with the specialized business of being funny. Joe was married to Norma Talmadge, who, like her sister Constance, was a popular film star. Buster had been dating their younger sister, Natalie, who had worked as a script editor on Roscoe and Buster's short *Out West* back in 1918.

The newspapers reported that Natalie was being courted in New York by the son of a wealthy Chicago dairyman. I'm tempted to say he was trying to butter her up. This galvanized Buster into action, and he booked his train tickets. A third of the way into his journey, he wired ahead to New York: 'On my way for our wedding. Please set date. Wire reply.' Buster sent the wire from Albuquerque, New Mexico. He was in Amarillo, Texas, in the middle of a game of bridge, when he received the reply. He excused himself from the game and rushed back on his crutches to his compartment. Sitting on his bed he then opened the telegram. It read: 'Yes. Wedding here May 31.' Ten days

What would the Talmadge clan have to say about this? Were the mother and two other sisters standing beside the photographer saying, 'Come on Buster, smile, look happy, this is your wedding day'?

later, on that very date at the end of May, Buster and Natalie were married.

Several photos of the wedding have appeared in various biographies over the years, but in none of them is Buster smiling. His expression could best be described as solemn. Is this taking the onscreen image too far? What would the Talmadge clan have to say about this? Were the mother and two other sisters standing beside the photographer saying, 'Come on Buster, smile, look happy, this is your wedding day'? Photographers always ask you to smile, particularly at weddings, so I imagine there was some pressure brought to bear.

Perhaps Buster's unsmiling face shows that he'd worked out already that this threatened to be a problem marriage. The Talmadges looked down on Buster because of his perceived lowly status. He was regarded as a vaudevillian comic who made slapstick comedies – which he was. They would certainly have laughed at the notion that Buster would one day be recognized as a great artist. It can't have made for an easy relationship between Buster and his in-laws.

Shortly after his marriage, Buster began making *The Playhouse*, which was released on 6 October and which was, perhaps, his most personal film to date. During his enforced convalescence, Buster may well have reflected on Charlie Chaplin's massive hit, *The Kid*, which was widely praised for its autobiographical details. Chaplin's dramatic childhood was the very stuff of great storytelling, while Buster's own life story, compared to most, would be considered idyllic: a childhood on stage, huge laughs in large theatres, mixing with the other performers, summers at Lake Michigan and then his big break into the movies.

The Playhouse combines his love of theatre with his new obsession, film. Buster buys a ticket for the playhouse and enters. A conductor emerges from the orchestra pit. It is Buster. He attracts the attention of the musicians to his left. There are three of them, and they are all Buster. One plays the double bass, the middle one plays the cello, and the third plays the violin. The Three Keatons. On the conductor's other side there are another three Keatons, playing clarinet, trombone and drums. They all interact with each other. Today, this trick photography would be simple, but in 1921 it could be achieved only with the combined incredible skills of the camera operator and performer. Buster tops the effect by having himself as a stagehand raising the curtain on nine Buster Keatons standing in a row, all dancing in unison to the same beat.

This simple-looking effect was achieved in the most extraordinary way. First, Buster devised a mask that fitted over the camera lens. It had nine shutters, which could be opened one at a time.

Above **Buster conducts Buster: trick photography such as this (from a later film) is a hallmark of *The Playhouse.***

> It was hardest for Elgin Lessley at the camera. He had to roll the film back eight times, then run it through again. He had to hand-crank at exactly the same speed both ways, each time. Try it sometime. If he were off the slightest fraction, no matter how carefully I timed my movements, the composite action could not have synchronized. But Elgin was outstanding among all the studios. He was a human metronome. My synchronizing was gotten by doing the routines to banjo music.[2]

Perhaps even more startling is Buster's appearance as six other characters watching the show from their private boxes. First, there is Buster as he normally appears, sitting next to Buster as a beautiful young woman with bare shoulders, fluttering away with her ostrich feather fan. The male Buster studies the theatre programme: 'Buster Keaton Presents BUSTER KEATON'S MINSTRELS.' Buster's name is then listed over twenty-five times, responsible for everything from 'Electrician' to 'Original Songs & Music by'. In another box we see Buster as a nine-year-old boy sucking a lollipop, communicating with a grumpy old woman, also Buster. The next box shows an elderly couple. She shouts at him to wake up, and he instantly obeys and starts clapping.

Buster revives a gag he had tried in *Back Stage*, but it's more successful here. He wakes up in bed, and we learn it's all been a dream. Furniture is being removed, and it looks as if Buster is being evicted. Then the walls are lifted away, and we see that we are still backstage. The joke works here because Buster spends time establishing the room as a room. The irony is that, for Buster, theatre was real life; it was where he lived his childhood. We see him in a nostalgic mood finding a knothole in the stage and prodding it with a broom handle – the old stage act. Later, he does a hilarious impersonation of a monkey, standing in for the real thing that has escaped backstage. No doubt he was thinking of Peter the Great, the monkey act that had fascinated him back at the Palace Theatre, London, in 1909, when the Three Keatons had briefly appeared in the capital. (Audiences had been appalled by Joe's stage treatment of Buster, and the engagement was not a success.) This film is filled with Buster's memories. It's a celebration of existence, of a life free from trauma.

Buster's next two-reeler, *The Boat*, was released on 10 November. Although this has long been considered one of Buster's greatest shorts, I'm afraid I have to disagree, although there are wonderful things about it.

Buster has built a boat in the basement of his house, but, because he's built it too big, he demolishes the house while he's removing it. At the launch he stands proudly on deck, but as the boat slips down the runway and into the water, it just continues its downward path, sinking lower and lower beneath the water. Buster looks around bewildered just before his head sinks under the surface.

The Boat may well have been conceived as a sequel to Keaton's first massive

Below **It's a long time in coming, but the final joke in Buster's *The Boat* explains why his sailing vessel is called *Damfino*.**

Newspapers were full of lurid stories claiming that the movie industry was out of control. Some of the stars were blowing their fortunes on cocaine, unaware of its addictive nature

success, *One Week*. Sybil Sealey plays Buster's wife for the first time in six pictures. The couple have two boys, both of whom wear the familiar porkpie hat. The action finale of *One Week* (with the house spinning round and round) is echoed here by the boat continually turning over in the water, with Buster still inside. The gag lacks credibility, however: a house could possibly spin, but a boat couldn't continually roll over. It's not the big finish that Buster was always looking for.

The name of the boat is *Damfino*, and this provides the last laugh of the picture. Buster and his family step out of their lifeboat. They are in the dark but realize they are standing in only 2 feet of water. Sybil asks Buster where they are and, even without a title-card, we can clearly lip-read him saying 'Damfino'. I didn't understand this joke for ages because I thought the name of the boat was pronounced 'Dam fee no'. But, of course, the pronunciation is closer to 'Damned if I know'. When he signals for help in a storm, it's like a 'knock, knock' joke in Morse code: 'SOS ... Who is it? ... Damfino ... Neither do I.' The final gag is uttered with a cheeky twinkle. It would be some time before Buster was so carefree again.

The Boat was finished at the end of August. Meanwhile Roscoe Arbuckle needed a break from his gruelling work load – he had just made three features back to back – and so he invited Buster to join him in San Francisco for the Labor Day weekend. Buster was unable to go as he'd made other plans, but Fred Fischbach (a friend from Keystone days) was keen to tag along. Roscoe's decision to go away that weekend went against the wishes of Adolph Zukor, head of Paramount, who had wanted Roscoe to stick around to make a personal appearance at 'Paramount Week', a publicity campaign designed to boost box office receipts and help promote a good image of Hollywood. Zukor was not a man to cross. He was a cold and calculating businessman who insisted on exercising complete control of his stars. He resented having to fork out more than $1 million a year for Roscoe and was, no doubt, determined to make him work for it.

Zukor was all too aware that Hollywood's image was desperately in need of a boost. Newspapers were full of lurid stories claiming that the movie industry was out of control. Some of the stars were blowing their fortunes on cocaine, unaware of its addictive nature, and the drug was even sometimes the subject of film comedy. In *The Mystery of the Leaping Fish* (1916), for example, Douglas Fairbanks parodies Sherlock Holmes's habit of consuming the drug by playing an amateur

What happened next changed Arbuckle's life for ever, although few know the real story. The myths and distortions that were circulated by the press persist today

detective called Coke Ennyday. (The main joke is that he's taking it every thirty-five seconds and consequently does everything at great speed.) Paramount bore the brunt of the bad publicity, with a number of scandals in which its stars were implicated. Who better than Arbuckle, with his wholesome image, loved by adults and children alike, to help dispel this negative image of Hollywood?

However, on Friday, 2 September, Roscoe went ahead and checked into the St Francis Hotel with his travelling companion, Fred Fischbach. The weekend passed without incident, but, against Roscoe's wishes, Fred invited two women, Virginia Rappé and Maude Delmont, to join them on the Monday. Roscoe knew these two were trouble: Maude was a professional co-respondent, known to Californian police for her various forays into the world of extortion, fraud and bigamy; Virginia had a reputation in Hollywood for violent outbursts when under the influence of alcohol. And Fred had made sure that there would be plenty of that (having placed a large order for bootleg liquor). Prohibition had became law on 20 January 1920, but that never stopped people getting alcohol if they wanted it. Numerous guests poured in, and a party was soon under way.

What happened next changed Arbuckle's life for ever, although few know the real story. The myths and distortions that were circulated by the press persist today. The bare facts are that Virginia Rappé collapsed during the party. Three days later she was dead, and the cause of death was discovered to be peritonitis, brought on by a ruptured bladder. What was not clear, among all the vile rumour-mongering, was what caused the rupture in the first place. It is strongly suspected that Virginia was already ill before she attended the party, suffering from a botched abortion undertaken by a Dr Rumwell. This might explain why Maude Delmont dismissed the hotel medic and called in Dr Rumwell. It also might explain why Rumwell ordered a post mortem without the consent of the coroner's office. This was illegal. What's more, organs were removed and destroyed, effectively wiping out the 'evidence'.

Maude Delmont publicly claimed that Roscoe was responsible for Virginia's injuries after having attempted to rape her. Roscoe was charged with manslaughter. The press leaped on the story and began to tear Roscoe apart. A wave of hatred engulfed him, and the funny fat man became a sex monster who had crushed the life out of his victim. The media mogul William Randolph Hearst famously said, 'Fatty sold me more papers than the sinking of the *Lusitania*.' Roscoe was arrested on 11 September and charged with murder. The trial was scheduled to start on 14 November 1921.

From the outset, circumstances were stacked against Roscoe. San Francisco's District Attorney, Matthew Brady, was determined to get him. Local

Klux Rites Exposed Despite Threats

HERALD CHICAGO EXAMINER

FINAL EDITION

PRICE 3 CENTS

Today

Below

SATURDAY, SEPTEMBER 17, 1921

ARBUCKLE FACES GALLOWS

Today

An Important Birthday.
Breeding Better People.
A Serious Chill.
We're All Masked.

By Arthur Brisbane

AIR SERVICE CHIEF QUITS AFTER ROW

Gen. Member Resigns When Mitchell Charges He 'Sold Out.'

Guaranty Bank of N. Y. Cuts Its Dividend

IRISH DEMAND PARLEY WITH HANDS FREE

De Valera Explains Stand in a Telegram to Lloyd George.

Mystic Klux Rites Exposed in Spite of Death Threats

COMEDIAN MUST STAND MURDER TRIAL

Given Five Days to Get Case Ready; Forced to Stay in Jail.

BRYAN ATTACKS HEAD OF U. OF W.

LOOP MAY SEE KU KLUX PARADE

Secrets of Kloran, 'Book of the Invisible Empire,' Safeguarded by Direst Penalties

Above One of the scandals that rocked Hollywood in 1921: the Arbuckle trial.

Right Roscoe Arbuckle's alleged victim, Virginia Rappé, whom Roscoe was accused of assaulting at a party in his hotel suite.

residents had been vociferously complaining about the conduct of film stars from Los Angeles coming to San Francisco and trashing their city. Brady was a self-serving, ruthless man with blinding ambition, whose sights were firmly set on becoming governor of California. Bringing down Arbuckle was the means to secure this all-important career move.

Charlie Chaplin was in Britain at the time of Arbuckle's arrest. When he was asked by the British press about the accusations flying around in the more lurid American newspapers he dismissed them as 'preposterous', but his opinion was not reported in America. Indeed, when Roscoe's friends in the US tried to speak favourably about Roscoe to the press, they were ordered by studio bosses to keep quiet. Buster Keaton wanted to go to San Francisco to testify on behalf of his best friend, but he was advised by Arbuckle's lawyers that there was already enough anti-Hollywood feeling in San Francisco.

Henry 'Pathé' Lehrman (Chaplin's and Arbuckle's first director at Keystone) gave an interview to the New York press in which he painted an image of Roscoe as a repulsive beast. The man who had adopted the name 'Pathé' (thinking it gave him class) said of Roscoe's situation: 'That is what results from making idols and millionaires out of people that you take from the gutter.'[3] In fact, Lehrman was widely known to be Virginia's lover, and he might have been hoping to cover up the suspicion that she had been carrying his baby.

While Arbuckle burned, on the other side of the Atlantic Charlie was experiencing a far gentler warmth from his fellow compatriots. He was home for the first time in nine years, and in London sixty policemen were needed to get him safely into the Ritz Hotel. While I was filming a television programme in the very room in which Charlie had stayed, I was told off-camera that the Ritz had been so appalled by the mob outside the hotel and the numerous complaints from the other guests, that the management privately informed the comedian that he would not be welcomed back should he visit again. The British press had whipped up the flames of interest, even photographing a maid preparing Charlie's room. To escape the crowds outside his hotel, Charlie sneaked out of a side entrance and took a cab back to his childhood across the River Thames.

Meanwhile, in Hollywood, feelings were running high. Roscoe Arbuckle's trial began on 14 November 1921, and two weeks later he took the stand and testified. Maude Delmont, whose vicious lies about the actor had started the virulent campaign against him, was considered such an unreliable witness by the prosecution that she was never called to give evidence. Three of the witnesses for the prosecution, Betty Campbell, Zey Prevon and Alice Lake,

Right **Home in triumph. Nine years after leaving England, Chaplin revisits his native land and gets a rapturous reception. Here the police struggle to restrain an enthusiastic crowd.**

Charlie Chaplin was in Britain at the time of Arbuckle's arrest. When he was asked by the British press about the accusations flying around in the more lurid American newspapers he dismissed them as 'preposterous'

Right Arbuckle in court, surrounded by his defence team. Throughout the proceedings he protested his innocence and he was eventually acquitted. The scandal, though, destroyed his career.

took the stand and revealed that Brady had coerced them into testifying against Arbuckle, threatening them with prison if they refused. The prosecution case fell apart, and yet the jury had difficulty reaching a verdict. After twenty-two ballots, they were hopelessly deadlocked at ten to two for acquittal. One juror, Mrs Helen Hubbard, stated that Arbuckle was guilty and she would maintain that position until hell froze over.

A second trial began on 11 January, and during its course Roscoe's defence team made extraordinary tactical errors. Not thinking it necessary for Roscoe to go over his story again, they didn't call him to the witness stand, and nor did they make the traditional summing-up speech to the jury. The jury took a dim view of this and were again deadlocked, this time at ten to two in favour of guilty. This extraordinary saga staggered on to a third trial.

Meanwhile, Hollywood was hit by two more scandals. On 2 February 1922 Paramount director William Desmond Taylor was found murdered at his bungalow. Then, in March news hit the press that Paramount star and heart-throb Wallace Reid was being treated for drug addiction. He had been pumped with morphine after an injury he had sustained while filming, the intention being to keep him on his feet and the film on schedule, but it resulted in an addiction so severe that he was confined to a sanatorium. Rumour has it that, the following year, when Zukor realized that Reid was washed up, he stopped paying his hospital bills. Reid consequently went into sudden withdrawal and died.

On 6 March 1922 Roscoe's third trial began. This time he took the witness box and clearly impressed the jury. Upon being asked to retire and consider their verdict, the jury were out for six minutes. They returned to the court-room and the foreman of the jury was given permission by the judge to read out the following statement:

> Acquittal is not enough for Roscoe Arbuckle. We feel that a great injustice has been done him ... He was manly throughout the case, and told a straightforward story on the witness stand, which we all believed. The happening at the hotel was an unfortunate affair for which Arbuckle, so the evidence shows, was in no way responsible. We wish him success, and hope that the American people will take the judgement of fourteen men and women who have sat listening for thirty-one days to evidence, that Roscoe Arbuckle is entirely innocent and free from all blame.

The foreman of the jury made the above statement on 12 April 1922. Roscoe's seven months of hell seemed to be over, but on 18 April, six days after he had been completely cleared of all charges, Roscoe Arbuckle was banned from the screen. The distributors of his pictures, the Famous Players–Lasky Corporation, made an announcement via Will Hays. Hays had been appointed by the studios to 'clean up' Hollywood, and Arbuckle was offered up as a sacrificial lamb. Throw Arbuckle to the wolves, and Hollywood would be seen as putting its own house in order. Will Hays's statement read:

> After consulting at length with Mr Joseph Schenck, the producers and Mr Adolph Zukor and Mr Jessy Lasky of the Famous Players–Lasky Corporation, the distributors, I will state that at my request they have cancelled all showings and all bookings of the Arbuckle films.

I have often wondered whether an elaborate practical joke, played a few years before, had any bearing on this inhumane blacklisting of Arbuckle. Shortly after Joe Schenck decided to sell Arbuckle's contract to Famous Players–Lasky, Roscoe read that his new boss, Adolph Zukor, was about to make his yearly trip to Hollywood from New York. Roscoe invited him to dinner at his house. Among the other guests was Sid Grauman, who owned the Hollywood movie palaces, the Egyptian and the Chinese, and four actresses, Harold Lloyd's female co-star, Bebe Daniels, Viola Dana, Anna Q. Nilsson and Alice Lake.

On the night of Arbuckle's party, Zukor and the other guests arrived and were soon enjoying several rounds of drinks. But the waiter committed a breach of dining etiquette by serving shrimp cocktails to the male guests first. This annoyed Roscoe, who followed the waiter out into the pantry and loudly remonstrated with him. The waiter wandered back out and attempted to rectify his error by taking back the men's half-eaten shrimp cocktails and giving them

Roscoe's seven months of hell seemed to be over, but on 18 April, six days after he had been completely cleared of all charges, Roscoe Arbuckle was banned from the screen

Arbuckle completely lost it. He grabbed the waiter and dragged him off to the pantry. He could be heard shouting, 'I'll kill you, you damned dumb bastard'

to the women. The waiter disappeared into the pantry and reappeared carrying a stack of soup bowls and a silver ladle. He put them on the table next to Roscoe and went to fetch the soup. A terrible din emerged from the kitchen. Completely soaked to the skin, the waiter re-entered the dining room and, without explanation, casually removed the soup bowls and ladle. In an attempt to pacify the furious Roscoe, Adolph told him that it was quite all right, he didn't like soup anyway. Roscoe complained about the quality of service and Adolph agreed that it was difficult to find intelligent servants. The main course arrived in the form of a twenty-four-pound turkey on a beautiful silver platter. But, true to form, the waiter dropped a napkin by the pantry door which, on opening behind him, propelled both waiter and turkey across the polished floor on a film of gravy.

Arbuckle completely lost it. He grabbed the waiter and dragged him off to the pantry. He could be heard shouting, 'I'll kill you, you damned dumb bastard.' Roscoe chased the waiter through the back door and into the garden, where he was eventually placated by the other guests. Adolph, in particular, was extremely disturbed by the night's events. This was the first time he'd met Arbuckle, his biggest star, and he appeared to be a madman. Roscoe finally calmed down. Luckily for the evening, he had ordered his chef to prepare two turkeys in case one was insufficient. Moments later the phone rang. It was Buster Keaton. He was going to be late but was sure that he could still make it. Buster arrived and joined them all at the table. One of the other guests started to tell him about the appalling waiter they had all suffered and, as Buster later recalled, went on to say, 'The odd part is that he looks very much like you.'

> That caused Mr Zukor to scrutinize me more closely. Then he got it but took it dead pan. His eyes moved from me to Roscoe, then back to me. Sid Grauman was the first to laugh. Pointing his finger at Zukor, he said derisively, 'Then came the dawn.'
>
> Zukor didn't smile, just said in an even tone, 'Very clever boys, very clever.'[4]

Not the remark of a man who finds the whole situation hilarious. He has spent a worryingly fraught evening being duped by Arbuckle and Keaton. Buster was still in his film infancy at this point, and so Adolph Zukor hadn't recognized him as the waiter. Did he feel humiliated, I wonder? Or did he simply think how very rude to be invited to somebody's house and then put through such unnecessary stress? Who exactly was the boss here?

Buster Keaton's next film, *The Paleface*, is the first he made after Roscoe's arrest. Immediately, we see the difference in Keaton the filmmaker. We start with a title-card, 'In the heart of the West, the Indian of today dwells in simple peace.' In previous films with Roscoe, Buster would no doubt have cut to Indians knocking the stuffing out of each other. But here there's no gag. Instead, we see rows of tepees nestling in a quiet reservation. The 'Indians' are not the villains in this film. It's the 'Oil sharks' from the Great Western Oil Company who are the baddies. They kill a member of the tribe and steal the lease to the land from him.

The tribe receive notice to vacate the land within twenty-four hours. The chief, played by Joe Roberts, informs the tribe: 'White man kill my messenger!' Joe Roberts, although wearing appropriately darker make-up himself, is surrounded by genuine Native Americans. The tribe is not played for laughs. This approach, with its straight portrayal of another race, was unusual in comedy films of the day. The tribe, as the innocent victims of an injustice, could have been suggested by the injustice of Arbuckle's arrest on a charge of manslaughter. Certainly, this is the first time that Buster has used drama to such a degree. In his autobiography Buster refers to Arbuckle's arrest as 'The Day the Laughter Stopped'. It's a full three minutes before the first gag appears. Joe Roberts points to the main gates and says, via a title-card, 'Kill first white man that comes in that gate.' Entirely innocent, Buster walks through the gate. His appearance is the first laugh in the picture. The second is when we see he is carrying a large butterfly net.

The serious tone in this film helps you to care more about the people on the screen. The film's humour stems more from Buster's ignorance than that of the 'Indians'. The tribe performs a war dance around him, but, totally oblivious to his predicament, he joins in the dance, adding a little flourish of his own. Finally realizing he's in trouble, Buster disguises himself as an 'Indian' but, once he loses the cloak, his plaits make him look more like a schoolgirl. He temporarily eludes his pursuers and finds refuge in a house, where he quickly makes himself a suit out of some sheets of asbestos that are lying around. Buster is eventually captured, and the Indians attempt to burn him at the stake. Thanks to the flameproof asbestos underwear, Buster emerges unharmed. They bow to him in reverence. Buster turns Native American and is initiated into the tribe. When Joe tells Buster, 'White man say we must leave,' Buster replies, 'Us Indians must stick together'.

They storm Great Western Oil's office and perform a war dance around the room. When one of the oil men escapes on horseback, Buster gives chase

The tribe, as the innocent victims of an injustice, could have been suggested by the injustice of Arbuckle's arrest on a charge of manslaughter. Certainly, this is the first time that Buster has used drama to such a degree

Right **Buster in *Cops*, with one of the many policemen to come his way.**

but is forced at gunpoint to put on the oil man's clothes. Seen from a distance, he is not recognized by his own tribe who start firing arrows at him. Is it too fanciful to suggest an Arbuckle echo here – a man previously adored who is then attacked by the same people. Outside the courtroom in San Francisco, men and women shouted 'beast' and 'monster' at him and called him a pervert.

Buster's next film, *Cops*, has often been singled out as his best short film, and it certainly has a lot to recommend it. Its central theme is that of an innocent man being hunted down by the forces of law. At one point, Buster is chased by thousands of policemen. The opening shot shows Buster behind bars: a condemned man from the start? In the run-up to the Arbuckle trial, a photograph of Roscoe behind bars appeared in several American newspapers, but few of their readers would have suspected that the photograph was a fake. The bars were superimposed over his face. Another faked photograph showed him holding a bottle of whisky and sitting alongside Virginia Rappé. At the time few newspaper readers would have been aware that such visual trickery was possible.

Buster is talking through the bars to his snooty girlfriend, played by Virginia Fox. We cut to a wider shot and see that Buster isn't in prison at all. He is actually standing in front of a pair of huge gates and behind them lies a posh drive. He's not so much locked in as locked out. It's as if being an outsider to her world – belonging to another class – is tantamount to being a criminal. Retreating up the long drive, she turns and tells him she won't marry him until he becomes a successful businessman.

As Buster walks away, he passes Joe Roberts hailing a taxi. Joe drops his wallet, Buster sees it and kicks it towards himself. He opens it, checks the

From the moment Joe Roberts drops his wallet in the street to the moment Buster is handed the address, each gag naturally flows into the next. Five and half minutes of sublimely linked comedy!

money and only then does he hand it back to Joe. Joe snatches it away from him and attempts to get into the taxi but falls over. Buster helps him up and into the cab. As it drives off, we see that Buster has the wallet again. In the back of the cab Joe realizes he is missing his wallet so he orders the driver to do a U-turn. As the car drives past Buster, Joe leans out of the window and grabs the wallet, not realizing he's left Buster holding the money. The car returns, and Joe gets out of one side and Buster gets in the other. The car drives off. Joe stands in the middle of the road and, as his jacket falls back, we see a police badge pinned to his chest. The whole sequence unfolds beautifully.

We are in a rougher neighbourhood than is usual in a Keaton picture. This is his *Easy Street.* A criminal type, played by Steve Murphy, catches a quick glimpse of Buster's bank roll, and seeing the chance for a quick con, he sits down on the kerb beside a mountain of household contents. A family is waiting for a removal man to come and take their furniture to their new address. Steve Murphy bursts into tears just as Buster passes by and tells him: 'I'm broke and they threw me out. If I don't sell my furniture my wife and babies will starve.' Buster is touched by his plight and resolves to buy the furniture in order to prove his worth as a successful businessman.

Wondering what on earth he's going to do with all this furniture, he spots a horse and cart for sale at the bargain price of $5. He hands the money to a man sitting on the kerb beside the horse, and leads the horse and cart away. He doesn't realize that the $5 price ticket is actually attached to a jacket outside a tailor shop.

Buster takes the horse and cart to the furniture but is rather amazed to find a bunch of strangers helping him load it up. They are, of course, the family who owns the furniture – a policeman and his family, as it later turns out. Just before Buster trots off, the man hands him the destination address, 4 Flushing Place. It means nothing to Buster, so he throws it away.

From the moment Joe Roberts drops his wallet in the street to the moment Buster is handed the address, each gag naturally flows into the next. Five and half minutes of sublimely linked comedy! It has to be said, though, that *Cops* then becomes slightly ordinary. Such is the fluidity of the early scenes that a scene with Buster going along slowly with a tired horse does lack a certain cinematic snap. Buster later explained the problem:

> There was a scene – before we stumble into the parade – where Onyx [the horse] slows down and can't pull the heavy load of furniture any longer. I'm to unharness him and lead him out from the shafts. Then it's to cut and show me,

> bit in mouth, between the shafts pulling the wagon. Then pan back and show Onyx up in the wagon riding.
>
> It was a good idea except that Onyx wouldn't go along with it. We wasted a day trying to get him up in that wagon ... We finally gave up and shot me pulling the wagon alongside of the horse. Not as good a gag, but it had to do ... Monday morning we saw the reason for it all. Onyx had a brand-new colt standing by her when we came to the studio. *Her*, I said.
>
> [Clyde] Bruckman [one of Buster's regular gag men] was just opening his mouth to say something. I could feel the word forming in his mind. I beat him to it. 'The baby's name,' I said, 'is Onyxpected!'[15]

Opposite When Roscoe Arbuckle's career fell apart in the wake of his trial, Buster Keaton stood by him. Over the next few years he found his friend film work, even though Roscoe had officially been banned by the studios.

Back to the film and, without realizing it, Buster is now riding the stolen horse and cart, piled sky-high with stolen furniture, into the largest concentration of policeman you could imagine – the annual police parade! At this point Buster's girlfriend, Virginia Fox, arrives and is introduced as the mayor's daughter.

The parade stops, and Buster pauses for a cigarette, but he hasn't got a light. An anarchist on a nearby rooftop lights the fuse on a bomb and throws it into the parade. It lands on the seat beside Buster. It's a black, round bomb with a lighted fuse sticking out of it. Buster picks up the bomb and lights his cigarette with it. This is exactly the same gag and pose that Harold Lloyd adopted to be photographed in, just over two years earlier, when the prop bomb exploded. Lloyd was incredibly lucky to survive, and here's Buster re-creating the moment simply for the purposes of a gag. Once he realizes it's a bomb, he tosses it casually aside. It explodes but has a comical effect: the policemen caught in the blast end up with tousled hair, blackened faces and their jackets on the wrong way. A very smart bomb: it doesn't harm people, it just rearranges their clothing.

The explosion is the motivation for Buster to be chased by every policeman in town. But why did Buster choose the gag of taking a light from a bomb fuse? Was it chosen to upset Harold Lloyd? Harold and Buster were friends, but the Arbuckle scandal may well have provoked a major argument. From this distance in time I can only wildly speculate, but let's do it. Harold was a lifelong teetotaller and could have antagonized Buster by suggesting that, if there hadn't been any alcohol at the Arbuckle party, a tragedy would have been avoided. Moreover, while it was said many times by Arbuckle's contemporaries that his friends never called him 'Fatty', in Harold Lloyd's autobiography, *An American Comedy*, published in 1928, he refers to Roscoe as 'Fatty'

The explosion is the motivation for Buster to be chased by every policeman in town. But why did Buster choose the gag of taking a light from a bomb fuse? Was it chosen to upset Harold Lloyd?

Arbuckle throughout. Perhaps Harold carried some lingering resentment at having been judged not good enough when he appeared in a couple of Arbuckle pictures in the early Keystone days.

The climax of *Cops* is highly distinctive. After some extraordinary acrobatic stunts – at one point Buster is whisked off his feet by a passing car – he runs into the police station and re-emerges dressed as a policeman. Not content merely to step into a policeman's uniform, he also steps into a policeman's role: he locks up the entire force and throws away the key. Virginia Fox, the mayor's daughter, walks by and snubs him. He is still socially inferior in her eyes. He retrieves the key, opens the door to the station and is dragged back in. A tombstone appears with Buster's hat on top. The tombstone is inscribed with the words, 'The End'. A very dark note on which to finish a comedy.

Below Buster's *My Wife's Relations* has a strongly autobiographical flavour: he plays an innocent man who accidentally marries in to an appalling family. Did his in-laws ever see the picture?

Charlie Chaplin's great leap into autobiographical filmmaking with *The Kid* had been initially prompted by the death of his first-born child, Norman. Buster's trauma in witnessing what was happening to his close friend Roscoe similarly led him into autobiographical material. That and events at home with the Talmadge clan.

In one, unfunny, moment Buster is lying in bed with his new wife and he punches her in her sleep. To be fair, she does later hit him over the head with a vase

I believe that Virginia Fox's character in *Cops* reflects the Talmadge family's disdain of Buster. He was an ex-vaudeville comedian, whose best friend was accused of rape and manslaughter. The title of Buster's next comedy tells you everything. For the one and only occasion in his silent film career, Buster used a possessive pronoun in a title: the film was called *My Wife's Relations*, and it was released in May 1922.

When Natalie had become pregnant, her mother, Peg, had moved in with the couple. Constance, her sister, who had recently divorced, moved in as well. And this is the basic storyline of *My Wife's Relations*: Buster accidentally gets married to a rather formidable-looking older woman, played by Kate Price, and then has to live with her and her awful relations (four brothers and a father).

They first meet when she mistakes him for a vandal, thinking he is responsible for breaking a window. With punishment in mind, she drags him into the building concerned, not realizing it's a Polish Registry Office. She attempts to report his crime to the registrar but, because neither of them speaks the same language, he ends up marrying her to Buster. He asks her, in Polish, 'Do you take this man to be your lawful wedded husband?' to which she nods: 'Sure! He broke your window.' It's a rather pertinent confusion of marriage vows with the handing down of a sentence.

When they reach her house her four hulking great brothers check his teeth, turn him upside down and generally inspect him like an animal. In one, unfunny, moment Buster is lying in bed with his new wife and he punches her in her sleep. To be fair, she does later hit him over the head with a vase. The family then discovers that Buster has inherited a fortune from his uncle, and there's a sudden change of heart: 'Her husband is rich – now we must be nice to him.' So they move into a mansion. In real life Natalie was constantly encouraging Buster to move to better and bigger houses. In *My Wife's Relations*, although the family live in a mansion, they still have very bad manners. It's the in-laws who have no class: Kate Price drinks her tea from a bone china saucer.

The in-laws decide to throw a party. Buster is instructed by his wife to 'put half a cake of yeast in the home brew', and he accidentally empties the whole packet into the barrel. The camera cuts to the guests who are arriving and then cuts back to the bubbling home brew starting to froth over. It cuts again to a medium close-up of one of the guests tapping Buster's wife on the back: she is wearing a cream-coloured dress with embroidery running over her shoulder (not too dissimilar to the bubbles in the previous shot). We cut back to the home brew, which is now rapidly spilling over, giving the barrel a frothy skirt. We cut again to Buster's wife in mid-shot, with the same shape and colouring

Buster walks towards the camera, yawning, and pulls down a blind with 'The End' printed on it, echoing the inscription on the tombstone in *Cops*. The romantic ending of his earlier pictures has gone

as the barrel in the frothy skirt. Buster is basically comparing his new wife to a big, bubbling barrel of yeast.

Both this and Buster's next two-reeler, *The Blacksmith*, were far from Buster's best. *The Blacksmith* is partly a remake of *The Garage* (the last Arbuckle–Keaton short) and was chiefly remembered by Buster, in later years, for a comic routine that didn't work. A customer drives his brand-new white Rolls Royce car into Buster's workshop. He wants the front bumper tightened. The next few minutes show Buster getting oily handprints all over the gleaming white car, accidentally pouring oil over the back seat and burning the paint off with a blow torch left lying around. He then hoists another car's engine into the air. This inevitably swings into the Rolls Royce, smashing two of the doors. Buster's boss, played by Joe Roberts, turns up in a foul mood. He rips one of the doors straight off the car before Buster manages to hook Joe up on the hoist. Joe inevitably falls on top of the precious Rolls, wrecking it further.

The trouble with this sequence is that audiences didn't find it funny because they're watching a lovely-looking, expensive car, an item that few could afford, being destroyed. This is a curious lapse for Buster, whose comedy instincts had been honed to perfection during his years of playing to live audiences. It's also puzzling because the business of something spotlessly white being sullied by oily handprints has already occurred earlier on in the film, to Virginia Fox's horse. It's not like Buster simply to repeat a piece of business to no comic advantage.

In Marion Meade's biography of Buster she states that Joe Schenck's wedding gift to Buster and Natalie was a white Rolls Royce. Unfortunately, she doesn't give a source for this, but if it's true the scene in *The Blacksmith* makes perfect sense – not as comedy but as anger. This may not be the same car, but it's certainly the same make and style. Was Buster so angry at this point that he was willing to antagonize his producer, who, after all, was one of the men who banned Roscoe from the screen? *The Blacksmith* was made shortly after the ban had been announced. Roscoe had been generous to Buster when he first started out in pictures, and Buster wasn't the sort of man to forget that. Perhaps this is the same white Rolls Royce. Is Buster destroying a wedding gift onscreen? Would Buster's budget for the two-reeler have covered the cost of buying and then wrecking such an expensive car? Buster said he knew the scene didn't work. So why didn't he cut it?

As if that wasn't enough, later we see Buster and Virginia Fox jump on a train together and a title-card reads, 'Many a honeymoon express has ended thusly.' We see a train falling off the bridge. It's obviously a toy train, and Buster walks into view and places it back on the track. We cut to Buster, Virginia and baby. Buster walks towards the camera, yawning, and pulls down a blind with 'The End' printed on it, echoing the inscription on the tombstone in *Cops*. The romantic ending of his earlier pictures has gone. I wonder what conversations were had between Joe Schenck and Buster. It has been suggested that Joe encouraged Buster into marriage with Natalie. If that's the case, Buster might well have considered destroying a wedding gift as ample pay-back.

Buster needed to cool down. There was a poisonous atmosphere in Hollywood, and not all of Roscoe's contemporaries stood by him, so when the idea came up for a spoof Western set in a snowy landscape at Lake Tahoe Buster probably saw this as a great opportunity to get away from it all. Even so, one comic dig in the film refers to the Arbuckle debacle. A very popular cowboy star of the day, William S. Hart, had been critical of Roscoe while he was chatting to Buster at a Hollywood party, and it's interesting to note that in this new film, *The Frozen North*, Buster parodies William S. Hart's oversentimental tendency to cry in his Westerns. Buster felt that this over-the-top habit was ripe for a kicking, and he later said that, after seeing the film, William S. Hart didn't speak to him for a year.

The Frozen North feels like a Keaton–Arbuckle collaboration, and Arbuckle probably co-wrote the story, such as it is, and supplied individual gags along the way (although Eddie Cline is the credited co-writer and co-director). It's possible that Roscoe joined the small unit in Lake Tahoe and co-directed some scenes, because becoming solely a film director was obviously the next best option for him. Buster was determined to get his friend up and working again, and the possible collaboration between Arbuckle and Keaton could account for the strong vein of misogyny that runs all the way through the picture. In one scene, where Buster returns home, his wife greets him with open arms but he pushes her away. He struts across the floor and tells her to shut up. She screams and is accidentally knocked out by a falling vase: her unconscious body slumps to the floor. A sheriff hears her scream and approaches the cabin. Spotting him,

Left Buster reaches the end of the line in *The Frozen North*.

Buster picks his up his wife and 'dances' with her. Once the sheriff leaves, Buster drops her to the floor without even looking at her. There's an element of dramatic parody here, but it still leaves a feeling of unease.

Later, a married man catches Buster flirting with his wife. He kicks Buster firmly up the arse, which could be an indication that Roscoe is involved in the writing/direction. Keaton is rarely kicked up the arse in his own films: it's not his style. He bares his teeth at the husband in a gesture of extreme hostility, and here we have Buster breaking his deadpan expression. More evidence of Arbuckle's contribution?

It was during this time that Joe Schenck was finally persuaded by Buster to allow him to move into features. Buster's last four shorts all have strong moments, but, overall, a sense of 'getting them over and done with' pervades. As in *The Frozen North*, they all involved time filming away from the Keaton Studio in Los Angeles.

Daydreams, released on 22 September, tells the story of a man's inability to meet the approval of his sweetheart's parents, which was something Buster knew all about! Many of the street scenes were shot in San Francisco at the time when the Arbuckle trials were under way, and there might well be a nod to Arbuckle in the scene where Buster plays Hamlet performing the 'Alas poor Yorick' speech, in which Hamlet is grieving over the fate of his good friend who was formerly a court jester ('a fellow of infinite jest, of most excellent fancy') but is now reduced to a worm-eaten skull. On a lighter note, in one scene there's a tailor's dummy with a bowler hat and toothbrush moustache that strongly suggests Charlie Chaplin.

Buster's next two-reeler, *The Electric House*, was released on 22 October. Buster plays a botanist who graduates from the People's University. Owing to a mix-up at the graduation ceremony, he ends up being awarded the Electrical Engineer's diploma by mistake. This results in his being asked to 'electrify' the Dean's house. With the help of a book, *Electricity Made Easy*, he gets started while the occupants are away. They return from their vacation to find all sorts of wonderful surprises: at the flick of a switch the bookcase automatically selects books; the pool table recycles the balls; the bathtub moves along a track from the bathroom to the bedroom (so you can fall straight out of bed and into the bath); and dinner is served on a miniature indoor train, which runs on a loop from the kitchen to the dining room. Keaton's love of mechanical wizardry is exploited to its full comic potential.

The real Electrical Engineer, played by Steve Murphy, turns up, intent on revenge. The job should have gone to him, but he was mistakenly awarded a diploma in Manicure and Hairdressing. He secretly crosses the wiring. Everything goes haywire, and this is when the madness really begins. Keaton is at his acrobatic best and funniest as he gets caught on the unstoppable escalator.

The Balloonatic, released on 22 January 1922, was largely shot on location with Phyllis Haver. 'The Balloonatic' was one of the many nicknames that Roscoe had been called during his screen career. (He was also known as 'The Prince of Whales'.) It seems likely that Buster's home life is again alluded to in this film. Buster is at the entrance/exit to an amusement ride called 'The

The real Electrical Engineer, played by Steve Murphy, turns up, intent on revenge. The job should have gone to him, but he was mistakenly awarded a diploma in Manicure and Hairdressing

House of Trouble'. A female passer-by decides to buy a ticket and go in. As is so often the case with Keaton, he's in the wrong place at the wrong time: when the woman is ejected from the house, she lands right on top of Buster and flattens him. The same fate awaits him later in the film, out in the wilderness, when Phyllis Haver dives on top of him as he's carried downstream. Buster proves himself to be totally useless at surviving out in the wild.

The Balloonatic was made closely after the birth of his first child when the house was overrun by his wife's female relatives, so maybe it's no surprise that this film features Buster being flattened and emasculated by women. Having said that, it ends on a wonderfully romantic note: lying in each other's arms in a boat dreamily floating backwards, the couple don't realize they're approaching a huge rushing waterfall. Then, in a magical shot, which sums up what it's like to be in love, they reach the edge of the waterfall, and instead of falling the boat continues to float out into mid-air, high in the sky. It transpires that the boat's awning has got caught up in a hot air balloon.

Large sections of Buster's last short, *The Love Nest*, were filmed at sea. Anything to get away from home. It begins with a beautiful, romantic shot of Buster and his sweetheart in silhouette beside a shimmering lake. However, she has her back to him and a title-card announces: 'The story of a young man who lost his interest in women – and everything else.' In an attempt to forget her, he sets off to sail around the world in a boat named *Cupid.* After a series of adventures at sea (which turn out to be a dream) he wakes to discover, 'there was neither land … nor food … nor water … in short, there was nothing at all'. He thinks he's dying, but then a woman swims past his boat and we discover it's still moored; he hasn't gone anywhere.

If Buster's last few short films don't necessarily show him at his best, Charlie Chaplin's final three short films are absolute triumphs. His first film after the enormous success of *The Kid* was *The Idle Class*, which was released on 25 September 1921 while Charlie was still in London. In this film he plays an absent-minded millionaire. In an early scene we see him crossing a hotel foyer, dressed immaculately – apart from the fact that he's forgotten to put on any trousers. It is beautifully choreographed. Nobody ever sees him in a trouserless condition. He has a hilariously ingenious way of getting round the situation: crouched behind a newspaper, he manages to shuffle out of the foyer without anyone spying his legs. In another scene we see Charlie with his back to the camera, apparently sobbing away after his wife has walked out on him. As he

Above Chaplin's versatility and confidence were such that he did not always feel obliged to play the Tramp, even though that was the role most people associated him with. In *The Idle Class* he's a millionaire married to Edna Purviance.

continues to shake, he turns and we realize he's not crying but making himself a cocktail.

Once the character of the Tramp became hugely successful, Charlie rarely played other parts. Here, his portrayal of the rich man reminds us of his versatility. He also plays the Tramp who, by chance, resembles the millionaire. The millionaire's wife, played by Edna Purviance, sees Charlie at her fancy dress ball and thinks he's her husband in disguise. There's a real spirit of playfulness.

When he returned from London knowing he had only two more films to make in order to fulfil his First National contract, Charlie got to work straight away, and *Pay Day*, released on 2 April 1922, is another gem, full of wonders. The first half of the film is set on a building site. There's lots of fun to be had with a wooden lift that keeps shooting up and down, whisking away people's half-eaten lunches. And there's a cunning use of camera trickery that makes Charlie look as if he's catching an endless stream of bricks. In reality, he's dropping them and the camera is being hand-cranked backwards. Later we see him and his workmates coming out of a 'Bachelors Club' highly inebriated. His brother, Syd, plays a fellow drunk, and in one playful moment Charlie attempts to push the cigar that's in his own mouth into Syd's mouth. You can briefly glimpse Syd stepping out of character and breaking into a grin.

By the time Charlie gets home to his wife, played by Phyllis Allen, it's five o'clock in the morning. He's getting undressed to get into bed when the alarm clock goes off. She wakes up, and Charlie pretends that he is, in fact, getting dressed to go to work. He crawls off to sleep in the bath.

His last short ranks among the very best he ever made. In his final Mutual film, *The Adventurer*, Charlie was an escaped convict invited to a country house and then chased away by the police. His last film for First National again featured him as an escaped convict. The opening moments of *The Pilgrim* are so economically crafted that they're a million miles from the long-winded deliberations of the Keystones. A prison officer slaps up a flyer offering a reward for an escaped convict; it features a picture of Charlie in convict garb. The following shot shows a man in a wet bathing suit picking up a convict uniform from behind a bush and looking perplexed. We cut to Charlie, dressed as a pastor, walking alongside a railway station. In three quick shots he has established his situation and got a couple of laughs while doing it.

In pastoral mode he is mistaken by Mack Swain for the Rev. Philip Pim, the town's new pastor. He's led to the church where the congregation await his arrival. When he enters, Charlie spots a dozen of the congregation in their pews and immediately imagines they're a jury. He is handed a Bible and mistakenly takes an oath on it. He then takes a swig of the holy wine and momentarily leans against the pulpit like a seasoned drinker holding up the bar.

The church elders hand round the collection boxes, and Charlie runs over and grabs them for himself. He weighs them both in his hands. One clearly weighs more than the other, and he smiles at the side of the church that was generous and scowls at the side that wasn't. Having established that this church is purely mercenary, Charlie makes his sermon. He offers a histrionic rendition of David and Goliath, finishing to rapturous applause from a small boy in the front row. Everybody else is glaring furiously. Totally carried away by the moment, Charlie returns for a couple of curtain calls. Suggesting that preaching is just another form of show business made *The Pilgrim* a controversial film in some American states.

Chuck Riesner, whom we last saw in *The Kid,* appears in this picture as a former cellmate of Charlie's. Chuck sees Charlie walking down the street and thinks to himself, 'I know that face.' A flashback shows Charlie and Chuck in convict gear, behind bars and sharing a rather thin cigarette. Chuck's son in real life, Dinky, plays a very young child who torments Syd Chaplin (playing his father) and Charlie while they're sitting politely on a sofa trying to eat tea and biscuits. This is the other side to *The Kid.* This one is an absolute monster. He

His brother, Syd, plays a fellow drunk, and in one playful moment Charlie attempts to push the cigar that's in his own mouth into Syd's mouth. You can briefly glimpse Syd stepping out of character and breaking into a grin

A title-card reads: 'Mexico – a new life – peace at last.' Suddenly a gun-fight breaks out and, with his back to us, Charlie runs away, keeping his legs straddling the border, one leg in the US and one in Mexico

Opposite Charlie adopts yet another guise in *The Pilgrim* where he plays an escaped convict masquerading as a pastor.

punches them repeatedly in the face, pours water over them from the goldfish bowl and prods them with a knitting needle. He steals Syd's bowler hat and places it over an identical-looking steam pudding. Not paying much attention and trying to assist Edna in the kitchen, Charlie smothers the hat in custard, whipped cream and cherries. He then takes it into the dining room. Everybody joins Syd in the search for his hat, none of them realizing it has become the pudding on the table. Only when Charlie has trouble cutting into it, is the truth revealed. 'Where did you find it?' asks Syd's wife. 'They were eating it,' comes the reply. Syd leaves in disgust. This is his last appearance in a Charlie Chaplin film, but he will continue to star in his own silent comedies for the rest of the decade. This is also Edna Purviance's last appearance in a Chaplin comedy. She had been a loyal friend and was bitterly upset when their romance ended back in 1917. She was with him as his fame accelerated around the world, and she may even have encouraged Charlie to soften the Tramp's original aggressive character.

The Pilgrim's last scene is set at the international border between the USA and Mexico. Charlie has been taken there by a kindly sheriff who tells him to go and pick flowers on the Mexican side. Charlie doesn't understand at first but then realizes that the sheriff is giving him a chance of freedom. A title-card reads: 'Mexico – a new life – peace at last.' Suddenly a gun-fight breaks out and, with his back to us, Charlie runs away, keeping his legs straddling the border, one leg in the US and one in Mexico.

With this, Charlie shuffles away from short comedies for ever. Earlier in the film, in a sweet acknowledgement of the Keystone days, Charlie enters a saloon disguised with a Ford Sterling-style goatee beard, but comparing *The Pilgrim* to early Keystone comedies is like hearing the difference between a Beethoven sonata and someone hitting a piano with an axe.

Harold Lloyd was the first comedian to pick up the challenge laid down by the huge success of *The Kid*, and his first feature, *Grandma's Boy*, was released eighteen months later, on 3 September 1922. It was a hard film to get right. Harold plays a lot of scenes with an old woman, Anna Townsend. Did the idea of an old woman appeal because she was the opposite of a very young Jackie Coogan? In the past Harold had claimed that he reversed Charlie's costume to create a character for himself. Was he now doing the same with Charlie's lead characters? Certainly, Charlie's influence is evident here. Following *The Kid*'s example, *Grandma's Boy* begins with babies. Two babies, in fact, just to trump Charlie. One of them is wearing a huge pair of horn-rimmed

Above Praised by Chaplin, and partly indebted to him, *Grandma's Boy* was Harold Lloyd's first feature film. Here he is being urged to chase a rather disreputable tramp away from the house.

glasses. Then we see Harold as a schoolboy, more plausibly wearing the same spectacles, being bullied by a smaller boy. We move forward to Harold as a nineteen-year-old man. His rival, played by Charles Stevenson, throws him down a well to see if his suit will shrink. It does.

Just as *The Kid* begins with a dramatic sequence of events, so does *Grandma's Boy*. Harold is laying the pathos on a bit thick, and it must be said that he doesn't have Charlie's light touch at this point in his career. In one scene, realizing that he is a coward, Harold sobs on his grandmother's shoulder. The moment was, no doubt, suggested by the Chaplin–Coogan scenes of weeping in *The Kid*, which were seen at the time as exploring an emotional depth new to screen comedy. Grandma tells Harold about his grandfather's exploits in the American Civil War. He, too, was a coward until he was given a magic talisman by an old gypsy woman who promised, 'Him as holds the mystic Idol is all powerful! He conquers. Nothin' can harm him. Nothin' – Nothin.' Armed with this all-powerful piece of wood, Harold's grandfather was able to capture a bunch of enemy generals. Grandma gives the talisman to Harold. Convinced of its power to make him all conquering, he captures a murderous tramp who has been

Onscreen Harold is an extremely likeable character, and we are pleased when he triumphs, but the audience didn't laugh. The film told a good story, but there were no gags in it. So Harold went back and shot more material

terrorizing the neighbourhood. He then has a fight with his rival, whom he defeats in a flurry of speeded-up action. Grandma finally reveals that the mysteriously all-powerful talisman is actually nothing more than her umbrella handle. Harold had simply triumphed because he believed he could.

Just like his screen character, Harold was determined, in real life, to conquer his inadequacies. Let's imagine how Harold must have felt seven years before when he was sacked by Mack Sennett from the Keystone studios and told that he wasn't funny and had to go. Hal Roach, his business partner, had the same low opinion of Harold's abilities as a comic. Hal always praised Harold as an actor, but he also said he didn't have a funny bone in his body. Audience previews of *Grandma's Boy* confirmed Hal Roach's opinion. Onscreen Harold is an extremely likeable character, and we are pleased when he triumphs, but the audience didn't laugh. The film told a good story, but there were no gags in it. So Harold went back and shot more material.

The film, as it is now, features an amusing sequence between Mildred Davies, the love interest, and Harold's rival, Charles Stevenson. The two men mistakenly swallow mothballs thinking they are sweets. The alternation from pained expressions to polite concealment each time Mildred looks at them is very funny, and the sequence represents the main comic element of the picture. There are other gags here and there, but they are no more than individual moments within what is otherwise a drama. The picture features a lot of fighting, indicating Harold's early aspirations to become a professional boxer, before his mother put her foot down.

Fortunately, the mothball sequence and other gags were enough to transform *Grandma's Boy*, and it was an instant hit with critics and audiences alike. The film took a long time to shoot – from 22 October 1921 to 14 March 1922 – but the effort was worth it. Charlie Chaplin, for one, praised the picture:

> It is one of the best constructed screenplays I have ever seen on the screen ... the boy has a fine understanding of light and shape, and that picture has given me a real artistic thrill and stimulated me to go ahead.[6]

The above quotation is dated 23 May 1922, so Charlie had obviously seen the film at a private viewing some four months before its official release. Harold was thrilled by Chaplin's praise.

His next feature, *Doctor Jack*, was released on 19 December, only three months after *Grandma's Boy*, and, like its predecessor, it was an enormous success at the box office. The public loved Harold Lloyd in *Grandma's Boy* and wanted

Safety Last!

1

2

3

In Harold Lloyd's first screen masterpiece, *Safety Last!* all the action leads up to the final, climactic twenty-minute scene where Harold climbs the Bolton Building. The cash prize on offer will smooth the path to future happiness with his sweetheart Mildred.

What's surprising to learn is that the climbing sequence was filmed before the early part of the film and with no clear idea of what the rest of the story would be. The sequence had been inspired by Harold watching Bill Strothers (who plays the part of Limpy Bill in the film) climb a building one day in July 1922:

> The higher he climbed the more nervous I grew, until, when he came to a difficult ledge twelve stories up, I had to cut around a corner out of sight of him and peek back to see if he was over the ledge. If it makes me this jumpy, what would it do to a picture audience I asked myself. The more I thought of it, the better I liked it.[7]

The climb took two months to shoot because filming was restricted to between 11 a.m. and 1 p.m. to keep the angle of the sun consistent. Once the climbing sequence had been mastered, the rest of the story was worked out by Harold, Hal Roach, Sam Taylor, the co-director and Tim Whelan, the writer.

In *Safety Last!* Harold Lloyd climbs to the top of his profession.

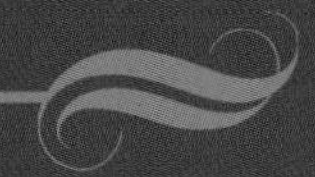

4

1 The climb is announced in one of a series of publicity shots for the film. 2 Harold starts the climb, hoping that his friend, Limpy Bill, will take over from him when he reaches the first-floor window. He doesn't. 3 He reaches the clock. Harold had actually lost the thumb and forefinger of his right hand in an accident, but here a clever prosthetic hides the injury. 4 Moment of panic. 5 Nearly there! 6 Harold's sweetheart gives him final encouragement.

5

6

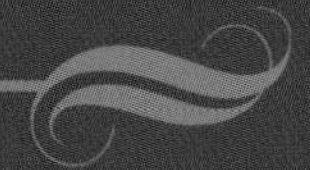

Doctor Jack outgrossed _Grandma's Boy_ at the box office, but its endless conveyor belt of comic devices betrays a lack of confidence in Harold's own comic ability

more of him. Sadly, however, *Doctor Jack* is not a good film. Again, it starts with a dramatic prologue. We see a young girl, with a haircut like Jackie Coogan's, asking for help from Dr Jack. The doctor has a good line in remedies: he believes in fresh air and love. An old woman is prescribed regular visits from her son. Another patient, reluctant to exercise, starts tapping his foot to music provided by the doctor. But then the film veers off into all kinds of sideshows. A small monkey appears, wearing matching gingham hat and coat. A comedy dog turns up, along with an escaped lunatic. Incident after incident is chucked at the screen. For the comic finale Harold leaps up and down with a cloak over his head, presumably attempting to spoof John Barrymore in *Dr Jekyll and Mr Hyde* (1921). It could be anybody under that cloak and maybe it is.

Doctor Jack outgrossed *Grandma's Boy* at the box office, but its endless conveyor belt of comic devices betrays a lack of confidence in Harold's own comic ability. Would Harold's shortcomings be exposed in feature-length films? Harold knew he had to do better next time.

His third feature, *Safety Last!,* was released on April Fool's Day, 1923, and it's Harold's first masterpiece. The film begins with Harold behind bars. He's copying Buster's opening gag from *Cops*, but he takes it further by featuring a swinging noose in the background. His sweetheart, Mildred, is present, along with a parson and a guard. He continues to milk the situation, until finally revealing he's really at a railway station and the swinging noose is actually a device that enables passing locomotives to pick up messages. Is Harold thumbing his nose at Buster for the gag in *Cops*, lighting a cigarette from a bomb fuse? I can't help but feel that there's some point being made here, but I just can't figure out what it is.

Harold is off to the big city to seek his fortune. Just as soon as he 'makes good', Mildred will join him and they will get married. A few months pass, and we see Harold and his roommate, Limpy Bill, avoiding the landlady when the rent is due. She knocks at the door, and the two men rush over to the corner of their sparsely furnished room where they each put on an overcoat. They hang up the coats and lift their legs out of sight. When we presented *Safety Last!* at the Colston Hall, Bristol, in January 2006, to an audience of over a thousand people, this overcoat gag got a massive laugh. As Charlie Chaplin once said about silent comedy: 'The whole thing is like a symphony in which the audience is as important as the screen.'[8] As the story unfolds, Harold bumps into his old friend Jim, now a policeman, whom he knew back in his home town. There's a bit of physical joshing between them, then Limpy Bill turns up and Harold decides to boast about how well he's in with the police. Seeing Jim on the phone, Harold

suggests to Bill that he push the policeman over. Bill takes some persuading and, by the time he agrees, Harold's friendly copper has been replaced by another on the same phone. This one is less than friendly and doesn't appreciate being shoved to the ground. Bill runs away and climbs up the side of a building to escape him. A small crowd gathers to watch. The policeman gives up the chase but warns that the next time he sees Bill he will arrest him. Harold later congratulates Bill on his climbing skills. Bill assures him it was nothing, he could climb a building sixteen-stories high while blindfolded.

Harold then enters a pawnshop to buy a decorative chain for Mildred. The pawnbroker is portrayed as a negative Jewish stereotype, much given to wringing his hands. In an earlier scene we saw an African-American man frightened out of his wits and made to act like a gibbering idiot. These characterizations were part of the comedy vocabulary of the day, but Chaplin never used this type of 'easy' gag, and Lloyd and Keaton phased them out towards the end of their silent careers.

Harold writes frequently to Mildred, telling her how well he's doing, and she decides it's time to visit him in the big city. Although Harold is actually working as a salesman in the cloth department, he manages to hoodwink Mildred into believing that he is, in fact, working at management level. This backfires on him when Mildred says, 'And just think – you've made money enough already for our little home.' Harold later overhears the real general manager declare, 'I'd give a thousand dollars – to anyone – for a new idea – One that would attract an enormous crowd to our store.' Harold immediately thinks of his friend Bill's extraordinary climbing skills, and he suggests a building-climbing stunt to the general manager who, after some persuasion, agrees. Harold offers Bill $500 to climb the twelve floors of the department store. Bill agrees, and the climb is scheduled for the next day when Harold, confident that he'll be $500 richer, promises to marry Mildred. Forty-five minutes into the picture everything hangs in the balance.

The following day the papers are full of the story: 'MYSTERY MAN IN DEATH DEFYING THRILL. To Climb Wall of Towering Skyscraper.' The paper features a photograph of Bill with his face blanked out. The policeman, who was (and still is) intent on arresting Bill, sees the publicity and realizes that it must be the same man. He makes his way to the Bolton Building, where the climb is to take place at two o'clock. When Harold spots the policeman, he tries to lose him, but to no avail. Then Bill has an idea: 'There's only one way out. You climb to the second floor, an' duck through the window. Then I'll put on your coat an' hat, an' go the rest of the way. They'll never know the difference.'

Forty-five minutes into the picture everything hangs in the balance. The following day the papers are full of the story: 'MYSTERY MAN IN DEATH DEFYING THRILL. To Climb Wall of Towering Skyscraper'

The last twenty minutes of *Safety Last!* are truly astonishing. Audiences are moved to heights of excitement punctuated by huge belly laughs. It's sublime alchemy

Left Even as late as 1928 a typical film crew for a silent feature film would number no more than half a dozen. This crew is at work on Harold Lloyd's film *Speedy*.

Harold is extremely dubious, but Bill assures him he only has to climb one floor. Remember, of course, in America the first floor is our ground floor. Harold is persuaded. He steps forward and announces that he is the Mystery Man. The policeman is immediately suspicious.

Harold starts to climb at exactly 53 minutes and 53 seconds into the movie. The policeman spots Bill and sets off in chase. Harold makes it to the second floor, but Bill tells him to climb one more floor; he just has to lose the policeman. However, Bill fails to shake off the copper, and Harold has to keep on climbing. As he does so, he encounters a comedy of obstacles, each destined to knock him (and the audience) off balance. The view behind Harold reveals that he's dangerously high. Having reached the penultimate floor, he scrambles onto a window ledge, but Bill accidentally knocks him off. Harold lunges for the hands of a large clock on the side of the building. The hands move from a quarter to three to half past two. The image of Harold Lloyd, with time on his hands, hanging from this clock, became famous throughout the world. It's an image that has come to define him. As a teenager in the late 1960s I had a poster of him, hanging from this clock, up on my bedroom wall.

With an enormous effort, Harold lifts himself onto the very top ledge of the building. Behind him we can see that he's hundreds of feet up. Mildred leans out of the window below and tries to warn him that there's a rather hefty-looking wind gauge spinning rapidly just inches above his head. Harold indicates that he'll meet her on the roof. He stands up and is hit by the wind gauge. Stunned and disoriented, he staggers perilously close to the edge. His foot gets caught in a loop of rope, sending him plunging over the edge. In a great arc he swings upside down and into mid-air. He swoops to the top of the building, where he lands in Mildred's arms. At this point the thousand-strong crowd in Bristol in January 2006 broke into spontaneous rapturous applause. Over eighty years after it was first shown, *Safety Last!* maintains its power to captivate an audience. The audience can see that he really is up that high. A slick gag finishes off this extraordinary picture. Harold walks across a large puddle of sticky tar. His shoes get stuck and he walks out of them. His socks get stuck and he walks out of those, too, without once breaking his stride. The last twenty minutes of *Safety Last!* are truly astonishing. Audiences are moved to heights of excitement punctuated by huge belly laughs. It's sublime alchemy. The combination of thrills and laughter rivals Chaplin's integration of laughs and sentiment for cinematic potency. On its release, *Safety Last!* was a massive success. And its thrill elements heavily influenced Harold's main rivals, Keaton and Chaplin.

Chapter 7
"Panning for Gold"

BUSTER KEATON

in

OUR HOSPITALITY

A METRO PICTURE
(IN 7 PARTS)

COUNTRY OF ORIGIN U.S.A.

Panning for Gold

Buster Keaton finally realized his ambition of releasing a feature-length film on 25 July 1923. The film was *The Three Ages*, and it was a parody of D.W. Griffith's mighty and lengthy epic *Intolerance*, which had appeared seven years before. Buster's film portrays three love stories set in different times: the Stone Age, the Roman Age and the Modern Age. The advantage of having the three different strands was that if the feature film didn't work out it could be edited into three separate two-reelers. Luckily, this wasn't necessary, but it reveals a certain lack of confidence, perhaps on producer Joe Schenck's part, in Buster's ability to make a feature.

Buster's first appearance in the Stone Age sequence is on the back of an animated dinosaur from the Plasticine Age. His rival for the attentions of the female lead is played by Wallace Beery, a noted character actor, while the female lead was taken by Margaret Leahy, who had won a competition in London that promised her a part in a new Norma Talmadge film. Unfortunately, when she arrived in Hollywood and started work on set, it soon became abundantly clear that she couldn't act to save her life. Joe Schenck, who had organized the competition, didn't want her messing up a Norma Talmadge picture, so he pushed her onto Buster, and although Buster complained he couldn't do anything about it. In her first appearance she's clearly ill at ease, and even the dinosaur is more animated than she is.

The same plot is acted out in each of the three ages, but the Roman section benefits from huge, impressive sets and small comic touches, such as when

Far left A very unlifelike lion considers Buster in the Roman sequence from *The Three Ages*.

Left Margaret Leahy and Buster in the last scene of *The Three Ages*.

Above **Buster, Wallace Beery and Margaret Leahy in the Stone Age section of *The Three Ages*. Leahy's performance is a revelation. It's dreadful.**

By its nature, *The Three Ages* is episodic, and Buster later recalled that they had to audience preview the film eight times, on each occasion going back to reshoot scenes

Buster emerges from an arched doorway and checks his sundial wrist watch. There are wonderful individual moments in the picture and far too many gags to record in exhaustive detail. One gag in particular, which required over fifty takes, looks very simple on the screen. Buster in caveman mode runs into a clearing, carrying a club; another caveman throws a rock at him, which he then hits back straight into his opponent's stomach. The action is filmed in one continuous take, because Buster hated faking gags. He could have filmed it by showing the caveman throwing the rock, cutting to himself hitting the rock and then cutting back to the rock hitting the caveman in the stomach. But he didn't and the real humour in the joke lies in the fact that the action happens for real in front of your eyes. An irregularly shaped rock makes it very difficult to stage the joke exactly as planned, but Buster kept shooting until the action was perfect.

By its nature, *The Three Ages* is episodic, and Buster later recalled that they had to audience preview the film eight times, on each occasion going back to reshoot scenes. Filming began in May, just a month after *Safety Last!* had been released, and Harold's film clearly inspired one of the moments in Buster's picture. Standing high on a rooftop, Buster is trying to figure out how to bridge the gap between his building and the building opposite. He spots a plank of wood and, using it as a springboard, dives across to the other building. The other building is far enough away to make it a bit of a stretch, and although he reaches the ledge he can't hold on. He drops 20 feet, bouncing against the side of the building as he falls, before landing in a safety net out of camera range. In reality, he was badly bruised.

The gag was dangerous but not as dangerous as it looked onscreen. A set consisting of two rooftops was built above the 3rd Street Tunnel in Los Angeles, and the camera was placed to capture Buster against the height of the other buildings with the street scenes way below, making it appear as if he's fourteen floors up. This is the same technique that Harold Lloyd used to such sublime effect in *Safety Last!*

Buster's co-director, Eddie Cline, who had been with him since *The High Sign*, his first two-reeler, suggested that the shot of him falling could be used as part of a new sequence. Buster agreed. In the finished film we pick up his descent from the building and see him fall through two awnings before the third finally catches him. He swings onto a drainpipe, which comes off the wall and deposits him through a window on the floor below. We cut to inside the building where Buster slides across a polished floor before disappearing down a fireman's pole. He lands with a bump at the bottom of the pole, sits down on the back of a fire engine and is immediately driven off to an emergency. His

Above Buster in *Our Hospitality* adopting a characteristic Keaton pose – shading his eyes while looking into the distance.

entire fall, up to the moment when the fire engine drives off, takes just fourteen seconds of screen time. Buster's accident has led to one of the biggest laughs in the picture.

His second feature film, *Our Hospitality*, was released on 20 November 1923, and it amply demonstrates that he had been studying the more successful features of both Chaplin and Lloyd. *The Three Ages* was fine, but Buster knew he could do better, and *Our Hospitality* is his first feature-length masterpiece.

The opening credits record that the film was co-directed by Buster Keaton and Jack Blystone, while Natalie Talmadge, Buster's wife, was cast as the heroine in an attempt to bring husband and wife together. It was to be a family affair. Joe Keaton, Buster's dad, played a locomotive engineer, and Buster's and Natalie's first child, Joe Talmadge Keaton, who had been born in June 1922, played a fifteen-month-old baby. Buster and his family had said that the boy must be called Joe because the first-born Keaton boy was always called Joe – it had been Buster's name until 'Buster' came along – but Natalie hated the name. She settled on Jimmy, and so Joe became Jimmy. Intriguingly, the child appears in the credits as Buster Keaton Junior. Was that done to annoy Natalie?

Like *The Kid* and *Grandma's Boy*, *Our Hospitality* starts dramatically:

Once upon a time in certain sections of the United States there were feuds that ran from generation to generation. Men of one family grew up killing men of another family for no other reason except that their fathers had done so. Our story concerns the old-time feud between the Canfield and McKay families as it existed about the year 1810. The humble home of John McKay – the last of his line, except his infant son.

A thunderstorm rages outside the simple house. Inside, Keaton Junior plays in his cot as his mother looks on. Her husband, John, arrives home with bad news: 'I just heard that Jim Canfield is in town – I'm afraid that means trouble.' Indeed it does. Jim Canfield turns up, and the two men shoot each other dead. Joe Roberts, playing Joseph Canfield, finds his dead son and carries him home, declaring: 'Now the feud must go on and on. My two sons must be taught to avenge this deed!' Keaton Junior's mother decides that her son would be safer at her sister's home in New York where he need never know about the feud. We are nearly eight minutes into the picture, and so far we have seen two murders with the threat of more to come. This dark prologue sets up the picture beautifully, and it's clear that Buster wants the audience to sympathize with his central character. In *The Three Ages* a lot of the cartoon gags were very funny but at the expense of character credibility. Is it possible to identify with a man who rides on top of an animated dinosaur?

Buster, playing the adult Willie McKay, receives a letter informing him that he has inherited his father's estate. His mother has died, and he knows nothing of the feud. He shows the letter to his aunt and imagines that he is to inherit a grand country house. Realizing that it's necessary to tell him the truth, his aunt explains about the feud.

The train that takes Buster south is a replica of Stephenson's *Rocket*: both comical and beautiful at the same time. It ambles along at such a leisurely pace that Buster's dog is able to keep up with it, and the track has been laid in an extremely bumpy and haphazard fashion, giving precedence to anything that lies in the way. At one point the train encounters a donkey on the track. The animal refuses to move, and in the end they decide to pull the track to one side and navigate around it.

Buster befriends the woman sitting beside him, who is played by his wife, Natalie. When they reach their destination, Buster is amazed to find his dog, which has run behind the train all the way, waiting for him. Natalie is greeted by her two brothers and her father: they are the Canfield clan. Buster asks directions to the McKay estate but makes the mistake of asking one of the Canfield brothers, who enquires why he's looking for the estate. He replies: 'It belonged to my father, and I've come to claim it.' When asked who his father is, he says 'John McKay'. The Canfield brother courteously asks Buster to wait and enters a store, saying to the shop assistant, 'Have you a pistol handy?' Luckily for Buster he hasn't. When he rejoins Buster, the Canfield man resumes his former display of politeness.

Buster would have analysed the reasons behind the huge success of *Safety Last!*, the last twenty minutes of which are among the greatest in the history of

In *The Three Ages* a lot of the cartoon gags were very funny but at the expense of character credibility. Is it possible to identify with a man who rides on top of an animated dinosaur?

cinema. As Harold climbs the building he is in a state of constant peril and is in danger of falling at any moment. The feud plot in *Our Hospitality* similarly places Buster in a state of constant peril. While the Canfield brothers go in search of some weapons, Buster wanders off and finds Natalie standing outside her family home. She invites Buster to supper. Buster wanders off again and sits on a rocky ledge. Some distance away a dam is blown up, causing a flood. Water starts to cascade over the ledge above Buster and turns into a torrent, which conveniently hides Buster from view the very moment the Canfield brothers rush by, intent on seeking him out.

The two brothers go back to the house. 'We'll hunt for him after supper.' Buster arrives for supper, and Natalie takes him by the hand and leads him into the grand living room. The two brothers and father are astonished to see their sworn enemy in their own home, and the brothers start loading their guns, but Joe Roberts stops them: 'Wait, boys! Our code of honor prevents us from shooting him while he's a guest in our house.' Buster overhears the brothers plotting: 'Father won't let us kill him in the house but wait 'til he gets outside.' Buster asks the butler whose house he is in. The butler replies, 'Canfield's'.

After supper, to which the local parson has also been invited, Buster is understandably reluctant to leave. He shakes everybody's hand twice. He throws his hat under the sofa and then tells everybody he can't find it. But his dog emerges from under the sofa with the hat in his mouth, so it's time for Buster to go. There's a storm raging outside, and as the parson is about to leave, Joe says to him, 'It would be the death of anyone to go outside tonight.' The parson is invited back into the house, and Buster takes this as his cue to stay the night too. The next morning Joe tells Natalie that Buster is the son of John McKay. She is shocked, but then doubly shocked when she realizes that her family fully intend to kill him.

Buster escapes from the house wearing a voluminous dress with a fetching bonnet. The father and brothers give chase, and in the distance they spot a dress and an opened black umbrella. Father raises his gun to shoot just as 'Buster' turns into profile, and we see that it's actually a horse with a dress and umbrella skilfully arrayed over its hindquarters. It's one of Buster's most celebrated jokes and always gets a massive laugh.

We see Buster running through the woods and scrambling down some rocky terrain. Then he slips and grabs hold of a jutting rock, hundreds of feet up in the air. Hanging from a rock is similar to hanging from a clock. Buster clambers around the cliff face, chunks of rock crumbling under his feet. He cries for help, and one of the brothers hears him. He runs off and finds an old man with a rope and a donkey: 'Lend me your rope – I want to swing a man over where I can get a better shot at him.' The old man agrees, and the brother ties the rope round his own waist and throws the rest down to Buster, who fastens it around his waist. Buster slips and accidentally pulls on the rope. We see the brother falling past Buster. Buster stands back against the cliff and looks straight into the camera. At us. He's tied to the guy who's just fallen off the cliff. As soon as the look registers, Buster is yanked out of frame by the descending brother. The two fall into a river, but Buster manages to clamber out, still tied to the baddie. The *Rocket* comes into frame, and it runs over the rope and severs the connection between the two men. The brother falls back into the river.

Buster steals part of the train to escape, but it hits an obstacle on the track and he falls into a fast-running river. Buster is sitting in a tiny box filled with logs. It floats, and he starts to paddle. Natalie is in tears on the riverbank as Buster glides by, up to his neck in water, and we see his head bobbing along.

The next sequence nearly cost Buster his life. In fact, he was attached to a wire so that he couldn't move too quickly for the camera that was tracking him, and this is what happened in Buster's own words:

> The wire goes pop, real soft and bang ... off to hell we go ... I'm hitting boulders now with my hip bones and knees, and a couple I hit so hard on my chest that I go clear up out of the water and over. The main thing is to keep from whirling. I'm fighting for breath and trying to remember how long the rapids are and how much of them are left. It starts to quiet down, and I think I've made it. Then suddenly I'm in foam a foot deep. You don't breath very well in foam, and you sure as hell can't swim on top of it. I later found out there was three hundred yards of that foam ganged up at the end of the rapids. It was a bend in the river that saved me. I couldn't have made ten yards more. I grabbed some overhanging branches, pulled myself out, feet still in the water and just lay on my face fighting for air.[1]

His distress is evident in the film, but the cameraman, Elgin Lessley, was under strict instructions to keep on filming, especially when things went wrong. Sometimes the mistake turned into something better than you had planned.

Back in the picture Natalie sets off to rescue Buster by boat, but that capsizes and she's now in the rapids. Buster grabs a floating log and ties the rope to it. He rests on it, unaware that he is heading for the waterfall. He goes over the edge, but the log gets stuck in some rocks and he holds onto the end of the rope, swinging above a massive drop to instant death below. The boat that

'It was a bend in the river that saved me. I couldn't have made ten yards more. I grabbed some overhanging branches, pulled myself out, feet still in the water and just lay on my face fighting for air' – Buster Keaton

Left One of Buster's finest stunts: the waterfall rescue in *Our Hospitality*. It's his version of Harold Lloyd hanging off the clock in *Safety Last!* and a superb bit of thrill comedy.

Natalie was in shoots over the edge of the waterfall and is smashed on the rocks below. And here she comes, helpless in the rapids, heading for the drop. Buster climbs onto a ledge, and as Natalie falls over the edge he swings out and grabs her arms, holding her above the raging torrent. It's a moment that makes audiences gasp and cheer. Buster drops Natalie to safety on a nearby ledge. It's a thrilling climax to a wonderful picture. The Canfields return home at nightfall, vowing to continue the search at dawn, but they find that Buster and Natalie have just been married by the local friendly parson. Big Joe realizes that for his daughter's sake the feud must end, and the three Canfield men put their weapons on the table. Buster shrugs in agreement and produces six revolvers from around his trouser belt. And a tiny gun from his boot.

Harold Lloyd's next feature was *Why Worry?*, which was released on 16 September, five months after *Safety Last!* Harold always had a strong work ethic and, with such a smash hit behind him, his confidence and energy were sky-high. *Safety Last!* was the fourth biggest box office hit of 1923. *Why Worry?* was the fifth, and it's easy to see why. It's a superb film but totally different from *Safety Last!* In later life Harold was occasionally dismayed that people remembered him chiefly for climbing buildings and nothing else – the price of the huge success of *Safety Last!* – so let's try to dispel the image of Harold hanging off that clock and focus on *Why Worry?*

Harold plays a millionaire, Harold Van Pelham, whose name was perhaps suggested by Buster's character in *The Saphead*, Bertie Van Alstyne. The film opens in the palatial grounds of a country club. 'Wealthy society idlers with absolutely nothing to do – come here to do it.' A newspaper report tells us:

The following scene shows an ambulance arriving at the dockside. Harold is stretchered out of the ambulance, puffing on a cigarette. He is a hypochondriac who 'has taken so many pills he rattles when he walks'

> Harold Van Pelham, the wealthy young clubman, is leaving the city this afternoon on account of the critical condition of his health. He is seeking seclusion in Paradiso, a restful little republic in the tropics, a spot almost unknown to American tourists.

The following scene shows an ambulance arriving at the dockside. Harold is stretchered out of the ambulance, puffing on a cigarette. He is a hypochondriac who 'has taken so many pills he rattles when he walks'. He is travelling with his nurse, played by Jobyna Ralston, and valet. Harold had married his previous leading actress, Mildred Davis, in February 1923, and she had immediately retired from his comedies. A title-card reads: 'His nurse – A loyal friend of long standing. She is putting her heart and soul in her work – especially her heart.'

Once on board ship bound for Paradiso, Jobyna continues her duties out on deck. She jumps in the air with surprise when the valet drops a tray of drinks, and lands on Harold's lap. They embrace until the excitement sets his heart racing and he has to take one of his pills. The scene ends on a charming shot of the two of them in silhouette against the setting sun. Tribute must be paid here to Harold's cameraman, Walter Lundin, who had been with Lloyd since his Lonesome Luke days. Lloyd, Keaton and Chaplin all had long working partnerships with trusted cameramen.

We cut to Paradiso, where everybody is very laid back. A sleeping man is conveyed along on a donkey-drawn cart. The donkey stops and jolts him awake, and he makes a delivery to a nearby building. Meanwhile, the donkey has a good look around. To its right is a sleeping old man whose beard is connected to the back of his chair by an elaborate cobweb. To its left, a man is asleep on his back and is snoring so hard that he's blowing the brim of his hat up and down. The donkey thinks and decides to lie down itself. Then we get a highly informative title-card introducing the villain of the piece:

> Jim Blake – An American renegade, who, to further his own financial interests, has lashed the riffraff of the Republic into an outlaw force – restless and eager to overthrow the government.

Opposite Harold Lloyd putting 8 foot 9 inch Norwegian Johan Aasen in his place in *Why Worry?*

Jim Blake, played by James Mason (not the British film star but another actor), looks down on the dusty main street and (via a double exposure) sees it literally in the palm of his hand. In a letter from World's Allied Bankers, Blake is told: 'We can no longer tolerate your continued interference with our

commercial interests in Paradiso. If you persist in this practice, we will send down an authorized representative to curb your activities'. Blake confers with his fellow outlaws, 'This letter came over a month ago. We'll make it hot – red hot – for this fellow when he shows up.'

We cut to Harold and his small retinue arriving in Paradiso, unaware that revolution is in the air. Jobyna is pushing him along in a wheelchair, but unfortunately, she accidentally lets go of the chair at the top of a steep ramp and it hurtles downwards. We cut back to where the outlaws are toasting the downfall of the republic. Harold bursts through the door at the back of the room and rolls gently to rest by the table, just as Blake's first lieutenant, Herculeo the Mighty, holds his glass out for the toast. Harold takes the glass and drowns the contents to help him swallow one of his pills. With cigarette in one hand and match in the other, Jim Blake menacingly stands up. Assuming it's for him, Harold takes the cigarette and lights it. Here is a man used to the world working entirely for his convenience. Everybody is his servant.

In a wonderfully funny sequence, Harold walks down the main street and sees charming village life everywhere he looks. In reality, people are being attacked all around him. A man, clubbed over the head, falls off a balcony and into a hammock. Harold assumes he's taking a siesta. Another man is hit on the head and falls forward in a bowing motion. Harold bows back. He applauds a couple for their passionate dancing whereas, in fact, the man is reeling back from a vicious attack and the woman is trying to stop him falling over. Harold is wandering through a comedy landscape as the gags happen around him. He wonders where his hotel is and seeks help from Jim Blake, who tells him that he will give him a military escort to the hotel. In reality, he tells his troops, 'Put the dog in jail, and keep him there!'

Thinking he's signing himself in at hotel reception, Harold unwittingly adds his name to a list of prisoners to be shot at sunrise. Much to his bemusement he is thrown into a cell, and finds himself sharing with a colossal figure in the shape of former circus giant, Johan Aasen. The Norwegian Johan was 8 feet 9 inches tall, and here he is cast as Colosso the Giant. He accidentally stands on Harold's foot. Harold retaliates by kicking him in the leg and giving him a stern telling off in the manner of a man rebuking his valet for laying out the wrong trousers. Colosso, who is suffering from toothache, is spellbound by Harold's natural air of superiority and immediately becomes servile.

Harold suggests that they should break out of prison, which they do, then he sets about curing Colosso's toothache by attempting to pull the tooth out. At one point he climbs up the giant by holding onto the rope that's attached to the

In a wonderfully funny sequence, Harold walks down the main street and sees charming village life everywhere he looks. In reality, people are being attacked all around him

tooth. Eventually the tooth comes out, and Colosso is so thrilled he bows down to Harold in supplication.

When Harold's valet appears in some state of disarray and explains that a revolution is in progress, Harold will have none of it: 'Well, tell them they'll have to stop it immediately. I came down here for a rest.' Harold enlists Colosso's help, and the giant easily overcomes the rebels. Harold then heroically rescues Jobyna from the unwanted attentions of Jim Blake and realizes that he enjoys protecting her. Thinking he's got a weak heart, he reaches for his medicine. Her disappointment is evident. Only later does the true nature of his 'ailment' hit him. He turns to her angrily and says: 'WHY DIDN'T YOU TELL ME I LOVE YOU?' He rejects all further medication.

We jump a year into the future and are back in America. A nurse is speaking to Harold on the phone, and we see Jobyna in bed with a newborn baby. Harold is told that he is the father of a little boy. He jumps for joy and runs out of his office and into a busy street, where he dodges in and out of cars. He runs to meet Colosso, who is now working as a traffic cop. Harold tells him the good news, and the two of them run off together, leaving traffic chaos behind them.

Above Jobyna Ralston, who appeared in six of Harold Lloyd's feature films.

Why Worry? is a triumph. The South American setting is fresh, and the jokes are on Harold rather than the indigenous population. If one is to be picky, it does run out of steam, treading water for the last ten minutes or so, but the pluses far outweigh the minuses. This is Harold's second smash hit in a row.

Ten days after the release of *Why Worry?* Harold attended the premiere of Chaplin's new feature film, *A Woman of Paris*, a drama starring Edna Purviance and Adolf Menjou. This would be Edna's last official appearance in a Chaplin film, and apart from a brief walk-on part, heavily disguised as a railway porter, Charlie himself does not feature in this picture. Critics raved about it, but the public weren't so enthusiastic, perhaps unsure about a Chaplin picture that didn't have Chaplin in it. The subtlety of the acting and direction drew huge praise from contemporary filmmakers, however, and Buster Keaton said:

> Charlie was one of the best directors ever in the picture business. *A Woman of Paris* with Adolf Menjou, his first motion picture ... for the first time on the screen, in that dramatic story, he kept doing things by suggestion. Well, every director in pictures went to see that picture more than once just to study that technique. He absolutely revolutionized the direction of pictures ... he wanted the audience to know that Menjou paid for the apartment that Edna Purviance was living in. And the way he did it was that he called on her one evening to take her out, give her a little bouquet or something like that, and he looked in a mirror and saw a spot on his collar. He took the collar off, went over to a bureau drawer, and took out a clean one ... That told the whole situation.[2]

In Charlie's own view:

> *A Woman of Paris* was a challenge. I intended to convey psychology by subtle action. For example ... Edna's girl-friend enters and shows her a society magazine which announces the marriage of Edna's lover. Edna nonchalantly takes the magazine, looks at it, then quickly casts it aside, acting with indifference and lights a cigarette.[3]

Her smiling face tries to convince that she is unconcerned, but her anger, pain and humiliation are clear as she repeatedly stubs out a cigarette. Such touches thrilled the critics. The *New York Times* declared that Chaplin's direction was 'bold, resourceful, imaginative, ingenious, careful, studious and daring'.

This was Chaplin's first film for United Artists, the company he had co-founded in 1919 with D.W. Griffith, Douglas Fairbanks and Mary Pickford. It was a revolutionary step, a production and distribution company owned by the stars themselves, and it led the head of Metro, Richard Rowland, to coin the now famous phrase, 'the lunatics have taken charge of the asylum'. United Artists was set up to give the producers of these films a bigger share of the profits they generated and to give them the artistic independence to make the type of films they thought would appeal to a mass audience.

Safety Last!, *Why Worry?* and *Our Hospitality* showed that Harold and Buster were more than capable of producing wonderful feature-length comedies. Charlie had serious rivals, and the three comedians were now pushing the art form to ever greater heights. The competition between them is illustrated by the fact that Buster's and Harold's next pictures were released within twenty-four hours of each other.

Harold was first with *Girl Shy*, which appeared on 23 April 1924, with Buster's *Sherlock Junior* following a day later. In *Girl Shy* Harold lives in Little Bend (in *Safety Last!* his home town was called Great Bend). He plays Harold Meadows, an apprentice tailor, who has a terrible stutter, which gets worse if he's near a woman, and the local girls tease him relentlessly. His uncle blows a whistle that breaks the stutter if it becomes persistent. On the night of the Saturday dance Harold locks up the shop and looks over at the dancing couples. He clutches a lamppost and starts tapping his foot, then his body swings to the rhythm of the music. It's a beautiful, charming moment. A passer-by asks him if he's going to the dance. Harold isn't. He's got to finish writing a book, entitled *The Secret of Making Love.* As he sits in his room working on the manuscript, he fantasizes about two distinctly 1920s types of women. First, the 'vampire'. Before the first Dracula film was released and cemented the definition of a vampire, the word was applied to women who exerted some supremely exotic power over men. Theda Bara, a film actress at her peak in the mid-1910s, popularized the image. On seeing her, normally sane men rushed to bestow lavish gifts upon her, gifts of such value that the men would be bankrupted. Harold's advice is to be indifferent to the vampire. The 'flapper' was a 1920s

Safety Last!, _Why Worry?_ and _Our Hospitality_ showed that Harold and Buster were more than capable of producing wonderful feature-length comedies. Charlie had serious rivals

type, a good-time party girl. In Harold's fantasy he believes that the caveman approach is the best way forward. He pushes her against a wall, and a shelf falls on her head. She then loves him for ever.

The next morning Harold boards a train with his completed manuscript. He meets Mary Buckingham, played by Jobyna Ralston, they strike up a conversation and hit it off. She is fascinated by the idea behind Harold's book, and later, when they meet again in the countryside, they fall in love.

The publishers think that Harold's book is a hoot, and Harold is mobbed by all the women in the office. He is teased relentlessly: 'I suppose you can look right into the depths of a woman's soul.' However, his meeting with the publishers quickly disillusions him, and they tell him his book is a joke. Harold is devastated. He meets Mary in the park but because his dreams of wealth will now not come true, he tells her 'it would be unfair to allow her to care any longer'. He puts her off because he's only a tailor's apprentice. He says he doesn't love her and never has.

By now the publishers are having second thoughts. If they publish Harold's work as a comedy, they might have a hit on their hands. Instead of a rejection slip the publishers send Harold a cheque for $3,000. Mary, meanwhile, is so upset at Harold's rejection that she accepts a proposal of marriage from her most persistent admirer, Ronald DeVore. The wedding date is set for Thursday, the 19th. Harold receives a letter from the publisher, but, expecting a rejection letter not a cheque, he tears it up without opening it. His uncle finds a piece of cheque on the floor, and the two of them quickly find the other scraps. Harold realizes that he's now in a position to propose to Mary, but a newspaper item catches his eye: 'Buckingham–DeVore Wedding Today.' A female customer walks in, reads the item and collapses into a chair: 'He can't marry again – I'm still his wife! Someone must stop it for the girl's sake.'

This is all the encouragement that Harold needs. He dashes off to the railway station but can't buy a ticket because of his stutter. He gives up and runs after the train but misses it. He tries to make a phone call, but his stutter lets him down. Then he switches to horseback, and the race is on. He falls off the horse and jumps on the back of a passing fire engine. He falls off the fire engine and steals a tram, which he drives super fast. He eventually gets to the wedding by means of a further combination of car, policeman's motorcycle and finally a cart, which is pulled by two horses in the style of a chariot race. Harold arrives at the top of the stairs in the hall where Mary and Ronald are about to be declared man and wife. He shouts stop, and everybody does. His stutter makes it impossible for him to be understood, so he simply picks up Mary and carries

Above **Actions speak louder than words. Having failed to articulate his feelings to Jobyna Ralston, Harold Lloyd steals her instead in *Girl Shy*.**

her off over his shoulder. Out on the street Harold tries to propose, but his stutter gets in the way. Mary blows a postman's whistle, Harold gets the words out and Mary says yes.

Girl Shy continued Harold's extraordinary run at the box office and was the eighth most popular movie of 1924. It was also the first film to be produced by the Harold Lloyd Corporation, and it marked the ending of his partnership with Hal Roach, who was too busy overseeing his other film ventures to devote much time to Harold. The split was perfectly amicable.

Buster Keaton's *Sherlock Junior*, released the day after *Girl Shy*, is simply one of the best comedies ever made, and it's a uniquely Keaton film. If you screwed up your eyes you could almost imagine Harold Lloyd in *Our Hospitality*, but only Buster could have produced *Sherlock Junior*. The plot is simple: Buster works as a projectionist/caretaker at a small cinema. (In the foyer we glimpse a Stan Laurel film poster advertising a movie called *Mud and Sand*, a parody of Rudolph Valentino's recent hit *Blood and Sand* .) He buys his girl (played by Kathryn McGuire) a box of candy for a dollar but changes the price to four dollars to make the present seem more impressive. His rival in love, played by Ward Crane, steals a watch from the girl's father and takes it to a pawnbroker so that he can buy a much more impressive box of chocolates.

The girl's father, played by Joe Keaton, notices that his watch has been stolen, and Buster, a keen amateur detective, looks at his 'How to be a Detective' book. Rule 1 is 'Search everybody'. Buster searches everybody, including the father. Ward Crane, who has dropped the pawnbroker's ticket into Buster's coat pocket, suggests that they search Buster, too. They find the ticket showing that a watch and chain have been pawned for $4, and Ward points out that Buster's box of chocolates cost that amount. Buster is told to leave and never come back.

Outside Buster consults his detective book: 'Shadow your Man Closely.' Ward leaves and Buster follows a few inches behind as Ward strides across the pavement. Ward pauses to pick up a cigarette. He smokes it and throws it over his shoulder. Buster catches it in mid-air, takes a quick puff and throws it away. Ward walks into a railway yard, and when he sees Buster he locks him in a large cargo container. Buster climbs out through a hole in the roof and emerges next to a huge water pipe, connected to a water tower. The train starts to move, and Buster, still on the roof, walks forward. He jumps over the gap between carriages, and as the last one disappears from under him he leaps onto the water pipe. At this point Buster could be forgiven for thinking that the most dangerous part of the gag was over. Far from it. As the pipe descended the sheer force of the water knocked Buster down onto the track, where the back of his neck smacked against a rail. He got up and continued the scene but suffered severe headaches for days after. Years later, in the 1930s, Buster underwent a thorough medical and was asked when he had broken his neck: an x-ray had showed that a callous had grown over a fracture near the top vertebra. Buster wondered if it might have been that time he'd grabbed a water tower pipe 20 feet up in the air before crashing onto the track below. The doctor thought it likely.

Back at the cinema Buster is in the projectionist's booth, and the movie *Hearts and Pearls* is being shown. He settles down next to one of the projectors, goes to sleep and begins to dream. His dream self rises from the projectionist's stool, leaving his physical body behind, and looks at the film. The actors onscreen merge into the other characters in *Sherlock Junior*, and Kathryn McGuire and Ward Crane are now onscreen in the cinema. The father in the film becomes Joe Keaton, here playing his most substantial role in a Buster picture. We cut to the interior of the cinema and see several rows of people and a pianist. Onscreen a woman enters the room. There is a jump in the film, and Buster suddenly appears, sitting at the back of the audience while a man

Years later, in the 1930s, Buster underwent a thorough medical and was asked when he had broken his neck: an x-ray had showed that a callous had grown over a fracture near the top vertebra

This stunning sequence was achieved by using surveyors' instruments to measure Buster's exact distance from the camera every time the location changed. It's an exuberant expression of Buster's love of cinema

suddenly appears onscreen. This jump appears in every available print of the film. Buster watches the action onscreen. He moves to the front row. He leaps up onto the stage in front of the screen – and he jumps into the film. He is immediately thrown out by Ward Crane, in a manner that suggests that he feels Buster has insulted him by jumping into his world. Buster jumps back in, but the shot has changed. He is now standing outside the imposing front door of an obviously large house. This next sequence is a cinematic tour de force, and at the time even Hollywood professionals were baffled about the way it was achieved. Buster steps off the front step of the porch as the scene changes round him and is now standing on top of a garden ornament in a walled garden. He falls off the ornament and sits down on it, but the background changes to a busy main road in the middle of the day. Buster falls back into the street. He gets up and walks away as the scene changes again: now he's in mountainous terrain about to step off a rock into a ravine. He looks over the ravine and suddenly he's in a lions' den. Then he's in a desert. He sits on a sand dune, and it changes to a rock in the sea. Buster dives into the sea, which becomes snow in a winter wonderland. (It's a genuinely snowy location – Buster would go to any lengths necessary to make a gag work.) He leans against a tree as the scene changes to the walled garden we saw before. This stunning sequence was achieved by using surveyors' instruments to measure Buster's exact distance from the camera every time the location changed. It's an exuberant expression of Buster's love of cinema – the stuff you can't do onstage.

Now the camera moves into the screen, and we become immersed in the film. Some pearls have been stolen, and Ward Crane is responsible. We see him slip them into the butler's hands, but he panics when he hears that Sherlock Junior has been hired. Buster is Sherlock Junior. A title-card introduces his assistant: 'His assistant – Gillette. A Gem who was Ever-Ready in a bad scrape.' (Buster's audience would have known that the actor William Gillette played Sherlock Holmes onstage to great effect for decades. Gillette is also the name of a manufacturer of razor blades, and a Gem and an Ever-Ready were types of razor blade. It may not make it any funnier for us, but at least we know what the gag is.)

Sherlock Junior and Gillette discover the crooks' hide-out. Gillette shows him two curious round hoops with paper centres about 3 feet across. Between them is a long, flowing dress and a bonnet. Buster arranges the dress and bonnet between the two hoops with their paper-covered apertures and places these over a window. So far we haven't got a clue what he's doing, but it becomes apparent in one glorious shot. He sets himself up to be deliberately captured by standing on the crooks' doorstep whistling. They pull him inside. One of the crooks is Steve Murphy, the ugly guy in *Cops* who had persuaded Buster to buy furniture that wasn't his.

One side of the house disappears in a blur of cinematic magic. Buster wants us to see this next gag in full. In one continuous take he grabs the pearls and dives through the window and through the hoops. He emerges wearing the dress and bonnet. He casually walks away as the crooks rush around looking for Sherlock Junior, while a figure in a long dress walks unchallenged among them.

Later he's riding to the rescue of Kathryn McGuire, sitting on the handlebars of a motorbike driven by his trusty assistant. They hit a large pothole, and Gillette falls off, unnoticed by Buster. He carries on, believing that someone else is steering. He weaves in and out of traffic. He disrupts Irish stag parties. We see him racing towards a railway line with a locomotive heading in his direction. He crosses the track just ahead of the train, missing death by inches. Or so it seems, because this sequence is actually a trick: the action was staged backwards with the camera operator cranking the camera the other way. Buster saves the girl, and they make their escape in the crooks' car.

Buster wakes up from his dream. Kathryn, who now knows the truth about Ward Crane having stolen the watch so that he could buy a box of chocolates, comes to see him in his projectionist's booth. We can tell that Buster wants to kiss her but doesn't know how. He looks to the cinema screen for inspiration. The man on the screen puts his hands on the woman's shoulders and holds her hand tightly. Buster does the same with Kathryn. He looks back to the screen eagerly. The man kisses the woman's hand and places a ring on her finger. Buster ditto. Then there is a passionate kiss between the onscreen couple. After

Left **Buster in one of his masterpieces, *Sherlock Junior.* His assistant Gillette is destined to fall off the back of the bike, but Buster will carry on – and he also plays Gillette's stunt double. Lurking in the background is Steve Murphy, a Keaton stalwart who also appeared in films by Harold Lloyd, Charlie Chaplin and Laurel and Hardy.**

Above In a dream state Buster watches the beginning of a movie before jumping into the screen in *Sherlock Junior.*

some deliberation, Buster pecks Kathryn briefly on the lips. Onscreen the picture blends into the happy couple one year later, with two young babies bouncing on their father's knee. Buster looks at the screen totally perplexed.

Although *Sherlock Junior* has a high reputation these days, in 1924 it was regarded as a rather problematic picture. It was not well received at its first preview, so Buster re-edited and previewed it again. For the second time the response was poor. After its third preview Buster re-cut it again and the film was finally released. At barely forty-five minutes long, it's by far the shortest of his features. Perhaps the audiences at the time found elements of it coldly mechanical. Buster standing in the middle of the frame as the landscape constantly changed around him is a brilliant thought, beautifully staged, but his audience possibly wanted a little more romance mixed in with their comedies.

One small element in the film seems to be a nod to Buster's past. In an early scene set in the cinema foyer we see Buster sweeping up with a broom and then standing on a piece of sticky paper. Brooms and stickiness featured in Buster's first ever movie appearance, in *The Butcher Boy*, and this may be a subtle allusion to Buster's early career with Roscoe Arbuckle. After the scandal that had

Although *Sherlock Junior* has a high reputation these days, in 1924 it was regarded as a rather problematic picture. It was not well received at its first preview, so Buster re-edited and previewed it again

enveloped Roscoe, Buster had urged him back into directing movies, and to show Hollywood the lead he employed Roscoe as co-director on *Sherlock Junior*, although admittedly under the pseudonym of William Goodrich. Unfortunately, the lead actress Kathryn McGuire kept bursting into tears under his direction, and he had to be fired. Roscoe was a very bitter man at this stage of his life and perhaps that bitterness was directed at Miss McGuire. Whatever the truth, *Sherlock Junior* carries Buster Keaton's name as sole director.

Buster's next feature, *The Navigator*, released on 14 October 1924, is often cited by critics and commentators as one of his best ever films, and he himself said it was one of his two favourite pictures and that he greatly enjoyed the experience of making it. Buster shared the direction credit with Donald Crisp, a veteran of D.W. Griffith's movies, who was brought in to direct the dramatic sequences.

The Navigator begins with a flurry of title-cards:

> Our story deals with one of those queer tricks that fate sometimes plays. Nobody would believe for instance that the entire lives of a peaceful American boy and girl could be changed by a funny little war between two small countries far across the sea. And yet it came to pass. The spies of the two little nations were at a Pacific seaport, each trying to prevent the other getting ships and supplies.

We find ourselves in a serious-looking room with serious-looking men. One of them says, 'Gentlemen, the enemy have just purchased the steamship *Navigator* ... It is our patriotic duty to destroy that ship. We will send her adrift in the fog tonight before the new crew goes aboard. The wind, the tide, and the rocks will do the rest.'

We meet the wealthy shipowner who has just sold the *Navigator*, played by an actor rejoicing in the name of Frederick Vroom, and his daughter, who is played by Kathryn McGuire in this, her second successive Keaton film. Buster plays an extremely spoilt, rich playboy called Rollo Treadway: 'Heir to the Treadway fortune – a living proof that every family tree must have its sap.' He looks out of his window and sees a married couple in a car. He looks at a photograph of Kathryn and says to his butler, 'I think I'll get married ... Today ... we'll sail for Honolulu tomorrow on our honeymoon – get two tickets.' He gets dressed, climbs into his chauffer-driven car and is driven in one smooth half-circle to the other side of the road. He gets out and walks up to Kathryn's front door. He goes into the living room and hands her some flowers. 'Will you marry

Buster plays an extremely spoilt, rich playboy called Rollo Treadway: 'Heir to the Treadway fortune – a living proof that every family tree must have its sap'

me?' 'Certainly not.' Buster leaves dejected. He refuses a lift back to the other side of the road, believing that a long walk will do him good.

When he gets home his butler offers his congratulations and hands him the honeymoon tickets, adding, 'The boat sails at ten in the morning, sir.' Buster replies, 'I don't get up that early – so I'll go aboard tonight.'

Buster goes to Pier 12, thinking it's Pier 2, so instead of getting on the Honolulu boat he mistakenly boards the *Navigator*. Frederick Vroom goes to the pier to pick up some papers from the *Navigator*, but before he gets there he is attacked by foreign agents. Hearing his cry for help, his daughter rushes onto the ship, which is cut loose from its moorings. She attempts to get off the ship but it's too late – the ship is drifting away from the pier.

A title-card tells us: 'The next morning found the *Navigator* drifting helplessly at sea.' Buster and Kathryn wake up on an otherwise completely empty ocean-going liner. At first neither is aware that the other is on board, but after many beautifully choreographed near misses they eventually meet up. They try to feed themselves in a kitchen designed to feed hundreds – all the pots and pans are way too big – but after a few weeks they have adapted quite nicely. Buster has built a complicated system of levers and ropes to help them cook breakfast. Then, as he is looking through the binoculars, Buster sees some black men in grass skirts looking agitated on a beach. He and Kathryn, without any evidence whatsoever, come to the only possible conclusion: they must be cannibals. They notice that the ship is drifting closer to the land, so they drop anchor, but this somehow causes the ship to spring a leak. Buster says it's only a matter of time before the ship sinks and that it can be repaired only from the outside. Kathryn notices a deep sea diving suit. He puts it on, jumps overboard and sinks to the ocean floor, where he puts up a 'Danger Men at Work' sign. A swordfish attacks him. He grabs it and has a sword fight with another swordfish that is looking for trouble. Meanwhile, the cannibals board the ship, grab Kathryn and take her back to the island. Things look grim until Buster, still in the diving suit, walks out of the sea and up onto the beach. This frightens off the natives. With Buster floating on his back and Kathryn sitting astride him, they paddle back to the ship. Suddenly the natives regain their courage and launch an attack on the *Navigator*.

Buster finds a tiny cannon, just a few inches long, which he points towards the island and lights the fuse. He walks away but catches his foot in a rope that is attached to the cannon. Wherever he goes now, the cannon follows him. As he falls over the cannon keeps coming at him. As it fires, he ducks out of the way and one of the natives is caught full in the chest. Then the ship is swarming

Opposite In *The Navigator* Buster and Kathryn McGuire play rich socialites who are the only two people on board an ocean-going liner drifting out to sea.

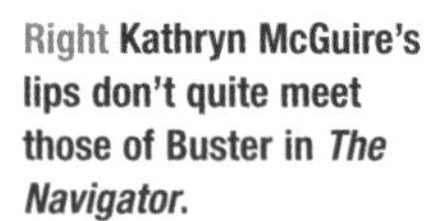

Right Kathryn McGuire's lips don't quite meet those of Buster in *The Navigator*.

with attackers, so Buster and Kathryn take their chances in the sea. They sink together beneath the waves but miraculously reappear. They are safe: they're standing on top of a submarine that is surfacing beneath them.

The idea for the picture originally came from Buster's technical director Fred Gabourie. He'd heard that a 500-foot-long ocean-going liner, *The Buford*, was available for hire, and Buster immediately hired it, before anyone had even thought of a story. And that's what's wrong with *The Navigator*. Although there are many good moments, the storyline is absolutely awful. Buster always wanted a measure of believability in his plots, but that has to be abandoned to accommodate the liner.

The first title-cards point out how incredible the plot is by their use of the

Buster and Kathryn take their chances in the sea. They sink together beneath the waves but miraculously reappear. They are safe: they're standing on top of a submarine that is surfacing beneath them

phrase 'Nobody would believe for instance ...' This doesn't make the plot any better; then there is a string of unlikely events. Buster and Kathryn end up on the *Navigator* at night just as foreign agents set her adrift. How far would a 500-foot liner drift from a pier? Let's be generous and accept that the next morning 'found the *Navigator* drifting helplessly at sea'. Why does nobody go to save them? Frederick Vroom doesn't appear to miss his daughter or do anything to find her. He just disappears from the film. He has to, or we'd be wondering why he's not rescuing his daughter from this abandoned ship, which is so big that surely it wouldn't be too difficult to find. They drift towards a land populated by cannibals. Where is that supposed to be? Have they drifted halfway round the world? The business with the boat apparently sinking doesn't make any sense either. It's included to get Buster underwater. *The Navigator* may be one of Buster's favourites, but he was often influenced by how enjoyable a picture was to make. The filming on board ship took ten weeks, mainly near Avalon Bay, off Catalina Island, which meant that Buster could spend a long time away from the less than happy family home. I also wonder how well he knew Kathryn McGuire. This is her second Keaton picture in a row, though it is also her last. From now on Buster's films would feature a different leading lady every time. Was that something that Joe Schenck insisted on?

There are too many flaws in the plot to include *The Navigator* among Buster's best, and it has more things wrong with it than any other independent Keaton feature. I may be flying in the face of eighty years' worth of critical opinion, but there we are. When it was first released, however, these flaws did not stop it from being a huge commercial hit.

Harold Lloyd's next feature-length film, *Hot Water*, was released on 2 November 1924, and it, too, is far from its maker's best. It runs for six reels but it's really three two-reelers stuck together. The first section concerns Harold's efforts to get home on a street car with lots of shopping and a live turkey that he's won in a raffle. The middle section, featuring Harold driving around in his brand-new car with the in-laws in the back, includes a lot of high-speed car action. The third two-reeler is the worst of the bunch. Harold is afraid of his mother-in-law, a stern prohibitionist. His neighbour advises him that the best way to deal with her is to get very drunk! Harold acts on this stupid advice and proves to be a not particularly convincing drunk. There is also some tedious stuff about chloroform and sleepwalking. Next to *Doctor Jack*, this is Harold's worst feature.

Above In *Seven Chances* Buster's business partner places an advertisement in the evening paper appealing for a bride for Buster, who needs to get married by seven o'clock if he is to inherit a fortune.

Buster Keaton's next picture, *Seven Chances*, was released on 16 March 1925. The idea for the film was not Buster's. It was based on a tired old theatrical farce, for which his producer, Joe Schenck, had bought the screen rights, telling Buster that this was to be the plot for his next film. Buster was furious, and it's quite possible that Schenck had spotted the massive holes in Buster's thrown-together plot for *The Navigator* and was determined that his star comic's next film would have a proper storyline. The plot of *Seven Chances* is plain old-fashioned melodrama. Buster is Jimmy Shannon, who learns that he must get married within seven hours in order to inherit a fortune. He proposes to his girlfriend Mary, but she thinks he's only doing it for the inheritance. She rejects him. He then goes round town asking every available woman he can find. None of them is interested.

So far Buster and his team of writers, Clyde Bruckman, Jean Havez and Joe Mitchell, have faithfully followed the stage play, but as they leave it behind the film grows wings. Buster's business partner puts an advertisement in the evening paper, appealing for a bride. He tells Buster to be at a particular church at five o'clock. Thousands of brides, one of whom is clearly a man, turn up at

Above **A little while later, Buster surveys the women (and one man) on offer.**

the appointed time, lured by the promise of marrying a millionaire. Buster makes his escape, and the chase is on. He learns from his general handyman, Jules Cowles, that his girlfriend does want to marry him after all. Cowles, an old vaudeville friend of Buster's in need of a job, is a white man, blacked up in this film for no good reason. Also in *Seven Chances* Buster stops a woman in the street and recoils in horror when he realizes that she's African-American. These blemishes aside, the rest of the film is great fun. The prospective brides chase him through cornfields and scrap metal yards and across rivers in a never-ending pursuit of their goal.

Buster clambers across mountain tops, dislodging rocks as he runs. The rocks dislodge boulders, that hit other, even bigger boulders. These rumble along after Buster as he races downhill away from them. The potential brides have gathered at the foot of the valley, and he faces a choice: brides or boulders. He takes on the boulders, and in a scene that was impossible to rehearse, he dodges the rocks and boulders that bounce towards him. One or two catch him. He gets to Mary's house just in time to marry her before seven o'clock. A happy ending tops off an exhilarating finale.

Almost unbelievably, the boulder sequence owes its entire existence to a stroke of luck. Initially it wasn't in the film, and when Buster previewed the picture he was convinced he had a turkey on his hands. But as they watched the scramble over the hilltops Buster and his gag men noticed a laugh that shouldn't have been there. The next morning they ran the film back and saw that as Buster was running he accidentally dislodged a couple of rocks that rolled after him for a moment or two. On the basis of that one laugh, Buster ordered his technical director Fred Gabourie to build hundreds of boulders out of papier mâché. Anything from the size of a grapefruit up to 'rocks' four times the size of Buster were constructed, then they went back on location and created one of the greatest sequences in silent comedy. It still works wonderfully with an audience. Dialogue would add nothing. Buster shouting 'hey' or 'watch out' would be desperately superfluous. Silence feels like an artistic decision.

Shortly after the release of *A Woman of Paris* in October 1923, Charlie began work on his second comedy feature, *The Gold Rush*, which was eventually released on 16 August 1925. The film begins with thousands of prospectors trudging through the snow. Then we see an icy, snowy landscape halfway up a mountain. Suddenly, round the corner and shuffling along a narrow path on the edge of a precipice comes the most famous figure in the history of cinema. He is up high and at risk of falling to his doom, a setting that could have been suggested by Buster's similar exploits along the cliff face in *Our Hospitality*. The exteriors of *The Gold Rush* were shot in Truckee near Lake Tahoe, a location also shared by *Our Hospitality*, and this may be why Charlie used the name Big Jim McKay for Mack Swain's character, McKay being one of the families in *Our Hospitality*. Charlie might be acknowledging Buster's achievement.

Charlie increases the Tramp's peril by having a huge grizzly bear suddenly appear on the path behind him. Immediately a thrill and a laugh. Charlie has absorbed the example of *Safety Last!* well. So often the pioneer, Charlie is for once a follower. Big Jim discovers a 'mountain of gold', but during a subsequent storm he and Charlie find themselves independently blown into Black Larsen's log cabin. In a fight Big Jim and Black Larsen grapple over a shotgun that, no matter where Charlie manages to hide, always ends up pointing directly at him. This is an adaptation of Buster's little cannon joke from *The Navigator*: no matter where you go, the barrel still points at you. Charlie takes the gag and humanizes it. The men draw cards to see who will go for food, and Black Larsen loses. Later, driven to the edge of starvation, Charlie and Big Jim try to feed

We see an icy, snowy landscape halfway up a mountain. Suddenly, round the corner and shuffling along a narrow path on the edge of a precipice comes the most famous figure in the history of cinema

Above **On location. Charlie Chaplin's *The Gold Rush* was filmed in Truckee, near Lake Tahoe – the same setting that Buster used in *Our Hospitality*.**

themselves by eating Charlie's old boots, which he has boiled beforehand. The sole is delicately removed from the boot in the fashion of a fish being filleted. The laces are eaten as if they were strands of spaghetti. The nails become wishbones. Later Big Jim hallucinates that Charlie is a giant chicken, and he chases him around the cabin until he comes to his senses. Once the storm is over, the two of them go their separate ways. Big Jim returns to his mountain of gold but is surprised by Black Larsen, who knocks him out. When he comes round, he has amnesia.

In a nearby town we see Georgia for the first time. She works in the Monte Carlo Dance Hall, and her first appearance is greeted by a title-card that simply reads 'Georgia'. This title-card appears three times, each time adorned with a single rose, a device that Buster would parody in his next picture. Charlie's usual leading lady, Edna Purviance, had retired from the screen by now, and Georgia is played by Georgia Hale. Initially the role had been given to Lita Grey, who had played the flirtatious angel in *The Kid.* When Lita learned that Charlie was looking for a new leading lady for *The Gold Rush*, she and a schoolfriend, Merna Kennedy, turned up at his studios requesting an audition. Lita knew Chuck Riesner, who was working as an assistant director for Charlie, and amazingly her plan succeeded. She was auditioned, hired and went on

The Gold Rush

A running gag in several silent films is the gun that accidentally follows you around. Buster Keaton features it in *The Navigator* when he lights the fuse of a tiny cannon but then finds that his foot has got stuck in a rope and that the cannon pursues him wherever he goes.

In *The Gold Rush* Charlie adapts the idea by having two men fighting over a loaded shotgun, which constantly points at Charlie no matter where he tries to hide within the log cabin. It's an extended sequence, which shows how brilliantly Charlie could build on what is, after all, a very simple idea.

1 Black Larsen seeks to reclaim his cabin from Charlie and Big Jim McKay who have taken shelter there. 2 Charlie inadvertently finds himself in the line of fire.

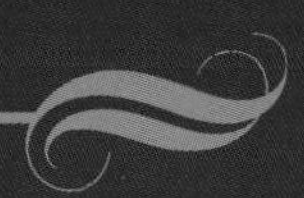

3

3 As Black Larsen and Big Jim fight, Charlie finds that wherever he goes the gun still ends up pointing at him. 4 Eventually it's agreed that Charlie and Big Jim can stay, and cards are drawn to see who will go off to search for food. In this publicity shot, Charlie draws the lowest card; in the film it's Black Larsen who does so.

4

I've sat in a packed auditorium and laughed and screamed and laughed again along with everybody else. It's a fantastic scene in a film full of fantastic scenes

location to Truckee, California. Charlie then made exactly the same mistake that he had made with Mildred Harris. He got involved with Lita, who was just sixteen years old, and she became pregnant. Her uncle was a lawyer, who threatened court action until Charlie agreed to marry her. The ceremony was quickly held in Mexico, but it was a desperately unhappy union, although it did produce two sons, Charles and Sydney. Lita's pregnancy ruled her out of *The Gold Rush*, and Georgia Hale, who had impressed Charlie in a film called *The Salvation Hunters*, got the part.

In the film Georgia fools the Tramp into thinking that she and her girlfriends will come to his log cabin for a New Year's Eve dinner. Charlie sets to work shovelling snow from the shop doorways to fund the party, but by the time New Year's Eve comes round, Georgia and the girls have forgotten all about the invitation, and we see Charlie sitting and waiting in the cabin he has so beautifully decorated with candles and Christmas crackers. Nobody arrives. He falls asleep and dreams of the party in full swing with everybody there. To entertain his guests he sticks forks into a couple of bread rolls. With his head just above them, the rolls dance. This is a beautiful elaboration of the joke that Roscoe Arbuckle briefly performed in *The Rough House* in 1917. Then, if you remember, Roscoe stuck two forks into two bread rolls and imitated Chaplin's walk. Here is Charlie developing that moment into an unforgettable routine. Perhaps initially conceived as a discreet tribute to Arbuckle, it stands out as one of the many highlights of *The Gold Rush*.

The comic climax of *The Gold Rush* features Charlie and Mack Swain waking up in their log cabin, completely unaware that during the night a storm has pushed their home onto a cliff edge. It's a situation initially inspired by the climbing sequence from *Safety Last!* – peril in high places. The men have no idea how close they are to disaster. The floor tips up steeply, and Charlie slides across it and through the back door. He grasps hold of the door and swings above the precipice. He swings himself back into the cabin and tries to reach the front door by crawling along the floor. As he and Big Jim seek to make their escape, the floor tilts alarmingly. The sequence runs for over eight minutes, and I've sat in a packed auditorium and laughed and screamed and laughed again along with everybody else. It's a fantastic scene in a film full of fantastic scenes.

Mack Swain finally rediscovers his mountain of gold, and he and Charlie become millionaires. We see them on board ship bound for America. They are wearing fur coats and are smoking big cigars, and a journalist suggests that Charlie should change into his old tramp's clothes for a photograph. Georgia happens to be on board, and when she sees Charlie as a tramp she assumes he's

Opposite Georgia Hale plays the saloon girl who toys with Charlie's affections in *The Gold Rush*.

Above **In *The Gold Rush* Mack Swain and Charlie discover the disadvantages of being in a cabin perched on the edge of a cliff.**

a stowaway. Once the mix-up is explained, the two of them kiss for the cameras. It's a lingering kiss.

On its release *The Gold Rush* was immediately recognized as a masterpiece. It retains that status today.

Harold Lloyd's new film, *The Freshman*, was released on 20 September, a month after *The Gold Rush*. He plays a character called Harold Lamb, who is nicknamed 'Speedy'. He is about to start college and has a naive, idealistic view of what life will be like. He practises a silly little dance as a way of introducing himself to people. He aches to play for the college football team but has no talent for the sport. Feeling sorry for him, the coach appoints Harold as a water boy. Harold believes he is on the team. He attends a big black tie social event wearing a suit that hasn't been properly finished by the tailor he's bought it from. The tailor attends the event to sew errant sleeves back on. In the end, Harold loses his trousers. Another student tells him that everyone at the college has been laughing at Harold and his silly little dance behind his back. Harold sobs in the lap of Jobyna Ralston, who plays Peggy, his landlady's daughter. She

The cheat points a pistol at Buster and says, 'When you say that – SMILE'. Here Keaton parodies his own style. The one thing he can't do is smile, so he uses two fingers to push his lips up at either end

gives him a pep talk: 'Stop pretending, Harold, be yourself.' At the big football game, Harold stands on the sidelines, desperate to get into the action. So many of his team are injured that he is thrown into the match as a substitute and subsequently wins the game. The college is thrilled, and Harold becomes a hero.

Although it made an absolute fortune in its day – it was the third most profitable film of 1925 – *The Freshman* hasn't aged particularly well. It's rather predictable, and the sequence with the suit falling apart seems to go on for ever. I've never seen *The Freshman* with a live audience, and it could well be that I'm judging it too harshly. An enthusiastic audience can make such a big difference to a silent comedy's appeal. There was a mixed critical reception at the time. On 12 July 1925 *Film Daily* proclaimed: 'Tops Lloyd's previous best for real laughs and pathos. Sets a new standard for well placed gags beautifully timed to collect 100% guffaws. A college comedy classic.' On the other hand, *Variety* magazine, then as now the showbiz bible, declared: 'Lloyd as a freshman at college has been over-boobed, made the boobiest sort of a booby boob, and in that they overdid it.'

Buster Keaton's next feature, *Go West*, released on 23 November, is a far more interesting picture and, in part, a parody of *The Gold Rush*. In it Buster plays a character called Friendless, who sells his few possessions before jumping aboard a train that, he hopes, will take him to a brighter future. He falls off the train and finds himself in the middle of a desert. It's the opposite landscape to the snowy terrain of *The Gold Rush*. Buster spots a beautiful Jersey cow, and a title-card appears. It says simply, 'Brown Eyes'. This is a parody of the title-card 'Georgia', which appeared in Charlie's film. Buster sees that Brown Eyes is limping, and he removes a stone from her hoof. In turn, Brown Eyes rescues Buster from an aggressive bull. Then Brown Eyes licks Buster's hand. Buster plays this moment absolutely straight – this is the first individual ever to have loved him. The cattle owner insists on including Brown Eyes in the mass drive to the slaughterhouse, and although Buster wants to buy her, he doesn't have the money. He enters a card game but spots that one of the players is cheating. The cheat points a pistol at Buster and says, 'When you say that – SMILE'. Here Keaton parodies his own style. The one thing he can't do is smile, so he uses two fingers to push his lips up at either end.

Having no luck in the card game, Buster joins Brown Eyes in the cattle truck bound for the stockyards. Armed cowboys stop the train and then set it off again at high speed with no one at the controls, but Buster runs along the

"I'm just a regular fellow – step right up and call me 'Speedy'"
The Glorious Art Film Co.
Presents
Lester Laurel
in
"The College Hero"

top of the train and stops it just in time. He realizes he's got to get the cattle to the stockyards and decides to herd them through the street. Naturally, they stampede and run into various shops, one of which is called 'The Pig and Whistle'. Buster runs in and shoos away the four cows that are in the shop. Intriguingly, there's a man in the background wearing a straw boater and attempting to climb up the shelves to get away from the cattle. His stance is highly reminiscent of Harold Lloyd climbing in *Safety Last!* Next, some of the cows run into a barber shop. Joe Keaton has an uncredited role here as one of the frightened customers. Buster passes a department store and spots a calf in the window. He goes in. The store is full of cows.

In the centre of the screen, but in the far distance, we see a plump woman wearing a big hat. She doesn't know that a herd of cows is approaching her. When she spots them she reacts with open-mouthed astonishment, but the action is so far away from the camera that it's very easy to miss. Why has Keaton, the consummate director, staged this bit of business in the deep background? The answer lies in the plump woman's reaction to the sudden appearance of dozens of cows. There is something very familiar about it. As the woman attempts to escape by getting into a lift we see her and her equally large companion, played by an actress called Babe London, in a much closer shot. We briefly glimpse the woman's profile: it's Roscoe Arbuckle in drag. Keaton has broken the ban on Roscoe appearing onscreen. It was a daring move. Also in this scene we have a man in a bowler hat trying on a pair of roller skates and then falling over in a manner reminiscent of Charlie Chaplin in *The Rink*. If Harold and Roscoe can make the party, there's no reason for Charlie to be left out. In this film parody, everyone gets a look in. I'm speculating about the Harold and Charlie look-a-likes, but Roscoe is definitely there, even though a later close-up in the lift substitutes an unknown actress for Roscoe just to throw people off the scent. 'That looked like Fatty Arbuckle.' 'No, look, it's nothing like him. Anyway he's banned from the screen.' It's an audacious moment in a film full of parody.

Left **'Lloyd as a freshman at college has been over-boobed, made the boobiest sort of a booby boob, and in that they overdid it.' Not everyone liked Harold's *The Freshman*.**

We briefly glimpse the woman's profile: it's Roscoe Arbuckle in drag. Keaton has broken the ban on Roscoe appearing onscreen. It was a daring move

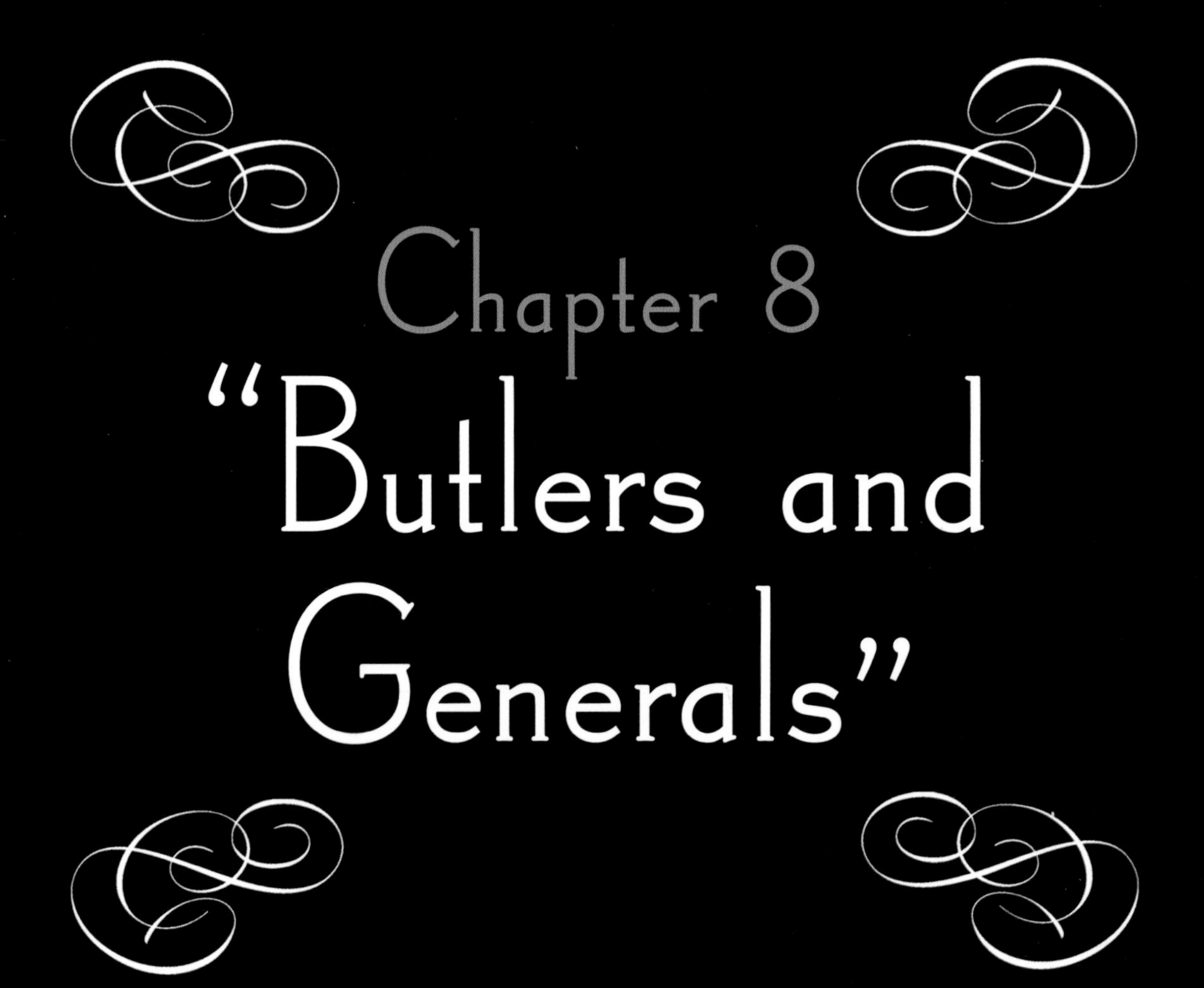

Chapter 8
"Butlers and Generals"

JOSEPH M. SCHENCK

presents

BUSTER KEATON

in

"The General"

·UNITED ARTISTS PICTURE·

Butlers and Generals

By 1926 Chaplin, Lloyd and Keaton dominated feature-film comedy. All three were on top form and would go on to make further highly successful films over the next few years.

1926 also saw the arrival of Harry Langdon into this august company. He had been spotted by Mack Sennett while he was performing his vaudeville act, Johnny's New Car, during which the car apparently fell apart in a humorous way. There's no record of the act, but I bet it involved Harry running up and down while holding on to the brim of his hat, something he does in all his films. His natural pace was slow, so it took a while for him and Sennett to get used to each other. Mack always liked his comedy fast and furious, and nothing about the 1920s was going to change that. It was, after all, the Jazz Age.

Harry's first Sennett picture, a two-reeler called *Picking Peaches*, was released on 3 February 1924, and it was a fast-paced romp with Harry, rather out of character, playing a flirt. The mature Langdon was far more child-like. As he made further films for Sennett, Harry set about slowing down the cartoon pace, and this creates a problem for modern audiences, because he goes to the opposite extreme. Some of his performances are very slow: once he stands still he has a tendency to gaze into the camera, and his reaction shots sometimes seem to go on for ever. Nevertheless, his popularity at the time justified a move into features, and, in fairness to him, in 1926, the year he established the Harry Langdon Corporation, he released two feature-length comedies within the space of six months that both show him to good advantage and that are by far the two best films he ever made.

The first, *Tramp, Tramp, Tramp*, deals beautifully with how to get around the problem of Harry's character just standing still: you enter him in a coast-to-coast cross-country walking race to win the first prize of $25,000. As usual, he plays a bit of a sexless simpleton, which creates an interesting tension between him and his girlfriend in the picture, who is played by the twenty-one-year-old Joan Crawford. She's clearly not happy in her role or in the film, and in one important scene with Harry she actually wears a hat that successfully obscures her face. She is not an actress who is going to regard working with Harry Langdon as a highlight of her career. Another member of the team was also to go on to enjoy future greatness. When Harry left Sennett he took his creative unit, and alongside his director, Harry Edwards, were two chief writers: Arthur Ripley and Frank Capra. Capra, who later claimed the credit for inventing Langdon's onscreen persona, went on to have an illustrious career, culminating in *It's a Wonderful Life*, which he directed some twenty years later.

In *Tramp, Tramp, Tramp* Harry, the son of a shoemaker, is madly in love

Right Harry Langdon. A major star of the mid-1920s. Less well known today.

To put it kindly, this sort of physical comedy did not suit Harry, who was, after all, forty when he made his leap to movie stardom. He lacked the athleticism of Keaton, Lloyd and Chaplin

with the billboard image of Joan Crawford that is being used to advertise Burton Shoes (she is the daughter of Mr Burton). He meets her at the starting line for the coast-to-coast walk, and she talks him into entering the race. As the competitors set off, Harry barges his way to the front, failing to notice that his fellow walkers have now veered to the right. Various misadventures follow, some of which smack of desperation – it's quite a stretch moving from two-reel, twenty-five minute comedies to an hour-long feature. In one scene, for example, Harry is lost in a field full of sheep, which he thinks are cows. There's a 10-foot-high solid wooden fence running along one side of the field, and ignoring the 'Keep Out' signs, Harry clambers over the fence but gets his jumper caught on a nail that's sticking out on the other side. This is just as well, because we can see that the fence has been built right on the edge of a cliff and that Harry is hanging above a sheer drop. This is a very clumsy attempt to get some thrill comedy into the picture. The idea of a terrifying drop certainly worked for Charlie Chaplin with his teetering log cabin scene in *The Gold Rush*, but here we are being asked to believe that somebody has built a 10-foot fence on the very edge of a cliff. Why? In addition, the pacing is wrong. Harry is hanging from a nail, but it's all happened so quickly that there's no sense of the tension you find in, say, *Safety Last!*

Things don't get any better as the scene develops. Harry slides down the cliff on a large piece of the fence, but it's clear that he – or rather, his much thinner stunt double – is now descending a far gentler slope than the one we saw just a second ago. A few small rocks roll past him, very much in the manner of Buster Keaton's *Seven Chances*. To put it kindly, this sort of physical comedy did not suit Harry, who was, after all, forty when he made his leap to movie stardom. He lacked the athleticism of Keaton, Lloyd and Chaplin. Sensibly, in my view, he steered away from thrill comedy after this sequence.

Once he has escaped from the cliff, Harry steals a chicken from a farmer, and before you know it, he's been imprisoned and given a ball and chain to carry about, although he escapes as part of a prison break-out. Later a cyclone blows into town, and Harry is blown in with it. He takes shelter in a building whose walls move backwards and forwards in the intense wind. Again, it's highly reminiscent of the teetering log cabin in *The Gold Rush*. At one point a building is lifted away, revealing Harry, who is now standing in the open air. This image would later be taken and much improved upon by Buster Keaton. At the finishing line, Harry runs in front of the only other competitor to have lasted the course – surely a flagrant breach of the walking ethos – and wins the big prize. He marries Joan Crawford, and one year later they have a lovely baby boy.

Left **Joan Crawford, around the time that she appeared in Harry Langdon's *Tramp, Tramp, Tramp.* In one crucial scene she wears her hat in such a way that it obscures her face. Was she less than enthusiastic about the film?**

It's Harry dressed as a baby in a giant crib, and it ought to be a quick gag to finish the film on. But the picture doesn't immediately end. We go on looking at Harry as a baby for a full minute and a half. He's muttering to himself, but there's no clue as to what he might be saying. Why is this joke extended way beyond its initial impact? The rest of the film is expertly made, so what went wrong here? Did Harry's ego demand a long, lingering shot on him? Am I being unfair?

Harry's second release of 1926, *The Strong Man*, appeared on 19 September and is generally regarded as his best film. It is also Frank Capra's directing debut. Harry is a Belgian soldier in the First World War who has been corresponding with an American girl, Mary Brown, but his war takes a bad turn

Right Masquerading as the Strongest Man in the World. Harry Langdon in *The Strong Man*.

when he is stuck in no man's land and is captured by a German soldier. Fortunately, he and the German become friends, and after the armistice they emigrate to the United States, where the German pursues his stage act – The Great Zandow, Strongest Man in the World – and Harry becomes his assistant. Harry is thrilled to be in America because he now hopes to meet Mary Brown.

Zandow gets a couple of gigs in a small town called Cloverdale, but when they arrive they find a town that is at war with itself. The town hall has been taken over by bootleggers who have transformed it into a bawdy music hall full of gambling and loose women. Opposed to them is the local pastor, who has led his outraged congregation in a march around the building that is intended to last seven days. They expect the building to tumble down on the last day like the walls of Jericho. When Harry arrives they are into the sixth day of their march and singing 'Onward, Christian Soldiers'. Harry very swiftly discovers that the pastor's daughter is Mary

There is a fair amount of Frank Capra in this story, particularly the triumph of small town values, but Harry integrates well into it, and he has several good moments, making this his strongest performance

Brown, and after some initial confusion he also discovers that she is blind.

Zandow, completely unprofessionally, gets drunk before his first performance. With an aggressive mob, otherwise known as the audience, demanding to see the Strongest Man in the World, Harry decides to go on in his place, and through a combination of trickery and sheer good luck he wins them over. Later, a riot breaks out among this, the most volatile of crowds, which Harry quells by firing an onstage cannon at them. This also causes the building to collapse, and its walls fall, just like those of Jericho. The criminal element flees, and the values of small town America are firmly re-established. In the end, Harry becomes the town policeman, and we see him walking arm in arm with Mary Brown.

There is a fair amount of Frank Capra in this story, particularly the triumph of small town values, but Harry integrates well into it, and he has several good moments, making this his strongest performance. *The Strong Man* was a huge hit in its day and was voted among the ten best pictures of 1926 in the annual film critics' poll.

Long Pants, Harry Langdon's third feature, released on 10 April 1927, is a bit of a disaster. His father, played by Alan Roscoe, has bought him his first ever pair of long pants (trousers), although his mother is against the idea because short pants have always kept him at home. This unpromising beginning sets up Harry as a rather creepy character. A chauffeur-driven car breaks down nearby. The passenger is Bebe Blair, who reads a letter warning her that smuggling 'snow' (cocaine) will lead to twenty years in jail. She sniffs as she finishes reading the letter, making it pretty clear where her own interests lie. Harry turns up on his bicycle, and to impress her he performs some tricks around her car. These are shown in long shot, but even so it's quite clear that a younger, thinner man is performing the tricks. This routine is so inexpertly filmed that I can't help but wonder if Frank Capra really is still directing at this point, in this, his last film with Harry.

Things deteriorate as the story becomes increasingly ridiculous. Bebe Blair drives off, unaware that she has dropped a note that promises marriage. Harry finds it, and in his own bone-headed fashion believes that it is addressed to him. He talks to his father about it – a father, incidentally, who appears to be exactly the same age as Harry. The father tells his son that he should marry Priscilla, the local girl (Priscilla is played by Priscilla Bonner, who had been Mary Brown in *The Strong Man*). On the day of their wedding Harry sees a newspaper headline: 'Bebe Blair in City Jail, Proclaims Innocence. Notorious Beauty Deserted by Former Pals.' This is enough for Harry to want to call off the marriage to

Frank Capra's opinion was that Harry Langdon thought he was much greater than he actually was, and in his autobiography paints a portrait of him as being as dumb in real life as he was onscreen

Opposite **In *Long Pants* Harry Langdon lures his fiancée into the woods with the intention of shooting her. Perhaps not the greatest idea for a comedy.**

Priscilla. His father asks him how he's going to get out of it, and Harry imagines taking Priscilla out into the woods and shooting her! And at this point any sympathy we might have had with Harry's character evaporates. To make things worse, he does actually entice his prospective bride into the woods with the sole purpose of shooting her. How could anyone have thought this was funny? And the whole ghastly scene goes on for nearly ten minutes. What happened to the smoother storytelling of *The Strong Man* and *Tramp, Tramp, Tramp?*

Long Pants never recovers from this scene. In fact, it gets worse. Bebe escapes from jail. She bumps into Harry. He hides her in a crate. An alligator is introduced into the film. We go to an oriental café. The film falls to bits.

Frank Capra's opinion was that Harry Langdon thought he was much greater than he actually was, and in his autobiography paints a portrait of him as being as dumb in real life as he was onscreen. He also claims that Harry's screen persona was created for him by a few talented writers and directors, Capra himself, Arthur Ripley and Harry Edwards being the principal architects. I suspect that there's a lot in this, and my own view is that Harry was obviously good enough to sustain a live career in vaudeville for twenty years – albeit working with a huge prop: a collapsible car – but doing precisely the same act for so many years does not indicate a fertile comic imagination. Harry's comedies were shaped by outside hands, and to expect a forty-year-old vaudevillian to be able to grasp the methods and possibilities of cinema would be expecting too much. Creating a story that successfully entertains an audience for over an hour is no easy task, and that's where *Long Pants* falls down. The story is ridiculous.

Harry directed his last three feature films himself. They are full of heavy pathos and scenes that go on for too long. Even before the coming of talkies Harry's time at the top was over.

Harold Lloyd's next feature, *For Heaven's Sake*, is a peach and shows precisely why he was such a major star, though, strangely, it was not among his most successful pictures at the time. It shows off to very best advantage Harold and his gag men's incredible ability to build a bravura comedy sequence packed with gag after gag after gag – as, for example, in the beautifully choreographed and photographed sequence where Harold gets the denizens of a pool hall to chase him, picking up passers-by on the way and leading them to a local mission hall. One of the thugs is played by Steve Murphy, whom we have previously seen as a con man in Keaton's *Cops* and as a broken-nosed crook in *Sherlock Junior.*

Harold plays more or less the same role he played in *Why Worry?*: an extremely wealthy man who believes that the world is full of his servants, though this time he is not a hypochondriac. The film really gets under way when he accidentally burns down Brother Paul's coffee wagon with a carelessly thrown lighted match. He asks Brother Paul how much it will cost to buy a new cart, and Brother Paul, thinking he's asking about the cost of a new mission hall, tells him that it will cost a thousand dollars. Harold is rather startled, but he writes the cheque anyway. He's even more startled when he reads in the newspaper that a mission has been named after him. He goes there to tear down the sign and is told off by Brother Paul's daughter Hope, played by Jobyna Ralston, who is not aware of his identity. Her father introduces them, and she realizes that this is their benefactor. In an absolutely charming scene, Hope walks Harold around the mission, and all the while he only has eyes for her.

Harold's next feature, *The Kid Brother*, which was released on 22 January 1927, benefits from a wonderful rural setting and begins with a beautifully composed opening shot. The sun, about to disappear between two very large hills, casts a golden light over a deserted ship that leans heavily to one side in a peaceful, placid bay. A horse-drawn caravan advertising 'Prof Powers' Original Mammoth Medicine Show' passes poetically along a path running down by the water's edge. The excellent Jobyna Ralston once again appears as the leading actress. This is her sixth and last feature with Harold, and as always she's very natural and brings great skill and a beautiful presence to the screen. Her character is called Mary Powers, and her father has died and left the medicine show to her.

We then cut to the ranch of Sheriff Jim Hickory and his two oldest sons, who are rugged, outdoor types. The sheriff is played by Walter James, who also played the father in Buster's film *Battling Butler*. Walter was impressive in that film, and he's equally impressive here. Harold plays the 'nerd' of the family. While the rest of his family is out, he fools around with a sheriff's badge, pretending to be important. The medicine show caravan turns up, and Harold signs a permit allowing the show to perform. Mary Powers is pursued by a grim-looking gent called Sandoni, who is played with genuine menace by an ex-wrestler called, deliciously, Constantine Romanoff. Harold comes across Mary in the woods as she is trying to avoid the ghastly attentions of Sandoni, and he bravely picks up a stick to frighten the thug. Sandoni runs away, but only because, unbeknown to Harold, there's a huge snake wrapped around the stick.

Harold and Mary shake hands and say goodbye, and Mary walks away, disappearing over the brow of a hill. A thought suddenly occurs to Harold, but

These beautiful visuals were achieved by using an elevator crane to follow Harold's tree climb. It's another example of Lloyd and his creative team continually looking for fresh methods to tell a story visually

Above Harold Lloyd rescues Mary (played by Jobyna Ralston) from the unwanted attentions of Constantine Romanoff in *The Kid Brother*.

Mary is out of view. He climbs 15 feet up a tree. The camera floats gently up with him. He can see her now on the other side of the hill, and he shouts out, 'What's your name?' She replies, 'Mary'. He smiles and waves goodbye. She wanders off down the hill and once again disappears from view. Harold climbs up another 15 feet, and the camera follows him faithfully. Again Mary is in view. 'Where do you live?' Harold shouts. Mary replies, 'With the medicine show – down by the river.' They again wave goodbye, and Mary carries on downhill and out of sight. Another thought occurs to Harold, and he climbs up another 15 feet. 'Goodbye,' he shouts to a just visible Mary in the far distance. 'Goodbye' comes back the reply in tiny letters. Harold is in love. So much so that he falls out of the tree, hitting every branch on the way down. He lands on the ground, rolls over and finds he is clutching a flower in his left hand. He slowly pulls off the petals one by one. She loves me, she loves me not. These beautiful visuals were achieved by using an elevator crane to follow Harold's tree climb. It's another example of Lloyd and his creative team continually looking for fresh methods to tell a story visually.

A dam is being built and the money that's been collected for the construction is in the safe keeping of Sheriff Hickory. Unfortunately, the money is stolen, and the sheriff becomes the chief suspect. He tells his two tougher sons to go looking for the two men who were with the medicine show.

Eventually Harold drops a dozen lifebelts over Constantine, rendering him immobile, then he sits astride him and paddles to the shore. Another triumph for Harold Lloyd

Harold wants to join his brothers, but his father says, 'Son you might get hurt, this is a man's job.' Harold goes outside and stands by a tree. Mary joins him and asks why he's not helping his brothers. Harold tells her that he's not as brave as she thinks he is. His father and brothers don't think much of him, and Harold shares their view. Mary counters this with a burst of positive thinking: 'No matter what anybody else thinks, have confidence in yourself and you can't lose.' This is Harold's own personal real-life philosophy in a nutshell, and in the film his character is galvanized by the words.

Three rough-looking men approach, believing that Harold is helping the girl from the medicine show to escape. Harold is knocked out and falls unconscious into a rowing boat. The boat is pushed out into midriver and floats away. The sons report back to the sheriff that there's no sign of the suspects.

We cut back to Harold in the boat, which has come to rest against the hull of an old shipwreck. He spots a tiny monkey wearing a little sailor's suit and cap scampering around on deck. The monkey throws down a scrap of paper, and Harold immediately recognizes it as a list of subscribers to the dam project. He climbs aboard the ship in time to witness the two men from the medicine show squabbling over the division of huge piles of bank notes. A fight breaks out, and Harold works a neat variation of Charlie's scene in *The Gold Rush* where he's desperately trying to escape from a gun that is constantly pointing at him. No matter where Harold hides in the room, the two assailants reveal his whereabouts, although they themselves never notice him. He hides under an eiderdown, but it's kicked away. He hides behind a tall writing bureau, but it's pulled down.

Constantine Romanoff wins the battle of the baddies and then spots Harold hiding under the bed. He chases Harold, who manages to elude him. Harold then has a brainwave. He puts a huge pair of boots on the monkey and tells him to walk along the deck. The baddie follows the footsteps while Harold grabs the money and stuffs it all into a bag. Romanoff discovers the deception, and a fight ensues between the two of them. Harold's initial inspiration for this scene was probably Buster's brutal encounter with Battling Butler at the climax of that film, but Harold makes much more of it. They fight in the depths of the stricken boat with the twist that Constantine can't swim added into the sequence. At the very bottom of the boat is a huge expanse of water, and Harold manoeuvres his foe into it and gains the advantage. Eventually Harold drops a dozen lifebelts over Constantine, rendering him immobile, then he sits astride him and paddles to the shore. Another triumph for Harold Lloyd.

At the end of *The Kid Brother* Harold sees a bullying neighbour who had given him a hard time at the beginning of the picture. The two square up to each other in a country lane. They circle each other, kicking up a storm of dust, which soon becomes a thick cloud obscuring them both from view. The dust settles, and we see the bully lying on the ground and Harold and Mary walking off together in the far distance.

The Kid Brother maintained Harold Lloyd's extraordinary run at the box office. Indeed, in terms of box-office popularity in the 1920s he was second only to Chaplin – their films made up to four times what Keaton's did. Whereas worldwide earnings for Buster's next picture, *Battling Butler*, were recorded at $749,201 (a lot by Buster's standards), Harold Lloyd regularly achieved earnings of two and a half million dollars a picture, and Chaplin was earning another million on top of that on each of his feature releases.

Lloyd made ten films during the silent era, each a huge success with critics and audiences alike, and his onscreen personality perfectly suited the 1920s. Breezy, optimistic, full of get up and go, he is the Jazz Age personified: skyscrapers, aeroplanes, motor cars, Harold Lloyd. Buster Keaton was even more prolific, releasing twelve feature-length comedies in the same period, but he did not enjoy the same popularity as Lloyd. Buster's films are darker in places and are less formulaic. Harold was much more of a crowd pleaser.

On 19 September 1926, the same day that Harry Langdon's *The Strong Man* appeared, Buster Keaton released his latest feature film, *Battling Butler*. As in *The Navigator*, he plays a spoilt millionaire, this time named Alfred Butler, who is sent on a camping holiday by his worried parents who want to toughen him up a bit. Alfred goes on the holiday in the wilderness but takes his valet with him. The valet, played by the diminutive character actor Snitz Edwards, sets up some excellent cooking facilities, arranges a bear rug on the floor of the tent and lays out silver cutlery – a luxurious form of roughing it.

Alfred and his valet attempt a spot of hunting, but as Alfred walks along, shotgun at the ready, various woodland animals appear gleefully behind him, while he remains unaware of their presence. Later, there's a hilarious sequence on the river where Alfred is completely bamboozled by a cheeky duck. Alfred capsizes his boat and finds himself drifting downriver with only his head visible above the water. As he passes Sally O'Neil, listed in the credits as 'A Mountain Girl', who is sitting on the bank, he politely raises his hat. The two of them arrange to have dinner that night, and she is amazed by his lifestyle: although they are in the open air, Alfred still dresses for dinner. They fall in love.

***The Kid Brother* maintained Harold Lloyd's extraordinary run at the box office. Indeed, in terms of box-office popularity in the 1920s he was second only to Chaplin – their films made up to four times what Keaton's did**

Above Buster Keaton proves that he's not a natural boxer in *Battling Butler*. It has to be said that his hair looks remarkably well groomed.

The following morning his faithful servant Snitz prepares a hot bath for Alfred and points out that their morning newspaper carries a story about a boxer called Alfred Butler. 'Some prize fighter has taken your name sir.' 'Arrange to stop it,' Alfred orders.

Alfred decides that he wants to marry the mountain girl and asks Snitz to arrange it. Snitz is rebuffed by the girl's family, who refer to Alfred as a jellyfish. Stung by the remark, Snitz boasts that they are mistaken and that Alfred Butler is, in fact, Battling Butler, the latest challenger to the current champion, Young Dorgan. Snitz shows them the newspaper with a photo of Battling Butler, who looks not unlike Buster. The family are convinced. Snitz tells Butler of the deception but says that the unfancied Battling Butler will lose the fight and disappear from view. This turns out to be a naive view. How green was this valet? Butler and Snitz attend the fight in person, while Sally and her family listen to it at home on the radio. Against all predictions, Battling Butler wins. Buster decides that he must go back to the mountains and tell Sally and her family the truth.

The real Battling Butler's training camp is also in the mountains, and both he and Buster travel there on the same train. The boxer is surprised to see the welcome committee at the station and even more surprised when they rush towards Buster and march him down the High Street with an accompanying

On the night of the fight Buster is in the dressing room, and Snitz has arranged for an ambulance to stand by. Sally turns up to wish him luck and to tell him that her father and brother are betting their life savings on him

brass band. They go straight to Sally's family home, through the front door and into the parlour. Sally's father, played with solid integrity by Walter James, greets Buster and introduces him to the other people in the room. Then he fetches Sally, who is in a bridal gown. The band strikes up 'Here Comes the Bride', a vicar appears out of nowhere, the couple say 'I do', and the two of them are married.

Somebody runs in with a newspaper. A headline screams: 'Battling Butler to Fight Alabama Murderer: Starts Training at Silver Hot Springs Tomorrow.' The article is written by Demon Onion, a pun on Damon Runyon, a legendary sports correspondent and short-story writer. Buster has to leave for training immediately, and, naturally, his new wife wants to come with him. He says, 'I want you to know me as I am … not the brutal, bloodthirsty beast that I am when fighting.' And he adds, 'Promise me you will never come near the training camp or to see me fight.' She reluctantly agrees. As they drive off, Snitz suggests to Buster, 'We'd better go to Butler's training camp, sir, so that you can answer her letters from there.'

They arrive, and Buster quickly makes entirely the wrong impression on Battling Butler when he appears to be flirting with the fighter's wife – in fact, the two of them are watching the boxer train when Buster's hand accidentally lands on Mrs Butler's hand. Battling Butler notices and is angry, but then Sally turns up, and Snitz asks the boxer to help the pretence that Buster is the real champion. Surprisingly, the boxer goes along with the deceit, but then he says to his trainers: 'If he wants to be Battling Butler, let him fight the Alabama Murderer, and he'll never flirt with anybody else's wife.' The boxer leaves, and his trainers have no choice but to train up Buster. He is hopeless. He is vulnerable. He rests his head on Snitz's shoulder. This is Buster post-*The Gold Rush*, and he's not afraid to use sentiment because he knows that it will enhance his story.

Buster trains hard for three weeks. On the night of the fight Buster is in the dressing room, and Snitz has arranged for an ambulance to stand by. Sally turns up to wish him luck and to tell him that her father and brother are betting their life savings on him. Snitz pushes Sally into a cupboard and locks the door. She can hear the crowd shouting for Butler through the wall, but she doesn't know that it's not Buster in the ring but the real Battling Butler. He knocks out the Alabama Murderer as Buster looks on bemused from the dressing room. The trainer roars with laughter: 'You didn't think we'd throw away a championship just to get even with you.' Snitz tells Buster that Sally didn't see a thing and runs off to let her out.

Buster thanks Battling for saving him, and Battling replies: 'I've been saving

Set during the American Civil War, *The General* was Buster's favourite among his own pictures. He loved trains, and in the film he plays Johnny Gray, a locomotive engineer

you for three weeks.' The boxer pushes Buster into the dressing room, where there's just the two of them. The boxer hits Buster with some force. He really hits him, and then he hits him again. Buster rushes to the door and opens it. Sally and Snitz are standing there. Buster takes more punches and sees Sally looking on puzzled. An inspiring determination settles upon him, and he fights back with new-found energy. The two men stand in the middle of the dressing room swapping punches, and in the flurry of fists, Buster knocks out the champion. The 'authenticity' of the fight has shocked some film historians, but I feel it's judged exactly right. Buster's bringing a different tone to the feature-length comedy. He knows that the audience will feel cheated if they're expecting Buster to fight the Alabama Murderer and then nothing happens. You can't really finish a picture like that. The fight with Battling Butler is unexpected, but it is dramatically very satisfying. The 'authenticity' makes Buster's triumph seem even greater.

Battling Butler was swiftly followed on 31 December 1926 by the first of Buster's films to be released by United Artists, and it is a film that is now widely regarded as one of the greatest comedies ever made. Set during the American Civil War, *The General* was Buster's favourite among his own pictures. He loved trains, and in the film he plays Johnny Gray, a locomotive engineer. 'The General' is his train, and he takes enormous pride in it. It's 1861, and the Civil War is raging. Buster is the first to try to enlist, but he is turned down because he's far more valuable to the South as a locomotive engineer. However, his girlfriend, Annabelle Lee, played by Marion Mack, is told by her father that Johnny didn't enlist. True, her father had seen Johnny refuse to join the line behind him, but that was because he had already been rejected twice. When Annabelle asks Johnny directly, she thinks he's lying when he says he was turned down.

A year later, and some Northern soldiers are plotting to steal a locomotive, which they do, but by chance they steal 'The General'. By further chance when the train is stolen Annabelle is the only passenger on board, and she is now effectively kidnapped. Buster gives chase on foot. He finds another locomotive and gives more effective chase in that. He sees a large, squat cannon resting on its own four-wheeled platform and hooks it up to the back of his train. He loads it with a cannonball and lots of gunpowder, hoping to fire it at the train he is pursuing. However, he gets his feet caught in a chain as he scrambles back to the locomotive. The angle of the cannon alters so that it's aiming straight at him. He throws a piece of wood at the cannon, but it's still pointing directly at him. Buster is saved by a bend in the track, and when the cannon fires he's no longer directly in front of it. This is a further adaptation of the joke that first appeared in *The Navigator* and then in *The Gold Rush*: the pointing barrel from which you can't escape.

Another celebrated gag follows almost immediately. Buster is riding on the cowcatcher at the front of the train. He sees a wooden railway sleeper lying across the track ahead of him, and because the train is moving slowly he is able to jump off and attempt to remove it. As he lifts up the sleeper the train catches up with him, and he is caught in the cowcatcher holding the sleeper. We see another railway sleeper lying across the track. In one continuous shot Buster throws his sleeper at the other one, hitting it on the end and causing both pieces to topple away from the track and down an embankment. It's a moment often greeted with audience laughter and applause. The gag is nothing special, but the execution is sublime. The joke could have been created by a mixture of close-ups and medium shots: close-up of a sleeper on track, medium shot of Buster throwing the sleeper out of frame, close-up of the sleeper hitting other sleeper, medium shot of Buster looking pleased with himself. The trouble is, it's not so funny. Authenticity – that's what Buster was after. The gag is only genuinely funny when you see him do it for real.

Buster rescues Annabelle Lee deep in enemy territory. He steals a locomotive, but now, in a lovely reverse of the previous action, he is the one being chased. Annabelle tries to help out by sweeping up as Buster is pushing the engine to maximum speed. She discards a piece of wood as unsuitable for

Below **A beautifully executed gag in *The General*. Buster prepares to throw one railway sleeper at another in order to get them both off the track.**

The General

Having initiated the idea of a gun that accidentally follows you wherever you go in *The Navigator* and seen it taken up by Chaplin in *The Gold Rush*, Buster went one better in *The General* and filmed the gag with an enormous cannon. He was concerned that the cannon might look like a prop he had invented, but it was actually copied from a genuine weapon from the American Civil War.

The gun may now be bigger, but otherwise the gag follows the usual path. Buster loads the cannon but gets his foot caught in a chain as he attempts to scramble back into the cab of his speeding locomotive. The cannon points right at him, and he's convinced he's going to be unable to avoid it when it goes off. Fortunately, the cannon fires as the train is going round a bend, so avoiding Buster and hitting the train in front instead. The publicity shots here show the gag being set up.

1

2

3

4

5

1 The gag that started it all. Buster in *The Navigator* accidentally tied to a gun. 2 The beginning of same gag in *The General*, but with a cannon. 3 Buster loads it. 4 He wonders why nothing is happening. 5 The fuse is definitely alight and he needs to get well clear…

Right The single most expensive joke of the silent era. A real locomotive crashes through a bridge in Buster's *The General*.

burning because it's got a knot hole in it. Buster offers her a slither of wood, which she throws into the fire. In furious disbelief he attempts to strangle her before kissing her gently. In the majority of Buster's features the love interest is often fairly useless and constantly gets in the way.

Buster had been impressed by *The Gold Rush*'s epic scale, and in *The General* he uses stunning exterior locations shot around Cottage Grove, Oregon, which again meant that he was spending a long time away from home. The area had parallel railway tracks that enabled him to achieve some beautifully smooth tracking shots, as a camera mounted on one locomotive filmed Buster scampering across another. Charlie had used some clever special effects in *The Gold Rush*, but Buster went one better and opted for complete authenticity.

One celebrated gag illustrates the point perfectly. A locomotive train attempts to cross a rapidly burning wooden bridge high above a placid river. To our amazement the train falls through the bridge and crashes to a watery fate several hundred feet below. It was a real, solid locomotive; not a model. The crash was filmed on 23 July 1926, and people came from all over Oregon to watch it. It's been estimated that this was the single most expensive shot of the silent era, costing $42,000. If you're not going to use miniatures you might as well not use miniatures in a big way. Incidentally, the superb Buster Keaton documentary *A Hard Act to Follow*, produced by Kevin Brownlow and David Gill, has some wonderful interviews with then surviving eyewitnesses to this spectacular event.

Unfortunately, the sheer cost of the film counted against *The General*. When it was first released it lost a great deal of money, and Joe Schenck, Buster's producer, decided that his next film would be much more tightly controlled and that there would be no expensive locations. The critics were not particularly impressed with the film, and many considered that it was in bad taste for a comedy to show soldiers dying in battles in the Civil War. *The General*'s reputation began to build only from the 1950s onwards, but at least Buster lived long enough to see it hailed as a masterpiece. In the 1960s he even toured Germany in a replica locomotive promoting the film's re-release. I first saw it in 1971 at the Academy Cinema, Oxford Street, London, my first experience of silent comedy in its proper context: big screen, live audience, live music. I left the cinema after the screening walking on a cushion of air. I floated down the steps of Tottenham Court Road tube station. Hearing the laughs that *The General* got that evening made me feel that I had brushed up against something immortal. Watching a film getting huge laughs nearly fifty years after it was initially shown made a big impression on me. This was screen immortality, and it deepened my appreciation of silent comedy.

The critics were not impressed with the film, and many considered that it was in bad taste for a comedy to show soldiers dying in battles in the Civil War. *The General*'s reputation began to build only from the 1950s onwards

Chapter 9
“Laurel Meets Hardy”

HAL ROACH
presents
STAN LAUREL AND
OLIVER HARDY
in LIBERTY
Directed by LEO McCAREY
A Metro-Goldwyn-Mayer Picture

Laurel Meets Hardy

In the late 1920s Harry Langdon had briefly challenged the dominance of Chaplin, Keaton and Lloyd, but his star faded quite quickly. In 1927, however, a new comedy duo were formed, who were to enjoy major success very swiftly and then go on to be among the comparatively few silent stars to have successful careers once talkies arrived. They were Laurel and Hardy.

Their double act came about thanks to the fact that both happened to be working for Hal Roach, whose career in filmmaking had continued to flourish, even after his main star, Harold Lloyd, struck out on his own. Hal's short films were doing well. His Our Gang series was extremely popular, and Charley Chase was making exceptionally fine comedies in collaboration with writer/director Leo McCarey, who had joined Roach in the early 1920s. Leo had a great sense of comedy, and by 1927 he was the overall supervising director at the Hal Roach studios. He had initially trained as a lawyer before entering pictures in 1918, and he was also a skilled pianist, who

Below left 'Put 'em both up, insect, before I comb your hair with lead.' Laurel and Hardy encountered each briefly in this 1921 film, *The Lucky Dog,* but there's no sign here of the comedy duo that would eventually emerge. Ollie plays a heavy – as he typically did in his early career.

Main image The Laurel and Hardy we recognise. Writer/director Leo McCarey had the inspired idea of putting them together.

loved to play on set while waiting for lighting changes or for inspiration to strike. He went on to enjoy great success as an Oscar-winning director in the 1930s, 1940s and 1950s and directed the most undiluted comic version of the Marx Brothers on film, *Duck Soup.*

As far as his early career was concerned, Leo McCarey always claimed that Charley Chase had taught him everything he knew. Charley specialized in middle-class comedies of embarrassment. In *His Wooden Wedding* (1925), for example, he's about to marry the girl of his dreams when a rival for her hand tells him that his bride-to-be has a wooden leg. They are kneeling together, and Charley reaches over and feels a wooden stick that has been placed there by his rival. He has a sudden vision of the future: his wife, children and pet dog are all sporting wooden legs. The roots of the middle-class television sit-com are here in Charley Chase's comedies.

But all that is nothing compared to Leo's inspired idea to put together Stan Laurel and Oliver Hardy. Ollie, a skilled actor and an effective heavy, had worked with Larry Semon for a while. Stan had enjoyed regular employment over the years but had never settled on a distinctive style, his best films tending to be parodies. His spoof of Jekyll and Hyde, *Dr Pyckle and Mr Pride*, for example, is very funny and has two hilarious transformation scenes. Curiously, though, the last film he made as a solo comic, *Should Tall Men Marry?*, features the Stan Laurel character we know from Laurel and Hardy, complete with huge, wide-mouthed grin and little cries of confusion.

Pairing Laurel and Hardy made a lot of sense – they were physical opposites, Ollie being large and heavy, while Stan was gloriously thin – but there was some initial resistance to the idea, not least from Stan, who was worried that his film career would move down a notch if he was no longer a solo act. I suspect that Hal Roach needed persuading, too. But Leo McCarey was the man to pull it off.

Their first film together, *Duck Soup*, was released on 13 March 1927. It shares a title with the Marx Brothers' film, directed by Leo, and it also shares the fact that neither film features duck soup. Laurel and Hardy's version was lost for nearly forty years until a copy was unearthed in a Belgian archive in the 1960s, and its rediscovery completely changed the perceived history of Laurel and Hardy. Until its reappearance, film historians assumed that although Laurel and Hardy regularly appeared in these early films nobody had yet had the idea of making

Ollie was happy to be an actor and to let Stan, Leo and a couple of gag men construct the storylines. Ollie loved playing golf and was good at it, so while the others worked up the material, he played eighteen holes

them a double act. But *Duck Soup* shows that they had and that the rapport between the pair is immediately obvious.

Our first sight of them as Laurel and Hardy is of the two of them, both shabbily dressed, sitting on a park bench and reading different sections of the same newspaper. Stan is wearing a bowler hat, whereas Ollie has adopted a big top hat, a monocle and a dark five o'clock shadow beard. Stan laughs uproariously at the cartoons, whereas Ollie is more interested in the serious news. Forest rangers are forcibly recruiting vagrants to fight forest fires. Yes, that's right. It doesn't sound very plausible, but it doesn't matter because it nicely sets up Laurel and Hardy's first piece of comic business together. A suspicious recruiting officer observes the two tramp-like characters on the bench. As the man approaches, Ollie, keen to establish his non-tramp credentials, removes a sad-looking cigar butt from a cigarette case and asks Stan to light it for him. Stan lights a match but holds it up to Ollie's eye by mistake. Ollie has moved his head at the crucial moment, and Stan wasn't watching what he was doing. The timing between the two actors is beautifully precise. This first gag tells you that this is already an exciting partnership.

They exit quickly, the two on one bicycle freewheeling down a steep hill. They crash near a mansion and have a look inside. From then on the film faithfully follows a sketch written by Stan's father, Arthur Jefferson, in 1905. *Duck Soup*'s writing credit reads: 'Story Based on *Home from the Honeymoon* by Arthur J. Jefferson'. Stan and Ollie are in Colonel Blood's house. The colonel is on his way to Africa, and a couple arrives at the front door, interested in renting the property. Ollie and Stan decide to pose as the owner and maid of the house. Seeing Stan Laurel in drag is one of the great joys in cinema. Colonel Blood returns unexpectedly because he's forgotten his bow and arrow, and farcical mayhem ensues.

After this extremely promising start Laurel and Hardy's next five films are disappointing. They were cast not as a double act but as part of an acting ensemble. In the next film, *Slipping Wives*, Ollie plays a butler trying to murder Stan, who plays a delivery boy who has been hired by a wife who is attempting to make her husband jealous. This and the next four titles, *Love 'Em and Weep*, *Why Girls Love Sailors*, *With Love and Kisses* and *Sailors Beware*, all had storylines written by studio boss Hal Roach, and it's pretty clear that somebody is deliberately not getting it. Roach was a stubborn man who regarded Oliver Hardy as a great heavy but just didn't see the double act potential. In some of these films Stan and Ollie barely meet.

The first official Laurel and Hardy release was *The Second Hundred Years*, which was filmed in June 1927 and released on 20 November. Hal Roach had left Pathé, his distributors from the beginning of his film career, and had signed up with the mighty MGM, which had been formed in 1925. The arrival of a brand-new comedy team was given a big publicity campaign by this new giant of the industry. Leo McCarey was back on board, and the promising work he had done with Stan and Ollie on *Duck Soup* was continued on this and the rest of their silent pictures. All twenty-one of them. From *The Second Hundred Years* on the standard of Laurel and Hardy films rocketed. Unlike all the other comedians discussed in this book, Stan and Ollie, once they were a proper team, made great films right from the outset. They had the advantage of knowing the movie industry inside out when they first came together – and they had Leo McCarey. Ollie was happy to be an actor and to let Stan, Leo and a couple of gag men construct the storylines. Ollie loved playing golf and was good at it, so while the others worked up the material, he played eighteen holes.

In *The Second Hundred Years* Laurel and Hardy are convicts, who are digging a tunnel with a pick axe. They successfully dig themselves all the way into the governor's office. Later they decide to escape by turning their coats inside out and pretending to be painters. They pick up some paint pots and brushes, and casually walk out of the main gates, but a suspicious policeman follows them. To allay his suspicions, Stan and Ollie paint everything in sight: they cover shop windows, handrails and cars with white paint as they stroll past the delightfully named ice cream parlour, Ice Cream Cohen. It's a sublime comedy sequence.

The Second Hundred Years was quickly followed by *Putting Pants on Philip*, which was released on 3 December 1927. Ollie plays Stan's uncle and glories under the name of the Honourable Piedmont Mumblethunder. Stan plays the

Left **Ollie as the Honourable Piedmont Mumblethunder, Stan as his kilt-wearing Scottish nephew Philip in *Putting Pants on Philip*.**

He emerges and briefly glances at the camera. He makes eye contact with us, and his expression says, 'Why me?' Ollie used this device sparingly but always effectively

Left **Everybody associates slapstick with custard pies, and here's the custard pie fight to end all custard pie fights in Stan and Ollie's 1927 film *The Battle of the Century.***

nephew, Philip, as a Scotsman and wears a fine kilt. This garment attracts great curiosity as soon as he gets off the boat. Mumblethunder is a pillar of the community and is intensely embarrassed to be seen walking next to a man in a skirt, so he tells Philip to walk several paces behind him. Philip initially obeys but quickly forgets and catches up with his repressed uncle, even linking arms with him. Philip is not Stan in a kilt; he is a different character altogether. Philip is an energetic woman-chaser – he sees a woman, and he chases her. Later he lays his kilt across a muddy bit of road and invites the young lady standing on the pavement to step on it to avoid getting her shoes dirty. She giggles and simply leaps over it. Mumblethunder laughs and steps on the kilt himself, completely disappearing from view into a muddy hole more than 6 feet deep. He emerges and briefly glances at the camera. He makes eye contact with us, and his expression says, 'Why me?' Ollie used this device sparingly but always effectively. He was an excellent actor, who provided Stan with a combined springboard and seesaw and always gave him a lot to react to. Stan later said that he preferred the team's silent films to their talkies, and the rush of excitement that he must have felt as audiences and critics acclaimed this new comedy duo would have been immense. He could hardly have expected such enormous success at this stage of his screen career.

Laurel and Hardy's last film of 1927, *The Battle of the Century*, was released on 31 December, and it brilliantly celebrates one of the iconic images of silent screen slapstick: the custard pie. The first reel features Stan Laurel as a not very good boxer, the Canvasback Clump, who is fighting Thunderclap Callahan, played by Noah Young. One of Thunderclap's cornermen is Steve Murphy, the broken-nosed character actor who specialized in playing characters with broken noses. Ollie is Stan's cornerman and manager, and Stan loses the fight.

Later the two of them are walking down the street past a pie shop. A man comes out of the shop carrying a tray of pies and slips over on the corniest prop imaginable: a banana skin. His pies fall off the tray. The man, played by Birmingham-born Charley Hall, looks at the banana skin and notices that Ollie is eating a banana. Putting two and two together, he throws a pie in Ollie's face. Ollie throws a pie at Charley, but Charley ducks. The pie hits a woman who is getting into a car. She throws a pie at Ollie and misses. It hits a man having his shoes shined. He comes over and starts throwing pies. Unfortunately, the L.A. pie company has parked a van nearby with a seemingly unlimited supply of chuckable dessert. Custard pies had long been considered old hat by the time *The Battle of the Century* was released, so the comic angle here is to have the biggest custard pie fight ever.

For Buster Keaton, there were problems. Never as popular as Chaplin or Lloyd, he had just released a picture, *The General*, that had met with indifferent reviews and that had proved massively expensive to make

Viewed now, the picture seems to be a rather rushed affair, but that's because there's about a third of it missing. The custard pie fight exists today primarily because film producer Robert Youngson used it in a slapstick compilation, *The Golden Age of Comedy*, released in 1957. The first reel, the boxing match, was only rediscovered decades after it was considered lost.

Incidentally Lou Costello, future half of Abbott and Costello, can be glimpsed as a ringside spectator.

Stan Laurel must have felt that, after long years of struggle, things were at last going his way. For Buster Keaton, there were problems. Never as popular as Chaplin or Lloyd, he had just released a picture, *The General*, that had met with indifferent reviews and that had proved massively expensive to make. Not surprisingly, his producer Joe Schenck insisted that the next picture should be commercial, and the result was *College*, which was released on 10 September 1927. This time Keaton takes a leaf out Harold Lloyd's book and the massive success he had had with his college campus film, *The Freshman*.

The film begins with a rainstorm. It is Buster's graduation day, and he and his mother are walking to the ceremony in a torrential downpour. Buster is concerned because he's wearing a fifteen dollar suit. At the ceremony he sits behind a radiator, and his wet suit starts steaming. And shrinking. Buster is awarded a diploma for being the most brilliant scholar, and he climbs onto the stage to receive his certificate. By now the arms of his jacket have shrunk almost to his elbows. One of the professors announces that 'Ronald will now speak on the curse of athletics', and as he lectures the sporty types in the hall, the buttons ping off his shrunken waistcoat. He looks down and realizes that his flies might be next. He stands behind a table on which is a strategically placed book. 'Where would I be without my books?' he asks.

The love interest, Mary Haynes, played by Ann Cornwall, confronts Ronald in the rain outside. 'Your speech was ridiculous. Anyone prefers an athlete to a weak-knee'd teacher's pet. When you change your mind about athletics, then I'll change my mind about you.' So our story is set up. It may be significant that the lead characters' names, Ronald and Mary, appear in Harold Lloyd's *Girl Shy*. This is Buster's way of gently indicating that he knows he's following Lloyd's lead here. Harold was always called Harold in his pictures, so Buster could hardly call himself that. Ronald was the chief love rival in *Girl Shy*, and the name sounds enough like Harold to make the in-joke work. The gag with the shrinking suit is probably inspired by the scene in which Harold's suit falls to bits in *The Freshman* or even Harold's shrunken suit in *Grandma's Boy*.

The shrinking suit episode is a brief funny opening to a film that is packed with gags. Ronald goes to Clayton College where Mary Haynes is studying, but he and his mother are poor and he knows he will have to work his way through college, so he gets a job behind the counter of a milkshake parlour. To impress Mary, Ronald has decided to excel at sports. His case is full of sports apparel, including boots, and booklets entitled *How to Play Baseball, How to Play Football* and *How to Sprint*. He plays baseball but completely ruins the game. In real life a fiercely keen baseball player, Buster has enormous fun playing the great incompetent.

One of Buster's most troublesome sequences is kicked off by a sign in a restaurant window, 'Wanted Coloured Waiter', and inside the restaurant we can see that all the waiters are African-Americans. Buster walks out of the kitchen with his thumb in a bowl of soup. He is blacked up. The African-Americans sharing the kitchen scenes with him are portrayed as real characters, not stereotypes, and Buster is very much the butt of the joke here. When half his make-up is wiped off his deception is discovered, and he is chased out of the restaurant by the irate kitchen staff.

The best sequence in the picture follows immediately. We see a variety of different track and field sports being practised by some of the college students: hurdling, sprinting, the high jump, throwing the discus are all being carried out efficiently by skilled athletes. Then we see Ronald having a go. For the next eleven minutes Buster delightfully finds funny slapstick gags within each

Below **Buster Keaton's take on Harold Lloyd's massively succesful college campus film *The Freshman*. In this scene from *College* there is a marked disparity between the enormous effort Buster puts in to throwing the javelin and the distance the javelin travels.**

sporting discipline. His attempt at throwing a javelin is marked by the enormous effort he puts into it and the low reward he gets out of it. The javelin lands 3 feet in front of him. In the film's finale Ronald saves Mary from the clutches of the college's star athlete, Jeff Brown, who is played by Harold Goodwin, and the film fades out as Mary and Ronald leave church having just been married.

Well, that's how Harold Lloyd would have finished it, but Buster includes a bitter epilogue. He shows Ronald and Mary with three children but they are ignoring each other. He's reading a newspaper, and she's sewing. We see Ronald and Mary in their eighties, sitting either side of a fire. He says something aggressive towards her, and she just sits there. We see two tombstones side-by-side in a cemetery. Up come the words 'The End'. Buster might have delivered the feel-good comedy his producer wanted, but it comes with an almighty sting in the tail. It's obviously a direct comment on Buster's continually disastrous shell of a marriage to Natalie Talmadge. How would she feel when she saw this deeply cynical view of wedlock? Did she even watch his films? *College* didn't do any better than *The General* at the box office, but at least it had cost a lot less to make.

Charlie Chaplin's long-awaited new feature, *The Circus*, was released on 7 January 1928. Since *The Gold Rush* in 1925 his personal life had been disastrous. His marriage to Lita Grey had imploded spectacularly, and her lawyers, led by her uncle, had attacked him with lurid and vicious accusations of his supposedly abnormal sexual desires. Highly personal details that would have destroyed a lesser individual appeared in newspapers, and Lita's lawyers tried to get their hands on *The Circus* just as Mildred Harris's lawyers had tried to get

Right For *The Circus* Charlie Chaplin actually learned to walk a tightrope. His perfectionism was such that he filmed over 700 takes before he was happy with this particular sequence.

Not only was Charlie's domestic life anguished, but the making of *The Circus* also proved very difficult. The first month's filming, for example, was ruined when a scratch was found to have damaged the negative

theirs on *The Kid*. The trauma of it all turned Charlie's hair grey within a matter of days.

Not only was Charlie's domestic life anguished, but the making of *The Circus* also proved very difficult. The first month's filming, for example, was ruined when a scratch was found to have damaged the negative, and everything had to be reshot. Signs of Charlie's perfectionism are everywhere. For one scene he learned to walk a tightrope, filming over 700 takes (although this figure is inflated by the need to reshoot the damaged footage). The sequence where Charlie is besieged by tiny aggressive monkeys while he is attempting walk the tightrope was shot originally over a two-week period in January 1926 – an extraordinary amount of time to have dedicated to a single scene. As with the log cabin on a precipice sequence in *The Gold Rush*, the climactic tightrope scene was designed to mix thrills with laugher, and it was, in fact, Charlie's first inspiration for the picture. He knew it was a winning recipe.

The film opens with a shot of a bareback rider in a circus. Her stepfather, the ringmaster and owner, pushes her around and then berates the disconsolate, useless clowns for their sheer unfunniness. It's a bold way to start a comedy. Outside among the sideshows a crowd has gathered by a large wooden ship with several lifesize mechanical figures sitting on it. A mechanical giraffe's head sticks its long neck out of a window. The Tramp enters, his back to the camera, just as he did in *The Gold Rush*, and he stands at the back of the crowd. The man next to him, played by Steve Murphy in his biggest role, picks the pocket of the man next to him. The individual whose pocket has been picked turns on Steve and demands that he return his wallet, pocket watch and chain. Behind his back, Steve Murphy places the items in Charlie's trouser pocket, which Charlie doesn't notice. Steve shows the angry man that he hasn't got his watch and wallet, and Charlie wanders off and attracts the attention of a child held over its father's shoulder. The child is holding a bun, and Charlie is starving. He smiles at the child and takes a bite from the bun. He quickly looks around to check that nobody is watching and spreads some tomato ketchup over the bun. He takes another bite. When the father turns round to see what's going on Charlie wipes the child's lips with a bib.

Steve Murphy reappears and is spotted by a policeman attempting to get the wallet and watch out of Charlie's trouser pocket. The policeman hands the items back to a completely baffled Charlie, who, after a moment's confusion, gladly accepts them. The policeman marches Steve away, but the pickpocket makes his escape while Charlie buys a bun. The man who had his pocket picked is standing next to him, and when Charlie consults 'his' pocket watch the man

The first year of the Academy Awards, yet to be called the Oscars, saw Chaplin receive a special award for writing, directing, producing and starring in *The Circus*

recognizes both it and the wallet that Charlie produces to pay for his meal. A policeman chases after Charlie, who runs around the corner and finds himself running parallel with Steve Murphy with the two policemen lagging behind. Charlie runs up the gangplank of the wooden ship and enters a maze of mirrors. The screen is filled with multiple images of the Tramp. He walks into a mirror, and his hat falls off. He tries to pick it up, but which hat is his? Steve Murphy runs into the mirror maze and tries to confront Charlie. But is he pointing at the real Charlie or at a reflection? Charlie escapes from the maze but only as far as the deck of the ship. He is standing next to a large mechanical figure when a suspicious policeman looks over to him. Charlie 'becomes' a mechanical figure himself, and his robotic turns are beautifully essayed. He continually clouts Steve Murphy over the head in a mechanical man type fashion, but the deception is uncovered when Steve collapses at his feet. This is the last time we see Steve Murphy – the only man to have appeared with Chaplin, Lloyd, Keaton and Laurel and Hardy – in silent comedy. A lovely double bill would be Buster Keaton's *Cops*, with Steve Murphy playing a con man, supporting *The Circus*, with Steve Murphy as a pickpocket. It would make a small part of both films seem like 'The Steve Murphy Story'.

Now a policeman chases Charlie into the circus ring. The two of them jump onto a large spinning disc, and no matter how fast they run, they stay in the same place. The audience, previously bored by some lame clowning, are immediately convulsed by these two newcomers. Charlie completely disrupts a magic act before finally making his escape. The entire sequence is nearly nine minutes of nonstop comic invention. The audience cries, 'Where's the funnyman?' and 'Bring on the funnyman', but the 'funnyman' has fallen asleep in an old cart around the back of the big top. The ringmaster eventually finds him and offers him a job. 'Be here in the morning and we'll try you out.'

The next morning Charlie meets the ringmaster's stepdaughter, who is played by Merna Kennedy. Born in 1908, Merna was a childhood friend of Lita Grey, who had arranged dinner so that Charlie could meet her. Hiring Merna for the female lead in *The Circus* made a lot of sense, because she had been onstage since she was seven years old in a song-and-dance act with her brother. And no doubt Lita could also trust Merna to keep her distance from her husband.

The ringmaster auditions Charlie in the circus ring as a handful of clowns look on. 'Go ahead and be funny,' instructs the ringmaster, who, with his grey moustache, reminds me a little of Henry Lehrman, Chaplin's first director at Keystone. Trying to be funny, Charlie does a daft walk, only for the ringmaster to say, 'That's awful'. This may be an echo of Lehrman's brusque manner to the young comic back in 1914. Even before Charlie is hired, he is fired – he hasn't got the making of a circus clown. The property men go on strike, and Charlie is rehired as a property man. He is carrying a huge tower of plates when a mule decides to chase him into the circus ring. The audience bursts into uproarious laughter, as indeed did cinema audiences in 1928. With more gags than *The Gold Rush*, *The Circus* was very well received at the time.

The first year of the Academy Awards, yet to be called the Oscars, saw Chaplin receive a special award for writing, directing, producing and starring in *The Circus*, but after its initial successful release the film disappeared for over forty years, before Charlie rereleased it in 1969 with a musical soundtrack composed by himself. Even in his later years his creative urge and desire to work never left him, and he wrote musical soundtracks for every silent film he had made from *A Dog's Life* onwards. Although not a trained musician, he had a great facility for composition and could play the piano, violin and cello. Most of his scores work well, particularly those for *The Kid* and my own personal favourite, *The Pilgrim*. *The Pilgrim* soundtrack begins with popular British singer Matt Monro singing a Chaplin tune entitled 'Bound for Texas'. Singing over a silent film would still be considered sacrilegious by some devotees of the art, but here is Charlie in 1959 making a bold musical choice that works perfectly and helps the film to feel more 'modern'.

However, in *The Circus*'s musical soundscape there is a real problem with Charlie and the monkeys on the tightrope. A situation that should be full of tension is accompanied by a gentle tune that conjures up images of Edwardian ladies strolling through a London park. In an earlier scene Charlie finds himself locked in a cage with a lion. Here the music serves the film beautifully by heightening the tension, and we feel genuine relief when he manages to escape.

Left Charlie is threatened by the supporting act. Monkeys became something of a theme in films over the next few years. They appear, for example, in Harold Lloyd's *The Kid Brother* and Buster Keaton's *The Cameraman.*

In the tightrope scene monkeys bite his nose and his trousers fall down, but the music maintains the incongruous mood of a lovely summer's day and kills the tension. Perhaps having originally filmed over 700 takes of this scene Charlie couldn't face writing a more precise score. I have been lucky enough to attend a private screening of *The Circus* when the musical accompaniment was provided by two musicians improvising around Charlie's original themes. Seen under these circumstances the tightrope scene is a revelation.

The horrendous time Chaplin experienced during the making of *The Circus* left its mark on him. In his autobiography, published in 1964, he doesn't even mention the film, but, even if it is somewhat neglected, it's still a wonderful film.

On 6 October 1927 Warner Brothers released a film by the Broadway star and popular recording artist Al Jolson. It was called *The Jazz Singer*, and it had a musical soundtrack that featured Al singing a couple of his biggest songs. The vocal synchronization was exact, and the public was enthralled by Jolson's personality. It was the beginning of the end of the silent era, but happily the following year, 1928, proved to be the most artistically successful in the entire era of silent comedy. Each of the major comedians released films produced at the peak of their powers: Chaplin's *The Circus*; Harold Lloyd's *Speedy*; and Buster Keaton's *Steamboat Bill Junior* and *The Cameraman*. In addition, in the same year, Laurel and Hardy made ten superb shorts.

Speedy, Harold Lloyd's last silent feature, was released a few months after *The Circus*, on 7 April 1928. Harold plays Harold 'Speedy' Swift, who, in Harold's own words, is 'an irresponsible, flip, scatter-brained, baseball crazy youth of a kind the city breeds by the thousands'.[1] The city is New York, and Jane Dillon, Harold's girlfriend, played by Ann Christy, is the daughter of Pop Dillon, who runs one of the last horse-drawn trams in the city. Harold can't hold down a job, so he's not too bothered when he loses one. He gets a job as a drugstore soda jerk dispensing soft drinks, just as Buster's character did in *College*. (Harold would have picked up on the detail that the two leads in that film were named after characters in *Girl Shy*. Here he returns the compliment by adopting one of *College*'s settings.)

In his autobiography, *An American Comedy*, Harold describes the gag-writing process:

> The 'boys' are Johnny Grey, Howard Emmett Rogers, Lex Neal, Ted Wilde and Jay A. Howe, the story and gag men. I sit with them as frequently as possible. They may have agreed upon a story or have five more or less hostile plots, and I may like all or none, or parts of this and that. The result usually is a compromise so scrambled that no one and everyone can claim the authorship ... These sessions have been known to be heated and passers-by to duck in passing the gag room window ... Soon we have more gags – and good ones – than we possibly can crowd into the picture. Some we discard without trial, others will be edited out. Some were worked out in the gag room, others were born of spontaneous combustion in the midst of camera operations.[2]

Above Harold Lloyd in *Speedy*. This scene was filmed at Luna Park, Coney Island – always a popular filming venue.

This dedication pays off time after time in Harold's pictures. The high-quality photography, excellent gag construction and immaculate storytelling combine with Harold's winning performances to guarantee that his many great films work as entertainingly today as they did over eighty years ago. The luscious exterior shots of that most modern of cities, New York, play a large part in *Speedy's* still contemporary feel.

Buster Keaton's last independent feature, *Steamboat Bill Junior*, was released on 12 May 1928, and it is a strong contender for his best ever picture. It was filmed in the summer of 1927 almost exclusively on location on the west bank of the Sacramento River – far away from home. The story was brought to him by Chuck Riesner, who had recently directed some Syd Chaplin comedies after working as an assistant director on *The Gold Rush*. Buster plays Willie Canfield Junior, for some reason using the surname of one of the feuding families in *Our Hospitality*. Charlie, remember, had used the other family's name, McKay, in *The Gold Rush*. Buster is the son of Steamboat Bill, played by Ernest Torrence, but father and son haven't met since Buster was a baby. Father gets a telegram:

'From the very start I was against making the switch to MGM. When Joe continued to argue for it, I asked Charlie Chaplin what he thought. 'Don't let them do it to you Buster,' he said' – Buster Keaton

'Dear Dad, It was mother's wish that when I had finished school to pay you a visit. I think I arrive Saturday Ten A.M. You can't mistake me I'll be wearing a white carnation Regards William Canfield Jr.' The father approaches several individuals at the railway station but none of them is his son. He shouts 'Hey' at a smartly dressed figure bending over a suitcase. The man stands up revealing himself to be African-American. The actor stares back at Ernest Torrence with some bemusement. His reaction is nicely underplayed. The joke is on the father here.

When they do meet up, the father is horrified by his son's appearance – especially his headgear. Junior is proud of his French beret, but Senior is determined to get rid of it. They go to a hat shop, where a variety of hats is placed on Junior's head: bowlers, straw boaters and at one point his trademark porkpie hat from the two-reelers. Buster sees his reflection and reacts with alarm. He quickly takes it off his head and throws it away. It's a funny moment, but why is Buster alarmed? Perhaps he had decided to drop the porkpie hat after its last appearance in *Go West*. Maybe it felt old-fashioned. In his next two silent features, Buster wears the same dark hat. Finally, a hat is chosen, but as Buster leaves the store a gust of wind blows it clean off his head and into the river. He pulls the French beret out of his back pocket and puts it firmly on his head. The gust of wind is a foretaste of future difficulties.

Steamboat Bill runs a steamboat on the Mississippi and so does his great rival, the richest man in town, J.J. King. Marion Byron plays King's daughter. Against their fathers' wishes, Buster and Marion fall in love. Steamboat Bill Senior is locked up in prison for fighting J.J. King in the street, and Buster attempts to help him escape by hiding some tools inside a loaf of bread. Buster then gets knocked out and is taken to hospital. Meanwhile, a fierce storm is on its way ...

While the picture was being made Joe Schenck had some rather bad news for Buster. He had decided to give up independent production to concentrate on running United Artists, and his brother Nicholas at MGM was buying Buster's contract. Buster was not happy and made it clear that he had no intention of going to MGM:

> From the very start I was against making the switch to MGM. It seemed to me I would be lost making pictures in such a big studio. When Joe continued to argue for it, I asked Charlie Chaplin what he thought.
>
> 'Don't let them do it to you Buster,' he said, 'It's not that they haven't smart showmen there. They have some of the country's best. But there are too many

> of them, and they'll all try to tell you how to make your comedies. It will simply be one more case of too many cooks.'
>
> Harold Lloyd was of the same opinion. Both Charlie and he had retained their own units. Their pictures were first rate and were coining money.
>
> I was so impressed by what they said that I asked Adolph Zukor, head of Paramount, if he would be interested in releasing my pictures. I explained that I wanted to make them in my own studio.[3]

Ah yes, Adolph Zukor. The 'victim' of that elaborate dinner party practical joke staged by Roscoe Arbuckle and Buster Keaton all those years before. Buster's last two films, *The General* and *College*, had not been great box-office successes, partly due to poor distribution by United Artists, and Zukor wasn't interested in Keaton. He offered the lame excuse that because Paramount was already releasing Harold Lloyd's pictures it didn't make sense to have two comedians on their list. (United Artists had distributed both Charlie's and Buster's films at the same time without anyone thinking that it was odd.) I believe that Adolph still harboured some resentment towards Buster and found it easy to turn him down. The following year the Marx Brothers signed for Paramount, joining Harold Lloyd.

Joe Schenck, however, proved to be very persistent and Buster eventually weakened:

> In the end I gave in. Joe Schenck had never steered me wrong in his life until then. I do not think he meant to that time either. But letting him override my own instinctive judgement was stupid. As I have said, it turned out to be the worst mistake I ever made.[4]

In reality, Buster didn't have much choice.

Buster was furious, and in his fury he undertook the single most dangerous comedy stunt in the rich history of silent comedy. It took no great athleticism or timing: all he had to do was stand still while the front of a house weighing three and a half tons fell on top of him.

> First I had them build the framework of this building and make sure that the hinges were all firm and solid. It was a building with a tall V-shaped roof, so that we could make this window up in the roof exceptionally high. An average second-storey window would be about twelve feet, but we're up about eighteen feet. Then they lay this framework down on the ground and build the

'Joe Schenck had never steered me wrong in his life until then ... But letting him override my own instinctive judgement was stupid ... it turned out to be the worst mistake I ever made' – Buster Keaton

Above It still makes audiences gasp today. Three and a half tons of house crashes towards Buster Keaton in *Steamboat Bill Junior*.

window around me. We built the window so that I had a clearance of two inches on each shoulder and the top missed my head by two inches and the bottom of my heels by two inches. We mark that ground and drive big nails where my two heels are going to be. Then they put the house back up into position while they finish building it. They put the front on, painted it, and made the jagged edge where it tore away from the main building, and then we went in and fixed the interiors so that you're looking at a house that the front has blown off. Then we put up our wind machines with the big Liberty motors. We had six of them and they are pretty powerful: they could lift a truck right off the road. Now we had to make sure that we were getting our foreground and background wind effects, but that no current ever hit the front of that building when it started to fall, because if the wind warps her she's not going to fall where we want her, and I'm standing right out in front. But it's a one-take scene and we got it that way. You don't do those things twice.[5]

It's a staggering moment of cinema. In January 2007 at the Colston Hall, Bristol, I presented *Steamboat Bill Junior* to over 1,500 people on a big screen with superb musical accompaniment from Neil Brand and Gunther Buchwald. The

Above The front of the house clears Buster with only two inches to spare on each side.

house front falling towards Buster is a tiny moment in a cyclone sequence that runs for nearly fifteen minutes, but when the stunt happened the audience cheered and applauded spontaneously. A few days after this ecstatic response I heard the playwright Mark Ravenhill extolling the virtues of *Steamboat Bill Junior* on a BBC Radio 4 arts programme. I seem to remember that he had seen the film on a big screen at an open-air festival many years before. The other people in the studio, who sounded like professional critics, had each been given a DVD of the film to take home and watch. Their verdict was unanimous: it simply wasn't funny because in their view humour dates very quickly, and black and white silent comedy couldn't be more dated if it tried. How could they get it so wrong? Well, watching a silent film on a small television screen with inappropriate music as accompaniment can destroy the magic. It's easy to see nothing.

In the storm scenes Buster allows himself a few moments of autobiography. He seeks refuge in an abandoned theatre where he encounters a ventriloquist's dummy. In vaudeville as a seven-year-old-boy he planned to kidnap a dummy called Red Top, but the ventriloquist, Trovollo, got to hear of the plan. He hid backstage, and as Buster approached Red Top the ventriloquist animated the dummy who yelled, 'Don't touch me boy, or I'll tell your old man.' Buster

'The executives and studio big shots also turned into gag men overnight, adding greatly to the confusion … I began to lose faith for the first time in my own ideas' – Buster Keaton

fled from the theatre in terror. In *Steamboat Bill Junior* he sees a dummy resting against a wall. It's moved by a gust of wind, and its head turns and looks straight at Buster, who runs away terrified.

Steamboat Bill Junior was Buster's last independent feature, and it's among his very best. As a crowd pleaser I rate it above *The General*, but it didn't help him with MGM. They had a very different idea about how films should be made. 'The worst shock,' he recorded later, 'was discovering I could not work up stories the way I'd been doing, starting only with a germ of an idea … Slapstick comedy has a format, but it is hard to detect in its early stages unless you are one of those who can create it. The unexpected was our staple product, the unusual our object, and the unique was the ideal we were always hoping to achieve.'[6]

Buster experienced MGM's way of doing things straightaway when he embarked on his next film, *The Cameraman*. His idea was a simple one: to play a budding newsreel cameraman in New York trying to impress Sally (Marceline Day), who works for a newsreel camera unit. MGM's staff writers leapt on the idea, and before long Buster's plot was being swamped by story ideas. Gangsters, lady jewel thieves and Salvation Army bands were all dropped into the mix.

> And it wasn't only the twenty-two writers who were eager to help me out. The executives and studio big shots also turned into gag men overnight, adding greatly to the confusion. With so much talk going on, so many conferences, so many brains at work, I began to lose faith for the first time in my own ideas. Nevertheless, after eight head-busting months we did have a story written down.[7]

A clear indication of MGM's meddling can be seen in the title-cards. Buster has run off to film a big fire, but he's not sure which direction it's in. He runs into a policeman, played by Harry Gribbon. Buster says 'Where's the fire?' The policeman doesn't know what Buster is talking about. He says, 'In which house?' Buster must have been contractually obliged to reply, 'No! It's not in a which house … it's in a warehouse!' This leads to Harry Gribbon's total confusion. 'Where's the which house? I mean … which's the warehouse?' This dialogue would be fairly tough going if we could hear it. Written down it goes for less than nothing. Audiences just look at it without smiling, and I don't blame them. These corny puns would never have appeared in an independent Keaton feature.

Despite his misgivings, Buster, the director Eddie Sedgwick, the unit manager Ed Brophy, Marceline Day and the two cameramen Elgin Lessley and Reggie Lanning headed for New York to get some background shots, but

Opposite MGM's interference in the making of *The Cameraman* outraged Buster. However, when left to his own devices in the film, he came up with comedy gold.

Buster's fame made work impossible. Two cameras were hidden in the back of a big limousine to film Buster crossing the trolley tracks at Fifth Avenue and Twenty-third Street. As he crossed, a trolley driver yelled, 'Hey Keaton', and all his passengers started shouting as soon as they spotted Buster. Although the recognition was gratifying, it was also annoying. The same happened later at another location a few blocks away. Buster and his crew went back to their suite at the Ambassador Hotel.

> We called Irving Thalberg in Hollywood and told him we were unable to get the shots the present script called for. We did not have to remind him that so much of the story was built around the shots that without them we'd have no picture ... I got on the telephone, 'Like Chaplin and Lloyd, I never worked before with a script written on paper,' I said, 'and I don't have to now. All I ask is that you let me throw away this script and the shooting schedule and permit Sedgwick and myself to decide what to shoot here.' Thalberg agreed. He had no alternative with us 3,000 miles away and burning up more time and money each day ... the important job we did was simplifying the plot line from beginning to end. Our story also made it possible to shoot all but two of the New York scenes in Hollywood.[8]

One of those scenes filmed in New York perfectly illustrates Buster's creative intelligence. The problem was how can you get Buster and New York exteriors together in the same frame without overexciting the people of New York. The solution was ingenious. Buster turns up at the Yankee stadium to film the baseball game, but the Yankees are playing away. The stadium is empty. Buster walks out onto the baseball pitch and pantomimes his way through a game. It's a beautiful, graceful sequence staged by Buster in the heart of New York with no one else around. The Yankee stadium had also featured in Harold Lloyd's *Speedy*, released the month before Buster began filming. In addition, the crew managed to get some street shots of Buster and Marceline Day by filming them very early one Sunday morning. The magnificent shots of Buster running through traffic must have been filmed by hidden means. Any visible camera would have drawn a curious crowd.

In a gesture to Harold Lloyd, Buster shares a couple of scenes with Josephine, a small monkey. Harold worked with a small monkey in *The Kid Brother*, although, of course, Charlie Chaplin was there first with his monkey sequence in *The Circus*, filmed in January 1926. In the space of twenty-two months, then, each of the top three comedians worked with monkeys, and in

Buster's fame made work impossible. Two cameras were hidden in the back of a big limousine to film Buster crossing the trolley tracks at Fifth Avenue and Twenty-third Street. As he crossed, a trolley driver yelled, 'Hey Keaton'

'Like Chaplin and Lloyd, I never worked before with a script written on paper,' I said, 'and I don't have to now. All I ask is that you let me throw away this script and the shooting schedule' – Buster Keaton

The Kid Brother and *The Cameraman* it's actually the same monkey. Josephine plays a highly significant role in *The Cameraman*'s plot. Harold Goodwin, as he did in *College*, plays Buster's rival for the girl, and he takes Sally out for a ride in a motor boat. The boat capsizes, and Harold swims for the shore, ignoring Sally's struggles. Buster, who is on the beach filming, dashes into the sea and rescues the unconscious girl. He then runs off to get some help, and in his absence Harold comes back and takes the credit for rescuing the now recovered Sally. Buster returns and stands on the beach, watching the couple walk off into the distance. We see him in profile as he sinks to his knees, and the camera pulls back away from his misery. As the shot becomes wider we see Josephine cranking the handle on Buster's newsreel camera: she has filmed the entire rescue as it really happened. It's a wonderful shot combining sadness with an uplifting laugh.

There are other great moments, too. After the disastrous 'which house warehouse', for example, there is an inspired action gag. Buster spots the fire engine. Carrying his ancient camera he bravely runs alongside the engine and leaps on board. We cut to a wonderful full-frontal shot of Buster clinging to the speeding vehicle. He is looking straight at us with grim determination: he is going to capture this fire. The fire engine pulls into a fire station and Buster gets off embarrassed.

Another superb scene in *The Cameraman* is when the phone rings and Buster runs down three flights of stairs to answer it. A camera on a lift follows Buster as he descends the stairs of a house specially built in cross-section for the sequence. We follow him exactly as he passes the floors. The first time the phone rings, it's not for him. He wearily makes his way back up to the top of the house, the camera on a lift following him upwards. This technique may have been suggested by Harold's use of a camera lift to film him climb a tree in *The Kid Brother*. When he does at last speak to Sally she tells him that her other date is off. Buster drops the phone, runs out of the house and down the street, arriving at Sally's house just as she puts the phone down. 'I'm sorry I'm a little late,' he says. The device of the cross-sectioned house was used in Buster's first independent short, *The High Sign*, and is here again in this, his first non-independent picture.

Another reminder of the earlier picture occurs when Buster and Sally take a walk along the pavement and he slips over a banana skin. This was a hackneyed gag for 1928, but perhaps Buster is making amends for thumbing his nose at the audience in *The High Sign*. In that film he avoided the banana skin and thumbed his nose. Here he slips on the skin and that's all there is to it. 'This time,' he might have thought, 'I'm going to play it straight.' The character that Buster plays in this film is more akin to a Harold Lloyd type in that he is resourceful and energetic.

Film historian Glenn Mitchell highlights two occasions in the finished picture where Buster breaks into a broad grin. The first appears early on when he is pushed around by a large crowd as he attempts to take a customer's photograph. The second is when Buster is climbing a ladder in Chinatown with Josephine on his shoulder, and he can be glimpsed grinning broadly. We will never know what made him laugh. If I were to offer an opinion based on the visual evidence, I would cautiously suggest that Josephine farted.

In later years MGM would run *The Cameraman* for its newly signed comedians to illustrate how a comedy film should work. The irony was lost on them that this was much more a Keaton film than an MGM picture. *The Cameraman* was released on 22 September 1928 and was a success with critics and at the box office. Perhaps MGM wasn't going to be so bad after all.

Laurel and Hardy's first short of 1928 was *Leave 'Em Laughing*, released in January, and it not only maintained the high standards of its immediate predecessors, but it surpassed them. *Leave 'Em Laughing*'s plot can be written on the head of a pin in 10-foot-high letters: Stan has toothache, and Ollie takes him to the dentist. They inhale copious amounts of laughing gas, and then attempt to drive home. That's it. The last nine minutes show the two of them, constantly laughing, wreaking havoc as they attempt to obey the instructions of a traffic cop, played by Edgar Kennedy. On several occasions Ollie, who is driving, reverses into the car behind him. Each time he is laughing as he

Right Ollie looks very much the part of a caveman in *Flying Elephants*. Dorothy Coburn is doing the pleading.

crashes. Then he looks puzzled and turns around to see what he has hit. He sees it's another car and begins laughing all over again. I love that detail in Oliver Hardy's performance. Stan's uncontrollable laughter and the sheer pleasure it brings him are infectious. For their official film debut as a comedy team, *The Second Hundred Years*, both Stan and Ollie had shaved their heads. When Stan's hair grew back it had a fluffier, more stand-uppy look, and in *Leave 'Em Laughing* there are some lengthy close-ups of the sprouting thatch. It's a sublime film.

Flying Elephants, their next two-reeler release, is a throwback to the past and not just because of its Stone Age setting. Released on 12 February 1928, the film had actually been made in 1927 before Laurel and Hardy were officially a team. Hal Roach dropped Pathé as his distributor and replaced them with MGM. *Flying Elephants* was a Pathé release, and the company held on to it until Laurel and Hardy had become big box office. Comparing *Flying Elephants* to the films released around it shows how quickly Stan and Ollie developed once they were specifically teamed together. Stan and Ollie don't really have a great deal to do with each other in *Flying Elephants*, but there's much in the film that is delightful. Stan's character, Twinkle Star, is the most effeminate man in the history of the world, and his blond bubble-cut wig is worth the price of admission alone. Ollie plays a thuggish type called Mighty Giant. It's not particularly a comedy role, and the big black wig does sometimes hide his features from the camera. The title comes from an observation of Ollie's that the elephants are flying south, and thanks to some charming early animation we see three elephants flying away. Frank Butler was the credited director, but Hal Roach actually directed the film in the rocky landscape of Nevada. Hal also wrote the story, so it's tempting to blame him for not seeing the potential of Laurel and Hardy as an interacting double act. It may not be as simple as

Left Stan, complete with outrageous wig, seems more receptive to Edna Marion. As these two film stills show, *Flying Elephants* is a bit of a throwback to the past – a film that features Stan and Ollie as individuals rather than as a comedy duo.

At times the music and effects track is highly specific. When Stan suggests that the professor might be a trifle cuckoo, we hear the call of a cuckoo. Ollie's reply via the title-card is priceless: 'He is as sound mentally as you or I'

that. Perhaps Stan was also resisting the double act at this point. As Twinkle Star, he cavorts with great enthusiasm and is clearly enjoying his work and his screen time with all the cast, not just Ollie. In this light, *Flying Elephants* can be seen as the nearest we have to a Stan Laurel solo vehicle with Oliver Hardy as part of the supporting cast.

Two weeks after *The Cameraman*'s release, Laurel and Hardy released one of their very best silent two-reelers, *Early to Bed*, which is the only Laurel and Hardy film not to feature a supporting cast. Like their first picture, *Duck Soup*, it begins with Stan and Ollie sitting on a park bench, but now they are both wearing their familiar bowler hats. They have a dog called Buster. Ollie opens a letter and discovers that his uncle has left him a fortune. Stan worries about what's going to happen to him, and Ollie promises to make him his butler: 'And so it came to pass that Hardy Manor had a new butler.' The next title-card tells us that it's '3 a.m. The Master's birthday.' Stan is waiting for Ollie to come home. He tries a piece of the birthday cake he's baked, and we linger on a close-up of Stan enjoying its flavour. The Master arrives home drunk, and Stan is appalled that he should have taken alcoholic refreshment. The Master chuckles like a naughty child. Stan orders him to bed. The Master replies: 'I don't want to go to bed … I want to play.'

Eventually Stan gets to bed. He is woken up by Ollie, who wants to show him his new spring outfit. Stan quits, but Ollie won't let him. *Early to Bed* is a delightful variation on the usual Laurel and Hardy relationship. It has a string of inventive gags and a fast pace, which helps the comedy to zip along. Stan and Ollie lost all this speed once they transferred to talkies.

By now sound was well and truly on the way. *Habeas Corpus*, released on 1 December 1928, was Laurel and Hardy's first film to be released with a synchronized music and effects track. Ollie knocks on the door, and we hear the knock. Stan scratches his head, and we hear scratching. A mad professor has paid Laurel and Hardy to dig up a body that he can use for his experiments, but it's a pitch-black night and on the way to the cemetery they get lost. Stan spots a white signpost, which Ollie insists on climbing. At the top is a sign: 'Wet Paint.' Ollie climbs down. A white stripe runs down the front of his dark suit. At times the music and effects track is highly specific. When Stan suggests that the professor might be a trifle cuckoo, we hear the call of a cuckoo. Ollie's reply via the title-card is priceless: 'He is as sound mentally as you or I.'

The music and effects track for their two-reeler *Liberty*, which was released on 29 January 1929, has also survived. Stan and Ollie have escaped from prison, and they change out of their prison uniforms and into street clothes in the back

Opposite **Never climb a signpost that bears a 'Wet Paint' sign. Ollie incurs a hefty dry-cleaner's bill in *Habeas Corpus*.**

THIRD ST.
WET
PAINT
S14-9

1

2

3

Big Business

The central idea of *Big Business* is a simple one: Stan and Ollie want to sell a Christmas tree to Jimmy Finlayson, but he doesn't want to buy it – and things go downhill from there. Stan catches his overcoat in Jimmy's door, so has to ring the doorbell again. Irritated by his persistent visitors, Jimmy becomes aggressive and attacks the Christmas tree. Stan and Ollie reply in kind, and by the end of the film they have wrecked his house and he has wrecked their car. Eventually a policeman intervenes and tries to establish who started it all, but his questions simply reduce everyone to tears – including, in the end, the policeman himself.

The whole routine is superbly timed and worked out, making *Big Business*, to my mind, one of Stan and Ollie's finest comedies.

4

5

1 The hopeful salesmen arrive. 2 It soon transpires that Jimmy doesn't want to buy a Christmas tree. 3 Ollie bears the initial brunt of Jimmy's irritation. 4 The house wrecking gets underway. 5 By now, things are completely out of hand.

Above Stan and Ollie get confused in *Wrong Again.*

of a moving car. They jump out of the car, but unfortunately they've put on each other's trousers. A woman screams as she sees two grown men taking off their trousers in an alleyway, an action she thinks is capable of only one interpretation. Down another alleyway they try to change their trousers behind two large boxes of wet fish. A crab falls into the trousers that Stan is wearing, but Stan and Ollie start walking briskly down the street. The crab nips Stan. He stops immediately in his tracks and stares with bewilderment straight into the camera. It's a moment highly reminiscent of Harry Langdon.

If there is some of Harry Langdon in Stan, there's an awful lot of Harold Lloyd in the second half of *Liberty.* Stan and Ollie find themselves on steel girders hundreds of feet up in the air. It's a real novelty to see them there and a reminder that Harold Lloyd's thrill pictures inspired a great deal of comedy in others. *Liberty* is an excellent two-reeler. Laurel and Hardy were on a hot streak, and their next three shorts were among the best silent comedies ever made.

Wrong Again, released on 23 February, features Stan and Ollie as stable hands. A bystander reading a newspaper informs them that: 'The famous Blue Boy has been stolen. There's $5,000 reward.' Stan and Ollie look into a nearby stable and see a horse wearing a blanket with the name Blue Boy on it. Ollie learns that the owner lives at 46 Collingwood Place. We cut to an interior set where we see two suspicious types placing the framed painting of 'Blue Boy'

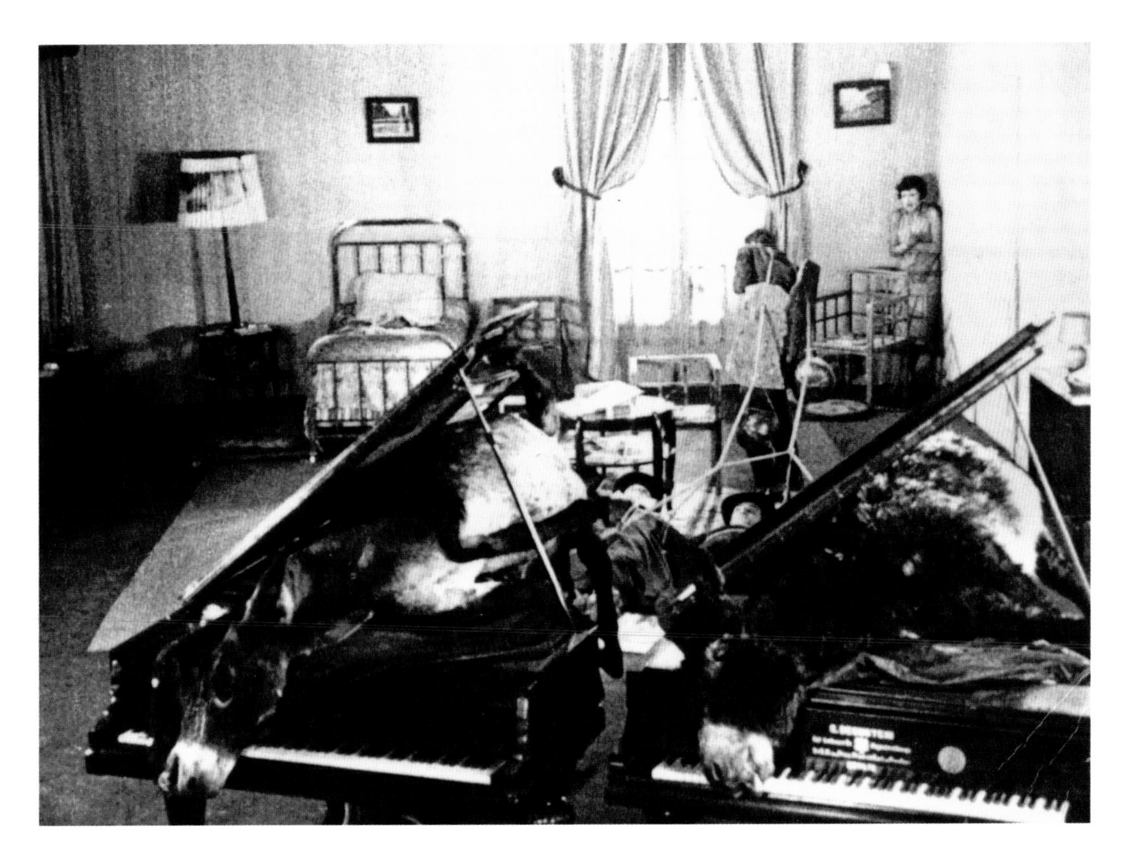

Above **The film that inspired the gag: Luis Buñuel's distinctly surreal film *Un Chien Andalou.***

against a wall. Two cops enter with guns. One policeman phones the owner to tell him his painting has been recovered. The owner says, 'Bring it right over.' In the meantime, Laurel and Hardy have turned up at 46 Collingwood Place with the horse called Blue Boy. The owner's about to take a bath, so he throws Ollie the front door key from a first-floor balcony and tells him to take Blue Boy into the house! Ollie takes a while to convince Stan, but eventually they take the horse into the house. Once inside the owner shouts down the stairs: 'Put him on top of the piano.' Stan and Ollie look at each other, but who are they to argue? They put the horse on the piano. The silent Laurel and Hardys set such a high standard that it's difficult to pick out individual favourites, but *Wrong Again* for its central surreal image of a horse on a piano is one of mine.

Leo McCarey directed *Wrong Again*, and its original music and effects soundtrack still exists. Many years later, in the mid-1960s, he was interviewed by Peter Bogdanovich, and revealed that Laurel and Hardy in their silent days had at least one very starry fan. When asked if he knew Keaton and Chaplin, Leo replied:

> Yes, particularly Chaplin. But we were all good friends, even though we were rivals, and we all met often. I very quickly allied myself with Chaplin, who particularly loved the Laurel and Hardy pictures.[9]

And so on to Stan and Ollie's next two-reeler, *That's My Wife*, which was released a month later on 23 March. Ollie's uncle has come to visit. He has never met Ollie's wife, but if they are both happily married he's going to set them up in a fine new home. That's great. The only trouble is that Ollie's wife has stormed out of the house because Stan won't leave it. He's been sitting on the sofa for two years. There's only one thing for it – Stan will have to drag up as Ollie's wife. He does.

Laurel and Hardy's last silent film release before their first talkie has often been considered their best ever. I've watched *Big Business* more than thirty times with a live audience, and the responses have been remarkably uniform. They always laugh in the same places with the same regular rhythm. Stan and Leo previewed their films in exactly the same way as Harold, Buster and Charlie, and the films were recut according to the audiences' reactions. That's one of the reasons they still work so well today.

In *Big Business* Laurel and Hardy are attempting to sell Christmas trees door to door. They try to sell one to Jimmy Finlayson, but he's not interested. The Hal Roach Studios had once sought to build a comedy trio out of Stan, Ollie and Jim, but three's an odd dynamic for a comedy team. As a solo performer playing opposite Stan and Ollie, however, Jimmy came into his own. He refuses to buy a tree, but Stan gets his coat caught in the hinges of Jimmy's front door, so he has to ring the doorbell again. Jimmy gets angry and cuts a Christmas tree in half with a pair of shears. Stan uses a pocket knife to strip some wood off the frame of Finlayson's front door. It's easy to lip-read his reaction, 'Vandals!' Jimmy smashes Ollie's watch. Stan and Ollie soak Jimmy with a garden hose. He throws a headlight into their car windscreen. A small crowd gathers as Stan and Ollie take Jimmy's front door off its hinges. He removes the steering wheel from their car. A policeman drives up and can't believe his eyes. The crowd has got bigger, running from the house back to the car to witness each fresh assault. At no point do Stan, Ollie or Jimmy attempt to protect their property. They watch each individual act of destruction, knowing it's going to be their turn in a minute.

Eventually, the policeman wanders over to interrupt proceedings. 'Who started all this?' he asks. Stan starts to cry, and Ollie joins him. The policeman, played by Tiny Sanford, turns to Jimmy: 'So you started this!' Jimmy tries to explain, but he starts to cry. We cut to Stan and Ollie in floods of tears. We cut back to the policeman, who is sobbing into a white handkerchief. We cut to the crowd who are consoling each other. Each one of these cuts provokes a huge laugh from a live audience. The editing enhances the inherent comedy in the situation, and it's a superb piece of filmmaking. Although *Big Business* was not their last silent movie – they released three others amid the six talkies released in 1929 – it does represent Laurel and Hardy at the peak of their silent craft.

Opposite **In *That's My Wife* Stan drags up as Ollie's wife and causes chaos in a fashionable nightclub.**

We cut to Stan and Ollie in floods of tears. We cut back to the policeman, who is sobbing into a white handkerchief. We cut to the crowd who are consoling each other

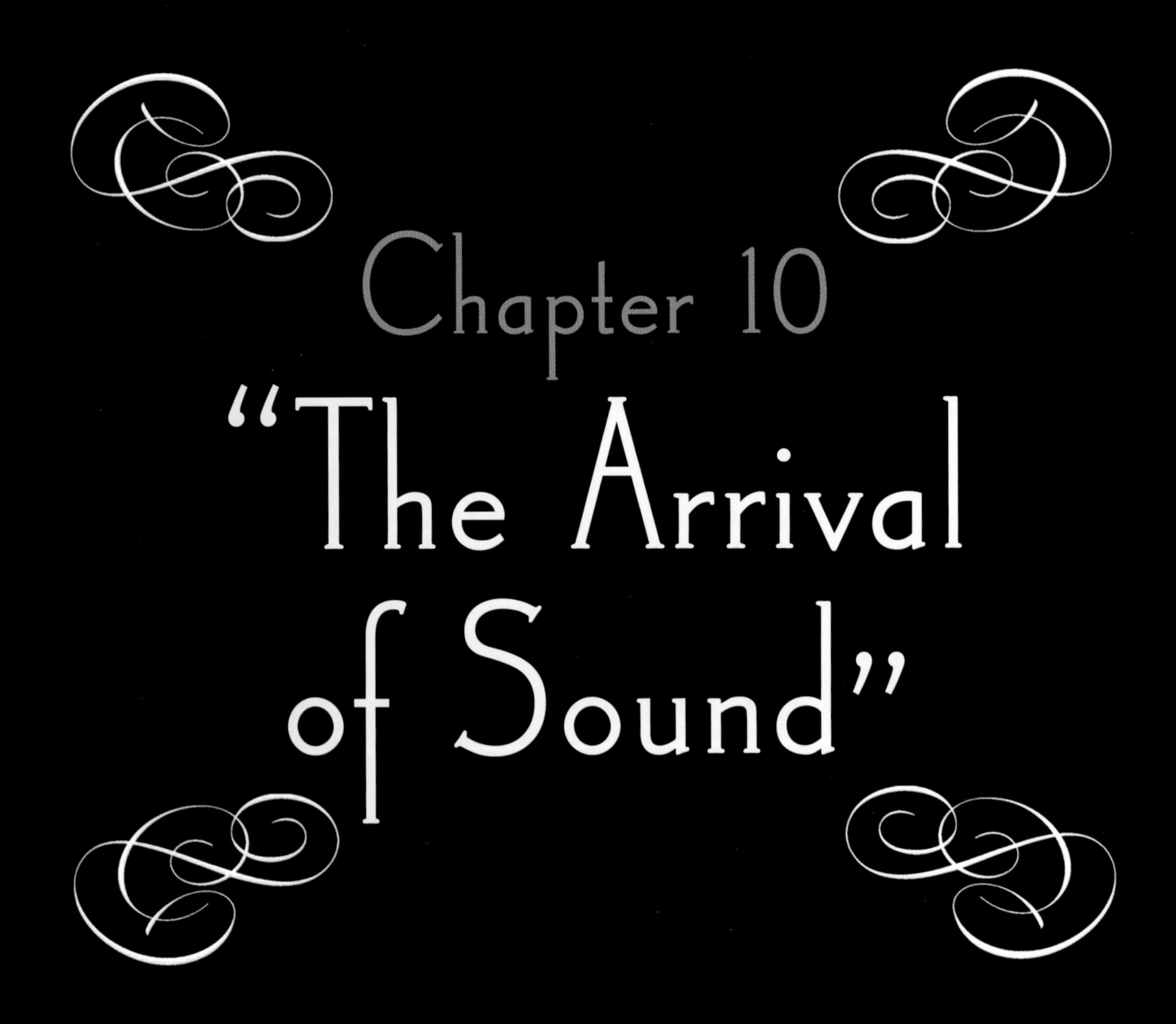

Chapter 10
"The Arrival of Sound"

Charlie Chaplin
CITY LIGHTS
DISTRIBUTED BY

UNITED
ARTISTS
WRITTEN · DIRECTED AND PRODUCED BY CHARLES CHAPLIN

The Arrival of Sound

The arrival of sound turned Hollywood upside down and changed the lives of many of the silent stars. A number failed to make the transition and disappeared from view, while European film stars who had flocked to America to appear in silent pictures mainly went back to their home countries. One glorious exception was Greta Garbo, whose MGM talkies continued the huge success she had established in her silent films. A whole new generation of screen entertainers appeared: the Marx Brothers, Eddie Cantor and Al Jolson were all vibrant vocal performers with musical skills aplenty.

Other things changed, too. Films now took longer to make. They were more expensive to produce. As a result the studios became increasingly powerful. Yet Buster Keaton, for one, always maintained that nothing about the talkies frightened him. He had used his voice throughout his stage career and knew he was perfectly capable of delivering dialogue. He made it clear that he wanted to make his next comedy, *Spite Marriage*, as a sound picture. However, comedy was not a priority at MGM – in late 1929 they had only one sound stage in operation and that was used for musicals. Consequently, the film was made as a silent movie, but it was released on 6 April 1929 with a synchronized soundtrack of music and effects. Buster had nothing to do with the compilation of this track, which was the responsibility of a separate department at MGM.

Spite Marriage was shot in just over five weeks, from 20 November to 29 December 1928, and it was directed by Buster's old vaudeville pal Eddie Sedgwick, who had directed *The Cameraman*. Buster plays Elmer, a besotted fan of the beautiful stage actress Trilby Drew, played by Dorothy Sebastian. Every night he sits in the front row, applauding her performance in an old-fashioned melodrama set during the American Civil War and hissing at the villains.

Trilby has an argument backstage with a fellow actor when he informs her he won't be taking her out that night because he has another engagement. Trilby storms out of the theatre just as Elmer is deliberately walking past the stage door, and, much to his astonishment, she decides to put her arm in his, though she then leaves him on the pavement when her taxi arrives. The next day Buster wanders backstage in the hope that he will meet her again. He recognizes an actor, Murphy, who gets the chance to kiss Trilby during the play, and tells him, 'I'd give anything in the world to play your part, Mister.' Then the police turn up. 'I want a guy working here by the name of Murphy.' Murphy takes Elmer to one side and says, 'Do you think you could play my part tonight?' Elmer knows he can do it – after all, he's seen the show thirty-five times.

He goes on and creates total havoc. It is a scene that perfectly illustrates Buster's favoured approach to sound filmmaking: dialogue cards where needed,

Above This production shot of the making of the 1935 Clark Gable film *Wife vs Secretary* shows just how much more complex filmmaking became with the arrival of sound.

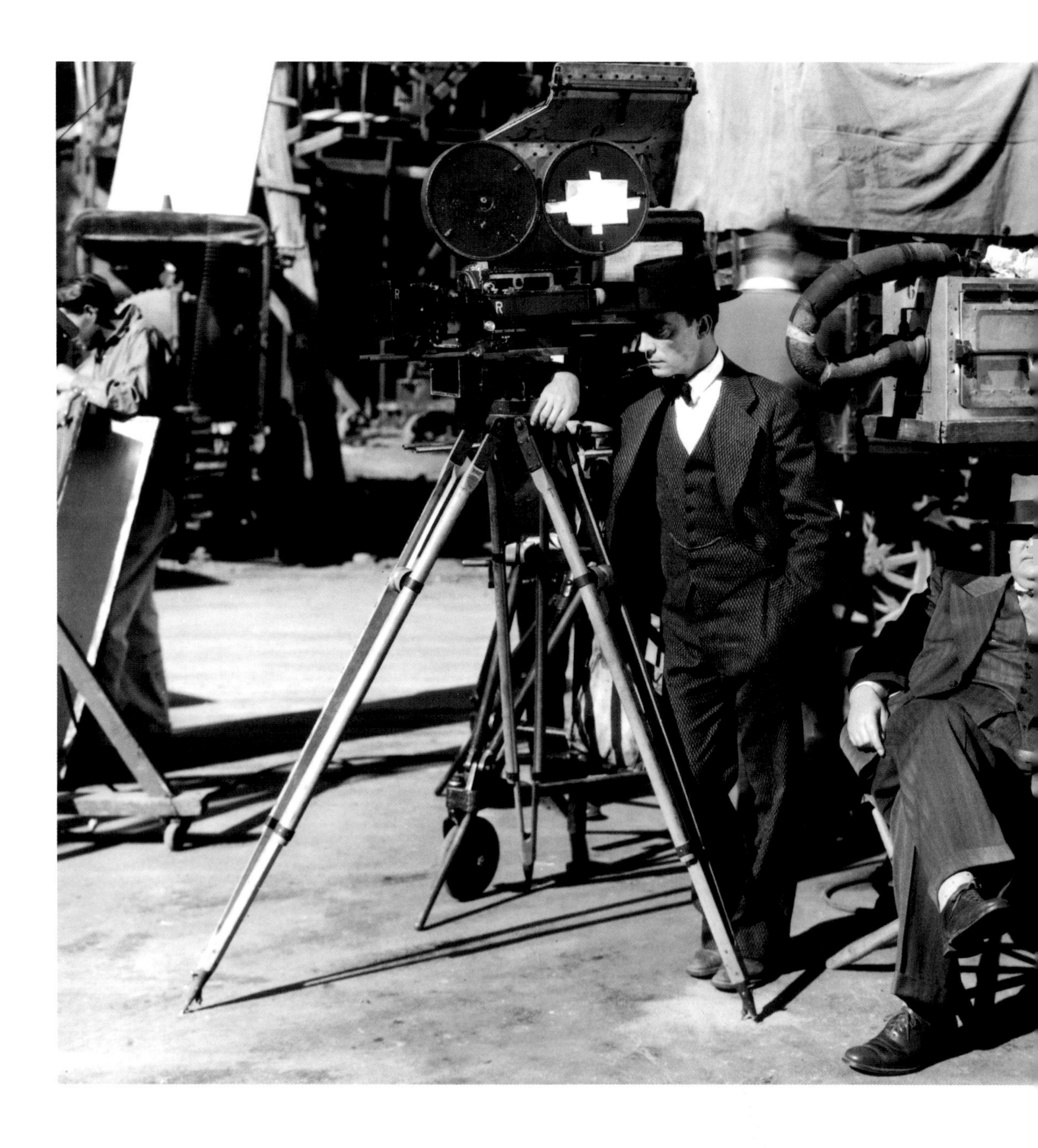

Spite Marriage **looks absolutely superb. The sets are lavish, with beautiful art deco designs by Cedric Gibbons. The photography is exceptional. Buster looks great and clearly relishes working with Dorothy Sebastian**

Left Buster Keaton on the set of *Spite Marriage*. Buster was becoming increasingly unhappy with his employers, MGM, but his last silent film is still a masterpiece. He is seen here with Eddie Sedgwick, the director.

but then a lengthy sequence of comic action. It's really the same way he made his silents. Most of the dialogue cards in his films appear in tight clusters, and for the rest of the time action predominates. *Spite Marriage* also shows him revisiting his previous films. A brutal fist fight between him and the villain is similar to that in *Battling Butler*, although this time the fight takes place aboard a luxury yacht. The sequence also recalls the vicious fight aboard the abandoned ship in *The Kid Brother*.

Spite Marriage has rarely been seen in the near eighty years since its release, and its critical reputation has suffered accordingly. It was felt that the difficulties Buster experienced during *The Cameraman* must have inevitably increased on *Spite Marriage*, his last silent, given that his talkie career with MGM was an unmitigated disaster. Certainly, that was what I thought when I attended a rare screening at the National Film Theatre in London in about 1995. However, I was wrong. I overlooked the effect of the intrusive film soundtrack on the audience that night: it distanced us from a silent film experience and dated the film horribly. I have now seen *Spite Marriage* on DVD on two or three occasions with the sound turned down, and I've substantially revised my opinion. *Spite Marriage* looks absolutely superb. The sets are lavish, with beautiful art deco designs by Cedric Gibbons. The photography is exceptional. Buster looks great and clearly relishes working with Dorothy Sebastian, who plays a much more rounded female character than is usual in Buster's films, which strengthens the romance. In fact, Dorothy and Buster were enjoying a secret affair during the filming of the movie, and their relationship continued for many years.

Spite Marriage, then, is a triumphant end to Buster Keaton's silent career. In terms of look and design it outshines many of his better known films, combining as it does the gloss of MGM with the heart of Buster Keaton, and I look forward to the day I present *Spite Marriage* to a live audience with a live musical accompaniment. It's Buster's last silent masterpiece.

Buster's first starring talkie at MGM was a long time coming. He made a brief appearance in *The Hollywood Review* of 1929, sharing the billing with many other stars, including Stan and Ollie, who performed a sketch with Jack Benny. Then came his first starring talkie, *Free and Easy*, a musical. He is cast as Elmer Butts, a bumbling public servant who is put in charge of the local beauty queen and her mother as they all journey by train to Hollywood. In this film Buster is just another actor. Although the film is terrible, it was a huge success at the box office. Audiences were immediately hooked on talkies and flocked to the movie houses to hear what their favourite stars sounded like.

The rest of Buster's MGM talkies are a rather sorry bunch with rare

On the days he didn't turn up for filming because he was too hungover, he cost MGM a great deal of money. His last film for them was called *What! No Beer?* And if there wasn't any it was because Buster had drunk it all

highlights here and there. The best, *Doughboys* and *Speak Easily*, have moments of magic, but they're not Buster at his best. The fact is, Buster couldn't fight MGM. Because these films were financially successful, the studio became ever more convinced that they were right about things and that Buster was wrong. Then Eddie Sedgwick, his director, was taken away from him, and the films got worse. To try to serve the huge foreign markets created by the universal comedies of silent cinema, Buster was obliged to remake each crummy film in at least two other languages, learning his lines phonetically, while Spanish, French or (on one occasion) German actors were brought in to shoot the foreign versions.

Not surprisingly, Buster felt incredibly low. He and Natalie, who had hated each other through most of their marriage, got divorced, and in his depressed state he let her have everything without a fight. The huge Italian villa with its lavish swimming pool and extensive grounds went to her, and later she legally changed their two sons' names from Keaton to Talmadge. *Spite Marriage* indeed. (Was that title chosen by Buster as another dig at Natalie? It surely must have been.) Buster also started drinking heavily, and it showed on film. On the days he didn't turn up for filming because he was too hungover, he cost MGM a great deal of money. His last film for them was called *What! No Beer?* And if there wasn't any it was because Buster had drunk it all.

Buster was sacked by MGM in February 1933, and the next two years proved to be the worst of his life. His misery was intensified by what happened to his great friend Roscoe Arbuckle. During Roscoe's screen banishment, good friends, including Buster and Charlie, had helped him financially – Charlie, for example, was one of the investors in Roscoe's nightclub venture in the late 1920s – and now, after more than ten years, this innocent man was finally forgiven by Hollywood. He made some sound two-reelers and then, in 1932, Warner Brothers, keen to promote Roscoe to features, offered him a contract, which he signed. He suffered a fatal heart attack in his sleep that very same night. But at least he died knowing he had been rehabilitated. He had returned to the big screen.

Roscoe's death was a hammer blow for Buster. He was taken to a psychiatric hospital in a straitjacket – from which he managed to escape – and he was subjected to the 'Keeley cure' for alcoholics, a type of aversion therapy that involved pouring copious amounts of different alcoholic drinks down the patient's throat until they threw up. This brutal treatment didn't work. During one long alcoholic haze, Buster married one of his nurses, Mae Scrivens, in a ceremony he could never remember. The marriage lasted a couple of years.

But Buster fought back. Just when it looked as if he was beaten, he made a spirited recovery, as in the finale of *Battling Butler*. Educational Films, a low-budget outfit, contracted him to make six two-reelers a year at $5,000 a film. Although they were shot quickly in four or five days, Buster was at least able to follow his own comedic instincts in front of the camera again. He didn't regard these shorts very highly, but then he was always a fierce critic of his own work. In fact, even allowing for the low budgets and the short filming schedule, moments of Keaton magic still shine through. These films put paid to the idea that Buster was ruined by the talkies. It was MGM's method that killed him off there. Away from their tyranny, he flourished in reduced circumstances. For example, his first Educational short, *The Gold Ghost*, which was released on 16 March 1934, features a piece of comic business that Buster had used in his first independent silent *The High Sign*. He aims his gun at one object but hits another. There are some dialogue scenes, but mainly we see Buster in action, unencumbered by speech. This was his method for sound films and it works.

By 1935 his worst days were behind him. He didn't touch another drink until 1940. In 1938 he met Eleanor Norris, a dancer at MGM, who was twenty years younger than him. They shared an enthusiasm for playing bridge, and they fell in love. They were married on 29 May 1940 and remained happily so. Throughout the 1940s Buster worked as a gag specialist on many MGM comedies, including two Marx Brothers films, and more closely with the comedian Red Skelton on a couple of remakes of Keaton originals. In 1947 he

Below Buster experienced a period of real unhappiness in the 1930s. His marriage fell apart, he was miserable at MGM and he was starting to hit the bottle. Things improved after he remarried in 1940. This photo shows him working as a gag writer for the Marx brothers.

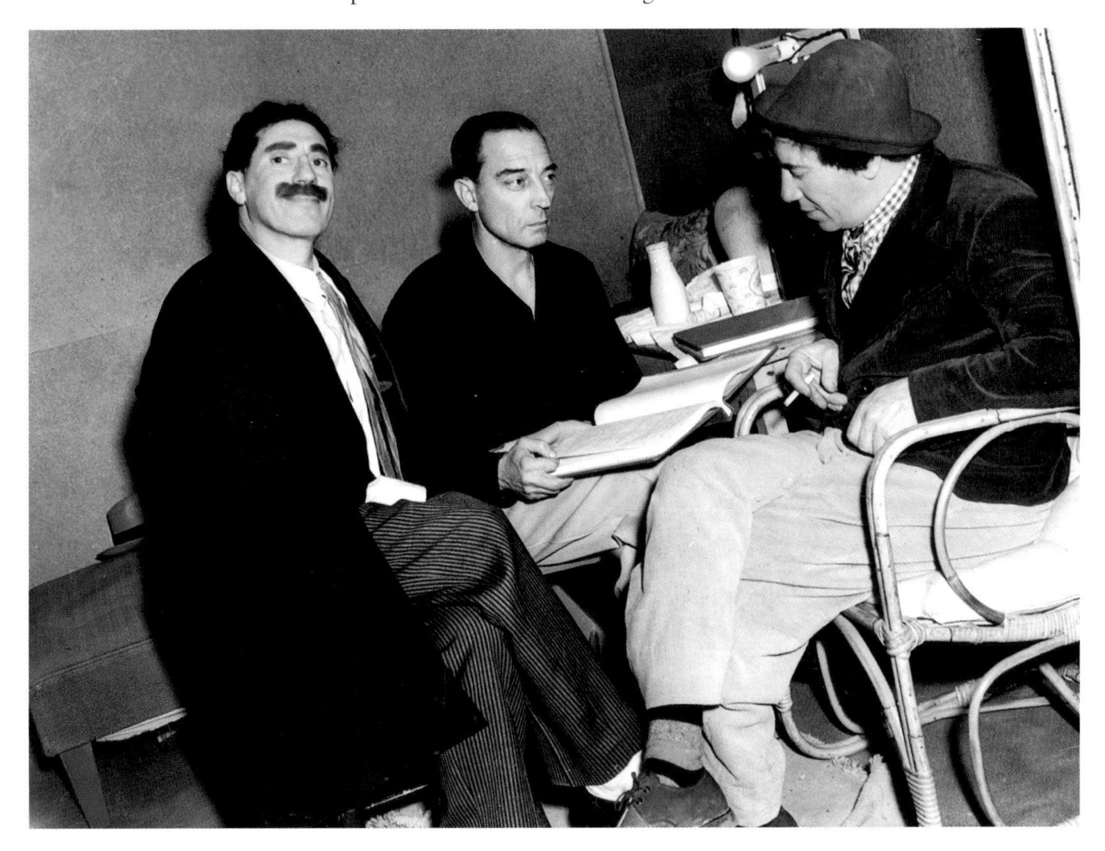

played with the Cirque Medano in Paris, and in the 1950s he enjoyed regular work in the new medium of television. He made two series of *The Buster Keaton Show* but found the constant demand for new material impossible to fill. He also made television commercials, appeared in stage plays and made cameo appearances in some prestigious films. His appearance in *A Funny Thing Happened on the Way to the Forum* was his last film role.

Buster was a successful working comedian his entire life. No matter what the medium, he conquered it: stage, silent films, talkies, French circus, television advertisements. In a precarious profession, Buster was very rarely out of work. He died on 1 February 1966.

Harold Lloyd's first talkie, *Welcome Danger*, had originally been made as a silent, but when Harold saw a sound film getting huge laughs because it featured such strange newly recorded sounds as eggs frying in a pan, he remade sections as a talkie and edited them into the previously completed film. The result, released on 12 October 1929, is a total mess, and there is no continuity between the two versions. It has to be said, though, that it was a massive financial success, making more money than any other of his films.

Harold's first proper talkie was *Feet First*, released on 8 November 1930,

Below More derring-do from Harold Lloyd in his first proper talkie, *Feet First*. Talkies didn't really suit his comic style, but he was able to retire a very wealthy man.

and it features him working in a shoe store. The challenges that sound poses, though, quickly become apparent. There is, for example, a nice sight gag with a lady's artificial leg, but the routine is rather pedestrian because it's shown in real time. Silent films could always speed up a little, but dialogue ties you to a realistic film speed. Moreover, at real speed Harold suddenly looks his real age – thirty-seven. Harold in *Speedy* was, well, far more speedy.

The last twenty minutes of *Feet First* amply illustrate the difference between Harold the silent comedian and Harold the comedian of the talkies. He is improbably hiding in a mail sack that is put onto a painters' scaffold and hoisted up the side of a very tall building. The sack gets caught on a hook and the scaffold returns to the ground, leaving Harold dangling in mid-air. From here on in we are in *Safety Last!* country. But in that film the building climb works so well because it builds to him getting up high. He starts from ground level, tentatively, and makes slow progress inch by inch. In *Feet First* suddenly, out of nowhere, Harold is up there. As he hangs off the edge of a building we hear him shout 'Hey' a number of times and grunt and groan, but there's no music on the soundtrack to help build an air of tension, and the scene ends up being dull. It seems to go on for ever. The same could be said of many a talkie released in 1930, although techniques were rapidly improving.

Harold's next talkie, *Movie Crazy*, is his best, but it was released in September 1932, during the depths of the Depression that followed the Wall Street Crash of 1929, and it didn't match the popularity of his silent films. Three further films followed in the 1930s, but they all confirmed that he was at his best on the silent screen. Harold was, however, fortunate. He was able to retire from Hollywood a wealthy man, and he then devoted his life to countless enthusiasms. He became a painter and studied colour theory. He was fascinated by 3-D photography, taking hundreds of thousands of photographs. In 1949 he was elected Imperial Potentate of the Ancient Arabic Order of the Nobles of the Mystic Shrine, a Masonic organization whose charity work included running hospitals for sick children. Harold was an enthusiastic Shriner and regarded his new title as a great honour.

In the 1960s he revived some of his films in two very well-received compilations. The first, *Harold Lloyd's World of Comedy*, released on 4 June 1962, was a big hit at that year's Cannes Film Festival and went on to play in London and Paris for four months each and in Tokyo for five. The second compilation, *Harold Lloyd's Funny Side of Life*, was released on 9 November 1966. In his last few years he particularly enjoyed showing his films to a new young audience. He died on 8 March 1971. His films survive him.

Three further films followed in the 1930s, but they all confirmed that he was at his best on the silent screen. Harold was, however, fortunate. He was able to retire from Hollywood a wealthy man

If Buster and Harold's fortunes in talkies were mixed, Laurel and Hardy marched triumphantly into them. Their first, *Unaccustomed as We Are*, released on 4 May 1929, is a complete success. Ollie seems a little uncertain on a couple of his early lines, but Stan is immediately in tune. His first words onscreen are, 'Any nuts?', and Ollie soon hits his stride with an impassioned, 'Why don't you do something to help me?' Thelma Todd is the next door neighbour who ends up with her skirt on fire and the same skirt being torn off by Ollie. Her delightful legs are a major distraction.

It has to be said that the pace of this talkie is rather slow, but that is generally true of all Laurel and Hardy's sound films, certainly when compared with the silent films they made. The sheer youthful exuberance of Stan Laurel in *Big Business*, marching across lawns and ripping up shrubs, contrasts sharply with the more sedate and middle-aged Stan we see in this and the rest of their talkies. Stan once admitted that he actually preferred their silent films. The period when he was working with Ollie and Leo McCarey and finally becoming a big star to rival his fellow countryman Charlie Chaplin must have been very exciting. The huge success of their talkies has sometimes hidden the achievements of their silent career, but, of course, it is the Stan and Ollie of the talkies that the world remembers with particular affection, and there is no doubt that their natural voices suited their comic characters.

Various figures from the silent era appear in the Laurel and Hardy's sound films. Charley Chase, for example, who had maintained a successful career in two-reel talkies under Hal Roach, makes a memorable guest appearance in Stan and Ollie's highly acclaimed feature *Sons of the Desert.* Jimmy Finlayson, one of the original Keystone Cops, was a Laurel and Hardy stalwart, his lovely Scottish brogue perfectly fitting his bendy-eyes disdain and explosive anger.

Right Stan reluctantly accepts the inevitable punishment in *Way Out West.*

Left **Stan and Ollie as less than brilliant scholars in *A Chump at Oxford*.**

His best role in a Laurel and Hardy sound feature must be in *Way Out West*, the film in which Stan and Ollie sing 'The Trail of the Lonesome Pine'. Even Ben Turpin makes an appearance (his last) in a Laurel and Hardy film, the 1940 feature *Saps at Sea*. As ever, his eyes are crossed. This one joke had kept his film career going since 1907.

Stan and Ollie's last great film is *A Chump at Oxford*, which was released in 1940 and produced, like all their best work, by the Hal Roach studios. Hal was a sympathetic producer who trusted Stan Laurel and his various gag men and directors to make successful comedies. The duo made over fifty sound films for him, including thirteen features. After the pair parted company with him in 1940 they made several films at other studios, but ended up being treated in the same way that Buster had been treated at MGM. Other people thought they could make better comedies. They wouldn't trust the comedians themselves.

Oliver Hardy was a wonderful comic actor whose unjealous support of Stan Laurel led to that rarest of beasts – a double act with two funny men. In cinematic terms they are the best double act there ever was

In their latter years Stan and Ollie twice toured the music halls of Britain and Ireland, but Ollie suffered a series of strokes and died on 7 August 1957. Stan, an enthusiastic letter-writer, enjoyed a comfortable life until his death on 23 February 1965. He lived in Santa Monica with his wife, Ida, in an apartment looking directly over the Pacific Ocean. Celebrity fans, including Peter Sellers and Dick Van Dyke, visited to pay homage. Stan enjoyed watching Laurel and Hardy reruns on television and frequently laughed out loud at Ollie's performances. Oliver Hardy was a wonderful comic actor whose unjealous support of Stan Laurel led to that rarest of beasts – a double act with two funny men. In cinematic terms they are the best double act there ever was.

Charlie Chaplin took two years to complete his last silent feature, *City Lights*, having embarked on it in 1928. He himself admitted that while he was making it he worked himself 'into a neurotic state of wanting perfection'. He rehearsed and filmed over and over again. The simple gesture of a blind flower girl offering the Tramp a flower, for example, took days. No matter how Virginia Cherrill played it, Charlie wasn't happy. He wasn't satisfied with the way Virginia held the flower and reshot the scene dozens of times. It is key moment in the film, and Charlie wanted to get it right.

To add to Charlie's concerns, *City Lights* was being made when sound was on its way, and the film was actually released, in February 1931, when talkies had taken over. Having dismissed sound's advent as a passing fad, he was now worried that his new film would immediately be condemned as old-fashioned. Was there still a place for pantomime? His friend and fellow actor Henry Bergman later recalled how nervous Charlie was before the film's premiere. Sound did mean, though, that Charlie could add a music track, which – to Hollywood's astonishment – he announced he would compose himself. Another discipline for Charlie's creative energy to tackle, though he was a keen musician, having taught himself the cello, violin and piano, as his Aunt Kate recalled in a 1915 interview:

> The cello was the instrument I think he loved best, 'because it was so plaintive,' he said. I took a delight in watching his changing expression and his small hand quivering as he touched the chords. It was almost a caress. It was only when he caught my eyes glistening that he would laugh and suddenly do some funny little movement or dash off a gay air. This would immediately change my sad mood to one scream of laughter.[1]

City Lights combines two storylines. Charlie as the Tramp saves a drunken millionaire from a suicide attempt and is immediately befriended by him, and he meets a blind flower-seller with whom he falls in love. The two narratives dovetail beautifully. While drunk, the millionaire is friendly and generous – in one scene taking Charlie to a nightclub where Charlie mistakes a paper streamer for spaghetti and attempts to eat it even as it trails towards the ceiling. When sober, Charlie's new friend unfortunately doesn't remember him. The blind flower-seller mistakenly assumes that Charlie is himself a millionaire, and Charlie undertakes a series of jobs to pay her rent. He becomes a street sweeper but walks the other way when he sees several horses trotting along – shovelling manure off the street is to be avoided. He is then astonished by the sight of a passing elephant. In a drunken moment, the millionaire gives Charlie the money that will pay for an operation to restore the flower-seller's sight. He then sobers up again, and Charlie is arrested for theft.

This is a film in which pathos and comedy are perfectly combined, as shown in Charlie's first encounter with the flower-seller. The Tramp quickly realizes that the flower girl is blind. He gazes at her wistfully, but unaware that he is sitting there looking at her, she inadvertently throws a cup of water in his face. The same technique is used in *The Gold Rush*: Charlie looks longingly out of the log cabin towards Georgia Hale and is hit in the face by a snowball. This handily undercuts a scene that might otherwise seem over-sentimental.

The final scene of the film has passed into cinematic legend. The flower girl has had her sight restored and notices a couple of small boys teasing Charlie. She doesn't, of course, know who he is until, taking pity on the Tramp, she goes to give him some money and recognizes the touch of his hand. 'You,' she says. 'Yes,' Charlie replies. It's a wonderfully poignant moment.

Left In *City Lights*, Charlie saves a drunken millionaire from a suicide attempt and wins his eternal friendship – eternal that is, until the millionaire sobers up.

Right Charlie's first encounter with the blind flower-seller Virginia Cherrill in *City Lights* was a scene that caused him enormous difficulties. It took five days to film a scene lasting just seventy seconds.

Decades later Charlie described the scene to Richard Merryman:

> I had one close-up once, in *City Lights*, just the last scene. One could have gone overboard ... I was looking more at her and interested in her, and I detached myself in a way that gives a beautiful sensation. In not acting ... almost apologetic, standing outside myself and looking, studying her reactions and being slightly embarrassed about it. And it came off. It's a beautiful scene, beautiful; and because it wasn't over-acted.[2]

The Hollywood premiere of *City Lights* took place on 30 January 1931, and it was a spectacular affair. The crowds were immense, and Professor Albert Einstein and his wife were the guests of honour. This is a measure of the status that Chaplin and his comedy had achieved: from Albert Austin to Albert Einstein. (In fact, Albert Austin plays two characters in *City Lights*, marking his last appearance in a Chaplin film. He is also credited as an assistant director on the film. Away from the Chaplin studio, Albert directed a couple of features starring Jackie Coogan, *Trouble* (1922) and *A Prince of a King* (1923).)

After the Hollywood premiere, Charlie attended the London premiere, his first visit to his birthplace since 1921. Then he had lacked the courage to visit the Hanwell Schools where he had spent the most miserable time of his childhood. Ten years later he felt up to the task. The *Daily Express* reported his visit:

> He entered the dining hall, where four hundred boys and girls cheered their heads off at the sight of him – and he entered in style. He made to raise his

> hat, and it jumped magically into the air. He swung his cane and he hit himself in the leg! He turned out his feet and hopped along inimitably. It was Charlie! Yells! Shrieks of joy! More yells! And he was enjoying himself as much as the children. He mounted the dais and announced solemnly that he would give an imitation of an old man inspecting some pictures. He turned his back and moved along, peering at the wall. Marvel of marvels – as he moved the old man grew visibly! A foot, two feet! A giant of an old man! The secret was plain if you faced him. His arms were stretched above his head; his overcoat was supported on his fingertips; his hat was balanced on the coat collar.[3]

Charlie later told the novelist Thomas Burke that it was the greatest emotional experience of his life.

> I wouldn't have missed it for all I possess. It's what I've been wanting. God, you feel like the dead returning to earth. To smell the smell of the dining hall, and to remember that was where you sat, and that scratch on the pillar was made by you. Only it wasn't you. It was you in another life – your soul mate – something you were and something you aren't now. Like a snake that sheds its skin every now and then, but it's still got your odour about it. O-o-oh, it was wonderful. When I got there, I knew it was what I'd been wanting for years. Everything had been leading up to it, and I was ripe for it. My return to London in 1921, and my return this year, were wonderful enough, but they were nothing to that. Being among those buildings and connecting with everything – with the misery and something that wasn't misery ... The shock of it, too. You see, I never really believed that I'd be there. It was thirty years ago when I was there, and thirty years – why, nothing in America lasts that long.[4]

Charlie's trip to London turned into a world tour that kept him away from Hollywood until 10 June 1932. While he was away he visited Berlin, Paris, Venice, Singapore and Tokyo. Having a huge hit with a silent film in the era of sound was an immense achievement and one that Charlie enjoyed to the full. During the production of *City Lights* Charlie had worked prodigiously and had not found much time for a social life. He was making up for it now.

Charlie Chaplin's last silent film is partly a talkie. *Modern Times*, which was released on 5 February 1936, had been in production since September 1933. The film opens with Charlie working on the assembly line in a massive factory. When he sneaks off to the washroom for a quick cigarette the boss appears on a large screen behind him, ordering Charlie back to work. There are shades of George

While he was away he visited Berlin, Paris, Venice, Singapore and Tokyo. Having a huge hit with a silent film in the era of sound was an immense achievement and one that Charlie enjoyed to the full

Right Charlie attends the Hollywood premiere of *City Lights* on 30 January 1931, accompanied by Mr and Mrs Albert Einstein.

Orwell's *1984* here, although that book was still twelve years away. *City Lights* is an urban fairy tale. *Modern Times* is an urban nightmare: we are in the real world now. Charlie's fourteen months away from Hollywood had stimulated his interest in politics, and he had met many intelligent and powerful people, including H.G. Wells, Winston Churchill, George Bernard Shaw and Mahatma Gandhi. He had considered the soullessness of massive industrialization: the modern world. In *Modern Times* the factory sets with their gigantic machines are a long way from the simple Keystone park comedies of twenty-two years before. The Tramp has walked through an ever-changing landscape. In his earliest incarnation on location shoots for Keystone he had sat on a park bench in a real park or hid around

In *Modern Times* the factory sets with their gigantic machines are a long way from the simple Keystone park comedies of twenty-two years before. The Tramp has walked through an ever-changing landscape

the back of a real bush. Now he is in a make-believe factory in the real world.

One thing hadn't changed, however. In 1936 the Tramp still doesn't speak – after all, he was a character created in silent motion. Elsewhere in the film voices are heard, but they are used sparingly. Charlie is ordered back to work by the boss who appears on a big screen behind him and booms out an order at him. A salesman plays a gramophone record extolling the virtues of an automatic feeding machine, which is designed to eliminate the lunch hour and is complete with an automatic soup plate and a revolving plate with automatic food pusher. The record says, 'Let us demonstrate with one of your workers because action speaks louder than words.'

This sets the scene for one of Charlie's finest comedy routines. He is volunteered to try out the automatic feeder machine, and a circular table is placed in front of him with a bowl of soup, a large creamy dessert, some chocolates and a corn on the cob fitted to a machine. The demonstration begins. The automatic food pusher pushes the chocolates into Charlie's mouth, and an automatic mouth wipe swings in and gently dabs his lips. The corn on the cob machine is next, holding the corn so that Charlie can bite into it. But then the machine goes haywire. The corn revolves rapidly causing Charlie to spit it out – a variation on the spluttering of biscuit crumbs gag from the Karno days. The soup plate upsets its contents all over Charlie's chest, but the automatic mouth wipe still swings in to dab his lips. This is one of Charlie's greatest ever props. In a later scene he jumps onto the conveyor belt and is dragged into the interior of the machine. Wheels and cogs propel him into the heart of the beast, where he performs another brilliantly realized routine.

Now Charlie is diagnosed as suffering a nervous breakdown, and he is taken off to hospital in the back of an ambulance. On his release a doctor tells him via a title-card: 'Take it easy and avoid excitement.' He walks out of the hospital and down the street. A lorry passes him, loaded with large pieces of wood and with a red flag resting on the back of the load. The flag drops off, and Charlie picks it up and waves it above his head, trying to catch the lorry driver's attention. Several dozen men on a march come around the corner holding placards that read 'Unite' and 'Liberty or Death'. The men fall behind Charlie, who is still waving the flag. The march is disrupted by police on horseback, and Charlie is arrested as the leader and sent to prison.

We are then introduced to Paulette Goddard's character: 'The Gamin – a child of the waterfront who refused to go hungry.' Charlie had actually met Pauline some months before filming on *Modern Times* began, at a yacht party thrown by Joe Schenck in July 1932, and the two of them had established an

Modern Times

Although *Modern Times* contains elements of sound it is fundamentally a silent picture, and it contains some of Charlie Chaplin's best comedy routines. In the early part of the film the factory worker, Charlie, driven mad by soulless repetitive conveyor belt work, jumps into the machinery and becomes part of it. He whirls around the cogs tightening nuts up as he goes, and then, in a deranged state, tries to tighten up everything else in sight, including other people. Not surprisingly, he ends up in hospital suffering from a nervous breakdown.

When *Modern Times* was released in 1936, many people commented on the film's 'message'. Were scenes such as this evidence of anti-capitalist sympathies on Charlie's part? Was he, in fact, a communist? The Nazis certainly believed so, and the film was later used against Charlie when he fell foul of anti-communist hysteria in America in the 1950s. But while Charlie was certainly concerned with the problems of the modern world, *Modern Times* is not a party political film: like so many of Charlie's earlier films it's really about the little man at odds with the status quo.

5-P-33

immediate rapport. They had both come from broken homes and had entered show business at an early age. They became inseparable, and in this new mood of domestic happiness Charlie re-established contact with his two sons by Lita Grey, Charlie Junior and Sydney. Charlie Junior later wrote about ecstatic weekends spent with Paulette and his father at the Chaplin home.

> That wonderful magical house on the hill, with the man who lived there, the man who was so many men in one. We were to see them all now: the strict disciplinarian, the priceless entertainer, the taciturn, moody dreamer, the wild man of Borneo with his flashes of volcanic temper. The beloved chameleon shape was to weave itself subtly through all my boyhood and was never to stop fascinating me.[5]

In *Modern Times* the Tramp and the Gamin first meet when she steals a loaf of bread from a baker's van. She runs into the Tramp, knocking him over. The Tramp has been released from prison but wants to go back to jail because the modern world is so noisy. He tells a policeman that he stole the loaf of bread, but the ruse fails when an eyewitness tells a policeman that it was the girl that stole the bread. Charlie then gets himself arrested by consuming a hearty three-course meal and then nonchalantly asking a policeman to pay for it. He is escorted into the back of a police van where he meets the Gamin properly for the first time. The two of them make their escape as the van swerves to avoid an oncoming car. They fall out of the back of it and run, eventually setting up home in a rather ramshackle wooden hut. One morning Charlie

Below **'Buck up – never say die. We'll get along!' reads the last title-card of Charlie's silent career as he and Paulette Goddard walk away at the end of *Modern Times* in a clear echo of the ending of his 1915 film *The Tramp*.**

It's gloriously fitting to see the two of them walking away from us down a road, hand in hand towards their future. Unlike the ending of *The Tramp*, Charlie is no longer alone. Together they walk towards the horizon

reads in the newspaper that factories are re-opening. He immediately runs to the factory and gets a job as an assistant to a mechanic, played by Chester Conklin, an old friend from the Keystone days.

The Gamin gets a job as a dancer in a swish café owned by Henry Bergman, whose first appearance in a Chaplin film had been in 1916's *The Pawnshop*. Then, at Paulette's suggestion, Henry Bergman hires Charlie as a singing waiter. As Charlie walks onto the centre of the floor he loses the lyrics and has to improvise the words. He sings gibberish while pantomiming the story of a rich old man, a pretty girl and a diamond ring.

It's understandable why Charlie should have decided that the Tramp should sing in *Modern Times*. He reasoned that the early talkies of Keaton and Lloyd had done very well at the box office because people were fascinated to hear what their favourites sounded like, and he believed that similar curiosity would bring them to *Modern Times*. Dialogue for the Tramp was unthinkable, but a gibberish song would not compromise his global appeal. The problem is that the scene doesn't work. As soon as he starts singing, the Tramp disappears and is replaced by a middle-aged Charlie Chaplin impersonator doing a turn at a friend's wedding. It breaks the spell.

This is the only scene that Charlie ever included for purely commercial reasons rather than artistic ones, but that nonsense ditty aside, the music composed by Chaplin for this film is exceptional. Many people know the song 'Smile', which has been covered by many performers over the years. Few know who wrote it. Its melody appears throughout the picture, and it became a huge hit as a song for Nat King Cole in the 1950s.

At the end of *Modern Times* the police arrive at the nightclub–café to arrest Paulette for vagrancy. This old charge doesn't really make any sense now that she has a home and a job, but it's a plot point that leads to the film's last indelible image. Charlie and Paulette escape from the police and flee from the nightclub. A title-card reads 'Dawn' and we find our couple by the roadside. The 'Smile' theme plays over the images as Paulette collapses in tears. 'What's the use of trying?' Charlie responds with: 'Buck up – never say die. We'll get along!' The last title-card of his silent career. He and Paulette resume their walking down the road. Charlie indicates that Paulette should smile. She does.

It's gloriously fitting to see the two of them walking away from us down a road, hand in hand towards their future. Unlike the ending of *The Tramp*, Charlie is no longer alone. Together they walk towards the horizon.

Charlie had been very nervous about *City Lights*, but he had no such worries about the merits of *Modern Times*, and the acclaim it received on its release

Buster was a late addition to the cast and was originally hired for just a couple of days. However, when the two men started to improvise together ideas began to flow, and the two-day engagement turned into three weeks

justified his faith in the film. It was a huge hit all over the world and has been constantly revived since. In China it is regarded as an anti-capitalist comedy.

All Charlie's films from now on were to be talkies. *The Great Dictator*, released in 1940, featured Chaplin as Adolf Hitler, a vain little man, terribly self-conscious about his height. The outside world had no knowledge of the Nazi death camps at this point, and Charlie later said that if he'd known about the Holocaust he would have never made the comedy. Nevertheless, it was Charlie's biggest ever hit. When the British Film Institute re-released it in 2003, I was quoted on the poster. 'When no one else in Hollywood dared, Chaplin used the one weapon every dictator fears – ridicule.' The framed poster is one of my proudest possessions.

Several films followed *The Great Dictator*. In 1947 came *Monsieur Verdoux*, a fascinating picture about a French bank clerk who murders rich widows for their money in which, in one of Charlie's finest performances, he convincingly ages twenty years with the minimum of make-up. Five years later came *Limelight*, which premiered in London on 16 October 1952. Charlie's last two films were *A King in New York*, made in England in 1957, and *A Countess in Hong Kong*, made nine years later. He was seventy-seven when he directed *Countess*, and incredibly it was his first film in colour. He played a tiny role, giving the main leads to Marlon Brando and Sophia Loren. The title tune, 'This is My Song', was a hit record for Petula Clark in the same year (1967) that the Beatles released *Sergeant Pepper's Lonely Hearts Club Band*.

Charlie's personal life during these years saw both highs and lows. In 1942 he met the seventeen-year-old Oona O'Neill. They were married a year later and had eight children in what proved to be a lasting and loving marriage. His relations with the United States, the country where he had made his career, turned sour, however. During the Second World War Charlie made a radio address to Russia at a time when Stalin was an ally. With the coming of the Cold War, though, his views and sympathies became suspect, and his radio broadcast was regarded as showing communist sympathies, and *Modern Times* was interpreted as a communist film. While he was on board ship to the London premiere of *Limelight* Charlie was informed that the US government had cancelled his re-entry visa. He was effectively exiled. Oona, being an American citizen, was able to slip back into the country, sell up the house and remove valuable assets.

During the last ten years of his life Charlie busied himself writing complete scores for such silent features as *The Kid*, *The Circus* and, finally, *A Woman of Paris*. He was eventually invited back to Hollywood in 1972, where he graciously accepted an honorary Academy Award. Buster, Harold and Stan

Above Two comic geniuses reunited. Buster Keaton and Charlie Chaplin in the 1952 film *Limelight*.

had already received theirs many years before. In 1975 he was knighted by the queen. On Christmas Day 1977 Sir Charlie Chaplin died in his sleep.

It seems appropriate to end with one of the great film triumphs of Charlie's later years, *Limelight*, because it is also one of his most autobiographical films and harks back to his early years in music hall. Essentially, it is a drama with occasional comic highlights, featuring a theme tune, composed by Charlie, that was a huge bestselling hit and is still recognized today as an easy-listening standard. The film probably features, too, a brief uncredited appearance by Charlie's first screen female co-star and former girlfriend, Edna Purviance as a lady in a hat sitting at the back of the manager's waiting room. Charlie looks in her direction and she tilts her head as the camera passes. She is expressing impatience perhaps. I think it's Edna.

And *Limelight* also features Buster Keaton. Buster was a late addition to the cast and was originally hired for just a couple of days. However, when the two men started to improvise together ideas began to flow, and the two-day engagement turned into three weeks. What emerged was a magical lengthy scene between Charlie Chaplin and Buster Keaton as two old comedians reuniting for one night, Buster as a near-sighted pianist and Charlie as a violinist with baggy trousers.

This really is our last image of silent comedy.

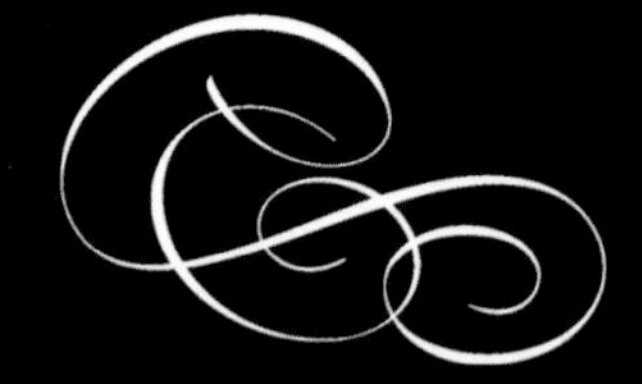

"Notes and Index"

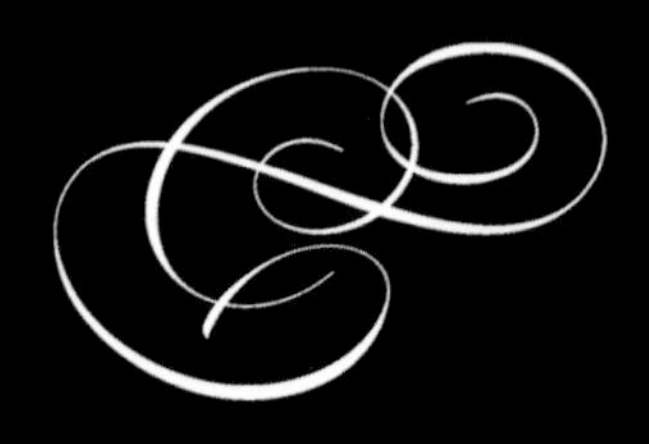
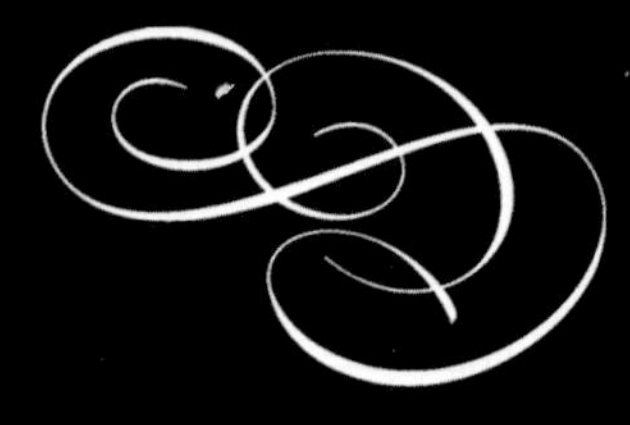

HAROLD
LLOYD

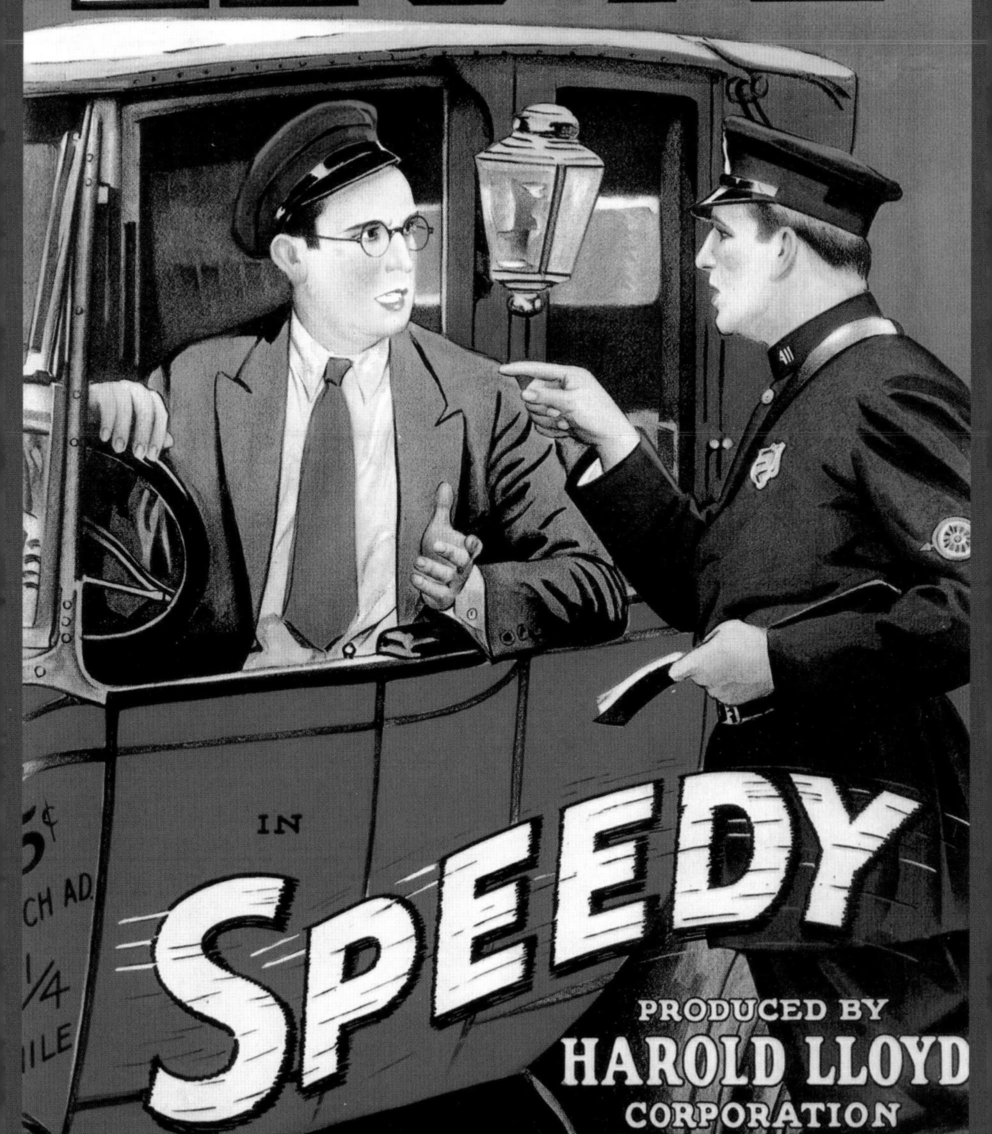

a Paramount Release

Notes

Introduction

[1] David Robinson, *Chaplin, His Life and Art* (London: Harper Collins 1985), 358.

Chapter One

[1] Charles Chaplin, *My Autobiography* (London: Bodley Head 1964; Penguin Modern Classics 1966), 15–16.
[2] Charles Chaplin, *My Autobiography*, 17–18.
[3] Charles Chaplin, *My Autobiography*, 18–19.
[4] Rudi Blesh, *Keaton* (London: Secker & Warburg 1967), 4.
[5] Patricia Eliot Tobias, 'The Buster Keaton Myths', *Classic Images* (Canada 1998), 281.
[6] Buster Keaton with Charles Samuels, *My Wonderful World of Slapstick*, (London: George Allen & Unwin Ltd 1960), 12.
[7] Buster Keaton with Charles Samuels, *My Wonderful World of Slapstick* 12–13.
[8] Buster Keaton with Charles Samuels, *My Wonderful World of Slapstick* 13.
[9] Buster Keaton with Charles Samuels, *My Wonderful World of Slapstick* 13.
[10] Charles Chaplin, *My Autobiography*, 20.
[11] Charles Chaplin, *My Autobiography*, 25.
[12] Charles Chaplin, *My Autobiography*, 27.
[13] Charles Chaplin, *My Autobiography*, 37.
[14] Charles Chaplin, *My Autobiography*, 39.
[15] Charles Chaplin, *My Autobiography*, 40.
[16] Charles Chaplin, *My Autobiography*, 67.
[17] Buster Keaton with Charles Samuels, *My Wonderful World of Slapstick*, 25.
[18] Buster Keaton with Charles Samuels, *My Wonderful World of Slapstic*k, 35.
[19] Buster Keaton with Charles Samuels, *My Wonderful World of Slapstic*k, 35.
[20] Rudi Blesh, *Keaton*, 78.
[21] Harold Lloyd and Wesley W. Stout, *An American Comedy* (New York: Dover Publications 1972), 3–4 .
[22] Harold Lloyd and Wesley W. Stout, *An American Comedy*, 4.
[23] Harold Lloyd and Wesley W. Stout, *An American Comedy*, 9.
[24] Harold Lloyd and Wesley W. Stout, *An American Comedy*, 13.
[25] Harold Lloyd and Wesley W. Stout, *An American Comedy*, 15.
[26] Harold Lloyd and Wesley W. Stout, *An American Comedy*, 17–18.
[27] Harold Lloyd and Wesley W. Stout, *An American Comedy*, 27.
[28] Harold Lloyd and Wesley W. Stout, *An American Comedy*, 33.
[29] Harold Lloyd and Wesley W. Stout, *An American Comedy*, 33–4.
[30] Harold Lloyd and Wesley W. Stout, *An American Comedy*, 34.
[31] Harold Lloyd and Wesley W. Stout, *An American Comedy*, 34–5.
[32] Charles Chaplin, *My Autobiography*, 99.
[33] Charles Chaplin, *My Autobiography*, 99–100.
[34] Simon Louvish, *Stan and Ollie: The Roots of Comedy* (London: Faber and Faber 2001), 19.
[35] Simon Louvish, *Stan and Ollie: The Roots of Comedy*, 19.
[36] Simon Louvish, *Stan and Ollie: The Roots of Comedy*, 24.
[37] A.J. Marriot, *Laurel and Hardy: The British Tours* (Blackpool, A.J. Marriot 1993), 18.
[38] A.J. Marriot, *Laurel and Hardy: The British Tours*, 27.
[39] Stan Jefferson in conversation with John McCabe.
[40] *Photoplay Magazine* 1936.
[41] Rudi Blesh, *Keaton*, 71.

Chapter Two

[1] Harold Lloyd and Wesley W. Stout, *An American Comedy*, 20.
[2] Harold Lloyd and Wesley W. Stout, *An American Comedy*, 21.
[3] Mack Sennett, *King of Comedy* (London: Taylor & Francis 1984), 65.
[4] Charles Chaplin, *My Autobiography*, 148.
[5] Charles Chaplin, *My Autobiography*, 160.
[6] Charles Chaplin, *My Autobiography*, 165.
[7] Harold Lloyd and Wesley W. Stout, *An American Comedy*, 39.
[8] Harold Lloyd and Wesley W. Stout, *An American Comedy*, 46.
[9] Mack Sennett, *King of Comedy*.

Chapter Three

[1] Glenn Mitchell, *The Chaplin Encyclopaedia*, (London: Batsford 1997) 203.

[2] David Robinson, *Chaplin, His Life and Art*, 172.

Chapter Four

[1] Buster Keaton with Charles Samuels, *My Wonderful World of Slapstick*, 91–2.

[2] Buster Keaton with Charles Samuels, *My Wonderful World of Slapstick*, 93.

[3] Buster Keaton with Charles Samuels, *My Wonderful World of Slapstick*, 92.

[4] Buster Keaton with Charles Samuels, *My Wonderful World of Slapstick*, 92.

[5] Charles Chaplin, *My Autobiography*, 188.

[6] *Chaplin Mutual Comedies: Chaplin's Goliath*, 90th Anniversary Edition (Film Preservation Associates 2006).

[7] Annette M. D'Agostino, *Harold Lloyd, A Bio-bibliography* (London: Greenwood Press 1994), 22.

[8] Charles Chaplin, *My Autobiography*, 208.

[9] Charles Chaplin, *My Autobiography*, 23–4.

Chapter Five

[1] Charles Chaplin, *My Autobiography*, 228.

[2] Charles Chaplin, *My Autobiography*, 235.

[3] Harold Lloyd and Wesley W. Stout, *An American Comedy*, 65.

[4] Harold Lloyd and Wesley W. Stout, *An American Comedy*, 75.

[5] Harold Lloyd and Wesley W. Stout, *An American Comedy*, 76.

[6] Harold Lloyd and Wesley W. Stout, *An American Comedy*, 78.

[7] Charles Chaplin, *My Autobiography*, 233–4.

Chapter Six

[1] Buster Keaton with Charles Samuels, *My Wonderful World of Slapstick*, 174.

[2] Rudi Blesh, *Keaton*, 168.

[3] Andy Edmonds, *Fatty: Untold Story of Roscoe 'Fatty' Arbuckle* (London: Little, Brown 1991), 172.

[4] Buster Keaton with Charles Samuels, *My Wonderful World of Slapstick*, 116–7.

[5] Rudi Blesh, *Keaton*, 203.

[6] Tom Dardis, *Harold Lloyd, the Man on the Clock* (New York: Viking Press 1983) 112

[7] Harold Lloyd and Wesley W. Stout, *An American Comedy*, 85.

[8] Glenn Mitchell, *The Chaplin Encyclopaedia*, 64.

Chapter Seven

[1] Rudi Blesh, *Keaton*, 233.

[2] Kevin W. Sweeney (ed.), *Buster Keaton Interviews* (Mississippi: University of Mississippi Press), 124.

[3] Charles Chaplin, *My Autobiography*, 295.

Chapter Nine

[1] Harold Lloyd and Wesley W. Stout, *An American Comedy*, 99.

[2] Harold Lloyd and Wesley W. Stout, *An American Comedy*, 98–9.

[3] Buster Keaton with Charles Samuels, *My Wonderful World of Slapstick*, 202.

[4] Buster Keaton with Charles Samuels, *My Wonderful World of Slapstick*, 202.

[5] John Gillett and James Blue, 'Keaton at Venice', *Sight and Sound*, 35, no.1 (January 1966), 27.

[6] Buster Keaton with Charles Samuels, *My Wonderful World of Slapstick*, 205–7.

[7] Buster Keaton with Charles Samuels, *My Wonderful World of Slapstick*, 208.

[8] Buster Keaton with Charles Samuels, *My Wonderful World of Slapstick*, 210.

[9] Peter Bogdanovich, *Who the Devil Made it* (New York: Random House 1997), 395.

Chapter Ten

[1] David Robinson, *Chaplin: His Life and Art*, 441.

[2] David Robinson, *Chaplin: His Life and Art*, 410.

[3] David Robinson, *Chaplin: His Life and Art*, 424.

[4] David Robinson, *Chaplin:: His Life and Art*, 425.

[5] Charles Chaplin, Jr., *My Father, Charlie Chaplin* (New York: Random House 1960; London: Longmans 1960), quoted in David Robinson, *Chaplin: His Life and Art*, 453.

Index

Text and Illustration Acknowledgements

The author is grateful for the following permissions:

Quotations from Rudi Blesh, *Keaton* © 1967 Rudi Blesh. First published by Secker & Warburg. By kind permission of the agent, Aitken Alexander Associates. Quotations from Charles Chaplin, *My Autobiography* © 1964 Charles Chaplin. First published by the Bodley Head. By kind permission of The Random House Group Ltd. All other quotations from Charles Chaplin reproduced by kind permission of The Chaplin Association. Quotations from Buster Keaton and Charles Samuels, *My Wonderful World of Slapstick* © 1960 Buster Keaton and Charles Samuels. First published by Doubleday. By kind permission of The Buster Keaton Estate. All other quotations from Buster Keaton by kind permission of The Buster Keaton Estate. Quotations from Stan Laurel by kind permission of The Stan Laurel Estate. Quotations from Harold Lloyd, *An American Comedy* © 1976 Harold Lloyd. First published by Arno P, NY. By kind permission of The Harold Lloyd Estate. Quotations from Simon Louvish, *Stan and Ollie: The Roots of Comedy* © 2001 Simon Louvish. First published by Faber & Faber Ltd. By kind permission of the author.

Illustrations
page
xiii Charlie Chaplin in *Kid Auto Races at Venice.* (The Ronald Grant Archive)
1 *The Kid* film poster. (The Ronald Grant Archive)
3 Hannah Chaplin. (The Kobal Collection)
3b Charles Chaplin senior. (The Bridgeman Art Library)
4 The Three Keatons. (© Bettmann / Corbis)
6 Buster Keaton as a small gentleman. (The Kobal Collection)
8 Lambeth Workhouse. (The Kobal Collection)
9 Charlie Chaplin at school. (The Ronald Grant Archive)
12 Marie Lloyd poster. (Getty Images)
13 *The Music Hall* by Walter Sickert. (The Art Archive / Musée des Beaux Arts Roen / Gianni Dagli Orti/© estate of Walter R. Sickert/DACS/2007)
13br Charlie Chaplin's contract of employment with Fred Karno. (The Bridgeman Art Library)
14 A vaudeville theatre c.1909. (© PEMCO – Webster & Stevens Collection; Museum of History and Industry, Seattle / Corbis)
17 Harold Lloyd as a child. (Getty Images)
21 Fred Karno. (The Ronald Grant Archive)
26 Fred Karno's troupe on board ship to the US. (The Ronald Grant Archive)
29 *Out West* film poster. (The Ronald Grant Archive)
30 Magic lantern. (© Michael Freeman / Corbis)
31 Engraving of a magic lantern show. (Getty Images)
32 Max Linder. (Rex Features)
34 Nickelodeon in Pittsburgh. (Granger Collection)
35 Inside of a 1920s cinema. (Granger Collection)
36l Mabel Normand and Mack Sennett. (© Bettmann / Corbis)
36r Mabel Normand and Ford Sterling in *Barney Oldfield's Race for a Life.* (Rex Features)
37tl Ben Turpin. (The Kobal Collection)

37tr Ford Sterling and Minta Durfee in *Dirty Work in a Laundry.* (© Bettmann / Corbis)
38 Mack Sennett. (© Corbis)
39 Scene from *The Birth of a Nation.* (© Bettmann / Corbis)
40 The Keystone Cops. (The Kobal Collection)
42 Charlie Chaplin in *Kid Auto Races at Venice.* (The Ronald Grant Archive)
47 Charlie Chaplin and Roscoe Arbuckle in *The Rounders.* (Keystone / The Kobal Collection)
50 Universal studios. (The Kobal Collection)
51 Group photograph including Harold Lloyd and Hal Roach. (Getty Images)
53 Ben Turpin and Charlie Chaplin in *His New Job.* (Rex Features)
54 Edna Purviance. (© Hulton-Deutsch collection / Corbis)
57 *The Vagabond* film poster. (© Swim Ink 2, LLC / Corbis)
59 Paddy McGuire and Charlie Chaplin in *The Tramp.* (Essanay / The Kobal Collection)
60 Charlie Chaplin in *The Tramp.* (BFI)
62 Charlie Chaplin and Chaplin doll. (Charles Chaplin / © Roy Export Company Establishment)
63 Charlie Chaplin in *A Woman.* (Essanay / The Kobal Collection)
66 Charlie Chaplin and Eric Campbell. (Charles Chaplin / © Roy Export Company Establishment)
67 Charlie Chaplin and Edna Purviance in *The Vagabond.* (Mutual / The Kobal Collection)
70 Roscoe Arbuckle. (The Kobal Collection)
71 Roscoe Arbuckle and Mabel Normand in *He Did and He Didn't.* (Keystone Films / The Kobal Collection)
72 Roscoe Arbuckle in *A Reckless Romeo.* (MPTV/LFI)
73 Charlie Chaplin in *One A.M.* (Mutual / The Kobal Collection)
75 Charlie Chaplin in *One A.M.* (Mutual / The Kobal Collection)
77 Charlie Chaplin and Albert Austin in *The Pawnshop.* (Rex Features)
78 Scenes from *One A.M.* (All Rex Features)
79t Charlie Chaplin and Eric Campbell in *Easy Street.* (© Bettmann / Corbis)
79b Charlie Chaplin and Eric Campbell in *Easy Street.* (Rex Features)
82 Charlie Chaplin and Edna Purviance in *Easy Street.* (© Bettmann / Corbis)
83 Street scene in Edwardian south London. (London Borough of Lambeth)
87 *A Dog's Life* film poster. (Getty Images)
89 Roscoe Arbuckle and Buster Keaton in *The Butcher Boy.* (The Ronald Grant Archive / Paramount Pictures)
94 Edna Purviance, Kitty Bradbury and Charlie Chaplin in *The Immigrant.* (Mutual / The Kobal Collection)
96 Charlie Chaplin in *The Gold Rush.* (Mutual / The Kobal Collection)
99 Eric Campbell, Charlie Chaplin and Edna Purviance in *The Adventurer.* (Mutual / The Kobal Collection)
101 Charlie Chaplin in *The Adventurer.* (Mutual / The Kobal Collection)
102 Larry Semon, Dorothy Dwan and Oliver Hardy in *The Wizard of Oz.* (© John Springer Collection / Corbis)
103 Larry Semon. (The Kobal Collection)
103b Larry Semon in *Spuds.* (Larry Semon Prods / The Kobal Collection)
105 Group photograph showing Oliver Hardy and Billy West. (The Ronald Grant Archive)
106t&b Harold Lloyd as Lonesome Luke and as the 'glasses character'. (The Ronald Grant Archive)
108 Postcard of Luna Park. (© Lake County Museum / Corbis)
109 Roscoe Arbuckle and Buster Keaton in *Coney Island.* (The Kobal Collection)
112 Edna Purviance and Charlie Chaplin in *A Dog's Life.* (Charles Chaplin / © Roy Export Company Establishment)
113 Charlie and Sydney Chaplin. (Rex Features)
115 Buster Keaton and Roscoe Arbuckle in *Goodnight Nurse.* (MPTV/LFI)
117 Douglas Fairbanks and Charlie Chaplin promote war bonds. (Getty Images)
118 Charlie Chaplin in *Shoulder Arms.* (Charles Chaplin / © Roy Export Company Establishment)

121 *Sunnyside* film poster. (AKG)
123 Charlie Chaplin and Mildred Harris. (First National / The Kobal Collection)
124 Charlie Chaplin in *Sunnyside*. (Charles Chaplin / © Roy Export Company Establishment)
127 Buster Keaton and Roscoe Arbuckle in *The Garage*. (The Kobal Collection)
128 Buster Keaton in *The High Sign*. (Comique Film Corporation / Album / AKG)
129 Buster Keaton as the three monkeys. (Ullstein Bild / AKG)
131 Buster Keaton in *One Week*. (Ronald Grant Archive)
132 Buster Keaton, Sybil Sealey and Roscoe Arbuckle. (© John Springer Collection / Corbis)
133 Buster Keaton in *The Saphead*. (AKG)
134 Douglas Fairbanks, Mary Pickford, Charlie Chaplin and his first wife, Mildred. (© Underwood & Underwood / Corbis)
135t Buster Keaton's house. (The Ronald Grant Archive)
135b Living room in Harold Lloyd's house. (Time & Life Pictures / Getty Images)
137 Buster Keaton in *Convict 13*. (The Ronald Grant Archive)
139 Buster Keaton in *Neighbors*. (Metro / The Kobal Collection)
140 Harold Lloyd in *Look Out Below*. (The Kobal Collection)
141 Mildred Davis and Harold Lloyd in *From Hand to Mouth*. (W & I Films / The Kobal Collection)
145 Jackie Coogan and Charlie Chaplin in *The Kid*. (Charles Chaplin / © Roy Export Company Establishment)
146 Jackie Coogan and Charlie Chaplin in *The Kid*. (Charles Chaplin / © Roy Export Company Establishment)
149 *Safety Last!* film poster. (Pathé / Aquarius Collection)
151 Buster Keaton with his in-laws. (Goldwyn / The Kobal Collection / Evans, Nelson)
155 Buster Keaton playing several musical instruments. (First National / The Kobal Collection)
156 Buster Keaton in *The Boat*. (First National / The Kobal Collection)
159c Newspaper reporting the Arbuckle scandal. (Rex Features)
159 Virginia Rappé. (© Bettmann / Corbis)
161 Charlie Chaplin in England. (Getty Images)
162 Roscoe Arbuckle in court. (© Bettmann / Corbis)
166 Buster Keaton in *Cops*. (Rex Features)
168 Buster Keaton and Roscoe Arbuckle. (© John Springer Collection / Corbis)
170 Buster Keaton in *My Wife's Relations*. (MPTV/LFI)
173 Buster Keaton in *The Frozen North*. (Buster Keaton Prod / Album / AKG)
176 Charlie Chaplin and Edna Purviance in *The Idle Class*. (Charles Chaplin / © Roy Export Company Establishment)
179 Charlie Chaplin in *The Pilgrim*. (Charles Chaplin / © Roy Export Company Establishment)
180 Harold Lloyd in *Grandma's Boy*. (Associated Exhibitors / The Kobal Collection)
182 Scenes from *Safety Last!* (All Hal Roach / Pathé Exchange / The Kobal Collection / Kornman, Gene)
183 Scenes from *Safety Last!* (All Hal Roach / Pathé Exchange / The Kobal Collection / Kornman, Gene)
186 Harold Lloyd filming *Speedy*. (Getty Images)
189 *Our Hospitality* film poster. (The Ronald Grant Archive)
190 Scenes from *The Three Ages*. (Both Metro / Aquarius Collection)
191 Buster Keaton, Wallace Beery and Margaret Leahy in *The Three Ages*. (Metro / The Kobal Collection)
193 Buster Keaton in *Our Hospitality*. (Metro / The Kobal Collection)
197 Buster Keaton in *Our Hospitality*. (The Ronald Grant Archive)
199 Johan Aasen and Harold Lloyd in *Why Worry?* (Hal Roach / Pathé Exchange / The Kobal Collection)
201 Jobyna Ralston. (© John Springer Collection / Corbis)
204 Jobyna Ralston and Harold Lloyd in *Girl Shy*. (Getty Images)
207 Buster Keaton in *Sherlock Junior*. (Metro / The Kobal Collection)

208 Buster Keaton in *Sherlock Junior.* (Metro / The Kobal Collection)
211 Buster Keaton and Kathryn McGuire in *The Navigator.* (Metro-Goldwyn / The Kobal Collection)
212 Buster Keaton and Kathryn McGuire in *The Navigator.* (Metro-Goldwyn / The Kobal Collection)
214 Buster Keaton in *Seven Chances.* (Metro-Goldwyn / The Kobal Collection)
215 Buster Keaton in *Seven Chances.* (Metro-Goldwyn / Album / AKG)
217 Charlie Chaplin filming *The Gold Rush.* (United Artists / The Kobal Collection)
218 Scenes from *The Gold Rush.* (All Charles Chaplin/© Roy Export Company Establishment)
219 Scenes from *The Gold Rush.* (All Charles Chaplin/© Roy Export Company Establishment)
220 Georgia Hale and Charlie Chaplin in *The Gold Rush.* (Charles Chaplin/© Roy Export Company Establishment)
222 Mack Swain and Charlie Chaplin in *The Gold Rush.* (Charles Chaplin/© Roy Export Company Establishment)
224 Harold Lloyd in *The Freshman.* (Pathé / The Kobal Collection)
227 *The General* film poster. (The Ronald Grant Archive / United Artists)
229 Harry Langdon. (© John Springer Collection / Corbis)
231 Joan Crawford. (© Underwood & Underwood / Corbis)
232 Harry Langdon in *The Strong Man.* (First National / Album / AKG)
235 Harry Langdon in *Long Pants.* (The Ronald Grant Archive / Harry Langdon Corporation)
237 Harold Lloyd and Jobyna Ralston in *The Kid Brother.* (The Ronald Grant Archive)
240 Buster Keaton in *Battling Butler.* (The Ronald Grant Archive / Buster Keaton Productions, INC / MGM)
243 Buster Keaton in *The General.* (United Artists / The Kobal Collection)
244 Buster Keaton in *The Navigator.* (Metro-Goldwyn / The Kobal Collection)
245tl Scene from *The General.* (Rex Features)
245tr&b Scenes from *The General.* (United Artists / The Kobal Collection)
247 Train crashes through a bridge in *The General.* (© Hulton-Deutsch Collection / Corbis)
249 *Liberty* film poster. (Rex Features)
250br Oliver Hardy and Stan Laurel in *The Lucky Dog.* (Metro / The Kobal Collection)
250 & 251 Laurel and Hardy. (The Kobal Collection)
253 Stan Laurel and Oliver Hardy in *Putting Pants on Philip.* (Hal Roach / The Kobal Collection)
254 Scene from *The Battle of the Century.* (Hal Roach / MGM / The Kobal Collection)
257 Buster Keaton in *College.* (The Ronald Grant Archive / Joseph H Schenck)
258 Charlie Chaplin in *The Circus.* (Charles Chaplin/© Roy Export Company Establishment)
261 Charlie Chaplin in *The Circus.* (Charles Chaplin/© Roy Export Company Establishment)
263 Harold Lloyd in *Speedy.* (Paramount / The Kobal Collection)
266 Buster Keaton in *Steamboat Bill Junior.* (The Ronald Grant Archive)
267 Buster Keaton in *Steamboat Bill Junior.* (The Ronald Grant Archive)
269 Buster Keaton in *The Cameraman.* (MGM / The Kobal Collection)
272 Oliver Hardy in *Flying Elephants.* (Hal Roach – Pathé / The Kobal Collection)
273 Stan Laurel in *Flying Elephants.* (Hal Roach – Pathé / The Kobal Collection)
275 Stan Laurel and Oliver Hardy in *Habeas Corpus.* (The Ronald Grant Collection)
276t Scene from *Big Business.* (MGM / The Kobal Collection)
276b Scenes from *Big Business.* (Both MGM / Album / AKG)
277 Scenes from *Big Business.* (Both MGM / The Kobal Collection)
278 Oliver Hardy and Stan Laurel in *Wrong Again.* (The Ronald Grant Archive / Hal Roach)
279 Scene from *Un Chien Andalou.* (Buñuel–Dali / The Kobal Collection)

280 Stan Laurel and Oliver Hardy in *That's My Wife.* (MGM / The Kobal Collection)
283 *City Lights* film poster. (The Ronald Grant Archive)
285 Production shot from *Wife vs Secretary.* (MGM / Album / AKG)
286 Buster Keaton and Eddie Sedgwick on the set of *Spite Marriage.* (The Kobal Collection)
289 Buster Keaton with the Marx brothers. (The Kobal Collection)
290 Harold Lloyd in *Feet First.* (Paramount / The Kobal Collection)
292 Oliver Hardy and Stan Laurel in *Way Out West.* (Stan Laurel Productions / Hal Roach – MGM / The Kobal Collection)
293 Stan Laurel and Oliver Hardy in *A Chump at Oxford.* (Hal Roach / UA / The Kobal Collection)
295 Charlie Chaplin in *City Lights.* (Charles Chaplin/© Roy Export Company Establishment)
296 Charlie Chaplin and Virginia Cherrill in *City Lights.* (Charles Chaplin/© Roy Export Company Establishment)
298 Albert Einstein and Charlie Chaplin at the premiere of *City Lights.* (Getty Images)
300 Scenes from *Modern Times.* (All Charles Chaplin/© Roy Export Company Establishment)
301 Scenes from *Modern Times.* (all Charles Chaplin/© Roy Export Company Establishment)
302 Charlie Chaplin and Paulette Goddard in *Modern Times.* (Charles Chaplin/© Roy Export Company Establishment)
305 Buster Keaton and Charlie Chaplin in *Limelight.* (Charles Chaplin/© Roy Export Company Establishment)
307 *Speedy* film poster. (The Ronald Grant Archive)

'Gags are done from inside. You must feel them, you must know how they are, you must time them, you must react to them'

– Harold Lloyd

‘In comedy, the most important person is the person you’re playing to – the person you’re trying to make laugh’

– Stan Laurel